STUDY GUIDE FOR THE TELECOURSE

FACES OF CULTURE

SIXTH EDITION

STUDY GUIDE FOR THE TELECOURSE

FACES OF CULTURE

SIXTH EDITION

Valerie L. Lee and Richard T. Searles

with Background Notes written by Mari Womack, Ph.D.

for

Coast Community College District
Costa Mesa, California

HARCOURT BRACE COLLEGE PUBLISHERS

FORT WORTH   PHILADELPHIA   SAN DIEGO   NEW YORK   ORLANDO   AUSTIN   SAN ANTONIO
TORONTO   MONTREAL   LONDON   SYDNEY   TOKYO

Coast Community College District

William M. Vega, Chancellor, Coast Community College District

Leslie N. Purdy, President, Coastline Community College

Peter Vander Haeghen, Administrative Dean, Office of Instructional Systems Development

Ira R. Abrams, Series Producer, original video programs

John Bishop, Producer, revised video programs

Arthur Barron, Creative Consultant, original video programs

Valerie Lynch Lee, Instructional Designer, revised video programs

Mari Womack, Content Reviewer, Sixth Edition

Randy Franz, Publications Assistant Senior

STUDY GUIDE CONSULTANT (ORIGINAL EDITION): Frances F. Berdan, Professor and Chair, Department of Anthropology, California State University, San Bernardino

MAP ILLUSTRATION: Kathy Strube, Coastline Community College

COVER PHOTO: Frans Lanting/Minden Pictures

Faces of Culture, a telecourse, is produced by the Coast Community College District and KOCE-TV in cooperation with Harcourt Brace College Publishers, in association with City Colleges of Chicago, Dallas County Community College District, Miami-Dade Community College, Southern California Consortium (INTELECOM), and State of Florida Department of Education.

The telecourse is distributed by **Coast Telecourses**
Coastline Community College
11460 Warner Avenue
Fountain Valley, California 92708
phone 714-241-6109 • *fax* 714-241-6286

ISBN: 0-15-503730-7

Printed in the United States of America

Address editorial correspondence: Harcourt Brace College Publishers, Suite 3700
301 Commerce Street, Fort Worth, TX 76102

4567 016 987654321

Preface

To the Student

Welcome to **Faces of Culture**, a telecourse that introduces the principles and information of cultural anthropology. Whether you are planning a career in anthropology or taking this course to gain insights into your own and other cultures, we believe that you will find it interesting, entertaining, and enriching.

Faces of Culture is designed according to the philosophy that culture as the expression of human values, behavior, and social organization exists in unique and varied forms throughout the world, in past and present times. The course attempts to document that diversity and demonstrate the inherent logic of each culture in light of the problems people need to solve and the environments to which they must adapt. Although some of the behaviors and customs you will see may, at times, strike you as odd or unpleasant, we urge you to try not to make value judgments about the cultures under study but to look instead for the purpose and function of the behaviors or customs within the context of those cultures and their values. At other times in this course, you will see human behavior that reflects universal needs and feelings, albeit expressed through diverse cultural customs and practices. Consequently, as you progress through this course, your own feelings will probably range from a sense of awe at the differences between people to a sense of respect for, and oneness with, people around the world. We hope that you will be touched by, and learn from, the people you will see and read about in this course.

Course Goals

The designer, academic advisors, and producers of this telecourse have specified eight major goals for students taking **Faces of Culture**. By the end of the course, you should be able to:

- Understand and appreciate the concept of culture from the perspective of anthropologists, as the adaptive mechanism that provides for survival of the human species.

- Recognize the underlying similarities as well as the wide range and variability of human cultures.

- Recognize and appreciate that there are a number of valid "cultural solutions" to living on Earth.

- Understand the relationship between culture and the individual.

- Understand the factors involved in culture change.

- Gain a broad cross-cultural background against which to view your own culture as well as contemporary social problems.

- Know the meanings of the basic concepts and terms used by cultural anthropologists.

- Understand procedures used by anthropologists in studying cultures.

Course Components

As with most classroom courses, *Faces of Culture* has a textbook, a study guide, assignments, and tests. The textbook is *Cultural Anthropology*, eighth edition, by William A. Haviland (Fort Worth: Harcourt Brace College Publishers, 1996). The book you are now reading, *Study Guide for the Telecourse Faces of Culture*, will guide your study through the course, providing reading and viewing assignments, study activities, and practice test questions. You may also be required to purchase and read additional books for this course—case studies that describe particular cultures in depth. In addition, *Faces of Culture* has a special learning element that most classes do not have: a companion half-hour video program for each of the 26 lessons in the course.

The components of *Faces of Culture* have been continually reviewed and refined. This study-guide edition, the sixth, reflects extensive updating of the textbook and the video programs. Since the telecourse was originally produced, three of the video programs have been replaced with completely new programs, four have been revised extensively, and ten have been enhanced with new narration, new footage, or both.

STUDY GUIDE

This study guide is your road map through *Faces of Culture*. It is a starting point for each lesson because it contains step-by-step assignments for reading, viewing, and doing related activities, overviews of the content of the textbook and the video programs, and a complete array of learning activities to help you master the learning objectives for the lesson. Each lesson in this study guide has the following components:

Assignments. Detailed instructions on activities and reading assignments to be completed before and after viewing each video program.

Overview. A brief discussion of the main points of the lesson, in both the textbook and the video program, along with a list of particular points to look for in the video program.

Learning Objectives. Statements of what you should learn from reading the textbook assignment, completing the activities in the study guide, and viewing the video program.

Study Activities. This section includes Vocabulary Check and Completion exercises to help you review and reinforce your understanding of important terms and concepts.

Self-Test: Objective Questions. A brief objective quiz that allows you to test your understanding of the material in the lesson.

Self-Test: Short-Answer Essay Questions. These questions enable you to check your comprehension of broad concepts presented in each lesson.

Suggested Activities. Suggestions for further study of anthropology. (Your instructor may also use these as assignments for extra credit.)

Answer Key. This section provides answers for the Vocabulary Check and Completion items and for the Self-Test Objective Questions and Short-Answer Essay Questions. Check your answers after you have completed each activity. If you have any incorrect answers, review the material.

In addition to the sections described above, twelve lessons in this study guide contain **Background Notes**, which are assigned in addition to the textbook material. The Background Notes contain information that supplements material presented in the video programs and textbook. Your careful study of the Background Notes is essential to your achieving the Learning Objectives stated for the lesson.

VIDEO PROGRAMS

The 26 video programs in this course incorporate films or portions of films showing many different societies and cultures. Many of the films have been photographed by or under the supervision of anthropologists, and some show people who seldom have been filmed. Other films come from Japanese and French anthropologists and filmmakers and have been seen rarely, if ever, in the United States. Thus, in this course, you have an opportunity to see authentic film of a wide variety of cultures and people from around the world. Because of this opportunity, you will be able to experience these cultures in a more thorough way than you could by just reading or hearing about them.

In the field of anthropology, a special kind of research has developed around the use of ethnographic filming—the recording on film of the lifestyles of people in one culture. Photographs and film allow anthropologists to document cultural practices, capturing visually all aspects of human behavior—including language, gestures, clothing, social interactions, rituals, and ceremonies—in a more complete way than a written record can do. This type of research has allowed the study of many cultures by many anthropologists and also permits recording certain practices and customs that, for one reason or another, are becoming rare, perhaps never to be repeated again. Much of the film you will see is ethnographic film, taken for the express purpose of being an accurate and authentic record of the people and practices of a specific culture in a particular place and at a certain point in time.

As part of the effort to be accurate and let the people of different cultures speak for themselves, many of the programs contain simultaneous English translations in the form of subtitles or narration. Because the subtitles carry important information, be sure your television set is clearly in focus so that you can read them.

One of the characteristics of culture is that it integrates all of the society. However, you will be studying various aspects of culture, such as political organization, religion and magic, family patterns, and the economy, as distinct and separate entities. Even though the video programs focus on distinct topics, remember that all parts of a culture work together. For example, when you watch the programs about political systems, you will also see practices that relate to a culture's patterns of marriage and family and kinship. So look beyond the specific focus of a program and be alert to the total pattern of a culture.

How to Take a Telecourse

If you are new to college courses, and to telecourses in particular, you might profit from a few suggestions offered by students who successfully completed other telecourses.

Telecourses are designed for busy people—people with full-time jobs or family obligations—who want to take a course at home, fitting the study into their own schedules. To complete a telecourse successfully, you need to plan how to schedule your viewing, reading, and study. Buy the books before the course begins and look them over; familiarize yourself with any materials supplied by your college and estimate the time needed to complete special tests and assignments for each lesson. Write the dates of midterms, finals, review sessions, and special projects on your calendar so that you can plan to have extra time to prepare for them. You may find it enjoyable and instructive to watch the programs with other people, but save talking and discussion until after the program so that you won't miss important information. The following suggestions about how to study and how to complete *Faces of Culture* have been compiled from students who completed telecourses successfully.

- *Do* buy both the textbook and the study guide for *Faces of Culture* or arrange to share copies with a friend. Do *not* try to complete this course without these books.

- *Do* watch each of the video programs. To pass the examinations, you will need to read and study the textbook and to view the video programs. At the end of each program, write a brief summary of what you have seen, the meaning of key concepts and terms, and the names of the cultural groups presented. If you have a videocassette recorder, tape the programs for later review.

- *Do* keep up with your work for this course every week. Even if you do not have class sessions on campus or assignments to turn in, you should read the textbook and do the assignments in the study guide, as well as watch the video programs. Set aside viewing, reading, and study time each week and stick to your schedule.

- *Do* contact the faculty member in charge of *Faces of Culture* at your college or university. The instructor can answer your questions about the material covered in the course. Your faculty member can also help you catch up if you are behind, advise you about additional assignments, discuss the type of test questions you can expect, and tell you where you can watch programs you missed or wish to review.

- *Do* complete all the Study Activities and Self-Tests in this guide. These will help you master the Learning Objectives and prepare for formal examinations.

- If you miss a program or fall behind in your study schedule, don't give up. Many television stations repeat broadcasts of the programs later in the week.Your college might have videocassette copies of programs available in the campus library or media center. And *do* call on your course faculty member or manager to help if you have problems of any kind. This person is assigned to help you succeed in *Faces of Culture*.

Acknowledgments

Producing the *Faces of Culture* telecourse was a complex team effort by many skilled people. Several of those persons responsible for this course are listed on the copyright page of this book.

In addition to those people, appreciation is expressed for the contributions of a number of academic advisors to the course. First, William A. Haviland, Ph.D., professor of anthropology at the University of Vermont and author of the textbook, served as a technical advisor to the series and helped in numerous ways throughout production of both the original and revised versions of the course.

Production of the original course was made possible with grants from several educational institutions. Each of them, in turn, provided a faculty advisor who helped to formulate the overall course outline and reviewed print and video materials as produced. These reviewers and the institutions they represented are:

Elvio Angeloni, M.A., Southern California Consortium (INTELECOM)

Richard Behnke, Ph.D., Pensacola Junior College
(Florida State Department of Education)

Marjorie Nam, M.A., Tallahassee Community College
(Florida State Department of Education)

Parker Nunley, Ph.D., Dallas County Community College District

Joseph Sasser, M.A., Florida Junior College, Jacksonville
(Florida State Department of Education)

Dennis Shaw, D.A., Miami-Dade Community College

Howard White, Ph.D., City Colleges of Chicago

Others also provided academic assistance for the course. Joe Filson, M.A., instructor at Golden West College, helped to formulate the course goals and instructional objectives. Frances Berdan, Ph.D., professor of anthropology at California State University, San Bernardino, reviewed the original study guide. Consultants provided specialized information used in several programs. Their names are included in the program credits.

In addition, appreciation is expressed to Richard T. Searles, M.Ed., educational materials writer and classroom teacher, who wrote the original study guide, and to Mari Womack, Ph.D. (anthropology), assistant professor of anthropology and writer and editor of educational materials, who wrote the Background Notes for this study guide, wrote the scripts for the revised video programs, and reviewed the content for this sixth edition of the study guide.

Administrative assistance was provided by J. Warren Binns, Jr., Florida State Department of Education; Sally Beaty, Southern California Consortium (INTELECOM); Rodger Pool, Dallas County Community College District; J. Terence Kelly, Miami-Dade Community College; and John H. Thissen, City Colleges of Chicago.

Appreciation is also expressed to Holt, Rinehart and Winston for their support of the original telecourse production. David Boynton, formerly their anthropology editor, provided a great deal of important advice and assistance during the planning stages of the original telecourse.

The original 26 video programs of *Faces of Culture* were produced by KOCE-TV in studios located on the Golden West College campus in Huntington Beach, California. An affiliate of the Public Broadcasting Service (PBS), KOCE-TV is owned and operated by the Coast Community College District. The revised video programs and this study guide and other materials for this course were developed by the Office of Instructional Systems Development at Coastline Community College (Fountain Valley, California), a member of the Coast Community College District.

Contents

The Nature of Anthropology 1

Assignments

Before viewing the video program	• Read the Overview and the Learning Objectives for this lesson. Use the Learning Objectives to guide your reading, viewing, and thinking. • Read the Part I Introduction, pages 2–3, and Chapter 1, "The Nature of Anthropology," pages 4–29, in the textbook.

View video program 1, "The Nature of Anthropology"

After viewing the video program	• Review the terms used in this lesson. Check your understanding of all unfamiliar terms appearing in the Learning Objectives and in the glossary notes in the textbook. • Review the reading assignments for this lesson. • Complete each of the Study Activities and the Self-Test in this study-guide lesson; check your answers with the Answer Key at the end of this lesson. • As a follow-up to the video program, you may wish to read brief descriptions of some of the anthropologists discussed in the video program. Check the index of your textbook for information about Franz Boas and Margaret Mead. • According to your instructor's assignment or your own interests, complete one or more of the Suggested Activities. You also may be interested in the readings listed at the end of Chapter 1 in the textbook.

Overview

This first lesson in *Faces of Culture* introduces you to the discipline of anthropology, or "the study of humankind," as anthropologists define it. The subject matter of cultural anthropology is shared with other social sciences, but anthropology differs from them in at least two significant ways. The first of these differences might be called the "focus of interest" of anthropology. Anthropologists take special interest in the wide diversity of human groups, including those groups that are distant both in space and time. The second way in which cultural anthropology differs from other social sciences is in its methods of research, or methodology. Investigators in this field seek knowledge of human activity from both the present and the past, using specially developed techniques. These techniques include sifting massive amounts of minute data in a search for patterns, conducting field research, and making comparative cross-cultural studies of specific aspects of culture. Anthropology gives us an opportunity to view humans and their societies from a new perspective, a wider view that can enable us to better understand people of remote places and times and, ultimately, to better understand ourselves.

You will see in this lesson that anthropology crosses the usual academic boundaries, extending into the realms of the sciences and the humanities. Like scientists in all fields, anthropologists gather information, develop explanations based on objective review of the data, then revise or even discard old explanations as new information is discovered. Moreover, the field of anthropology shares with the humanities a high regard for the arts and literature developed by people everywhere. And both anthropologists and humanists insist that other peoples' ways must be experienced and shared as much as possible.

In the lessons that follow, you will learn something about the many discoveries anthropologists have made in their studies of humans in a variety of times and places. After *your* studies, you will undoubtedly have a deeper appreciation for the creativity and adaptability that humankind exhibits everywhere, greater admiration for the drama of human life, and a clearer understanding of your own society and your place within it.

Video Program: This first video program shows a montage of peoples and lifestyles that will be explored more fully later in the telecourse. The presentation emphasizes the fundamental similarities of all members of the human race and the wide range of adaptations toward the common goal of survival. The anthropologist's goals of determining similarities and understanding diversity are reinforced in footage of Margaret Mead describing her work and her studies with Franz Boas. One theme of this introductory program is that the veil of ethnocentricity must be lifted to appreciate behavioral patterns unlike our own. The program also defines and describes anthropology, with emphasis on the discipline's holistic approach, scientific techniques, and assumption of the value of each society studied.

As you view the video program, look for:

- the manner in which anthropologists approach their studies of distinctly different cultures.
- the story of what happened to the Tasmanian aborigines as a result of British colonialization.
- the classic film taken of the war rituals of the Kwakiutl Indians of the Pacific Northwest of Canada.
- the return of the sacred pole to the Omaha.
- the reasons (told in the words of a Turkana leader named Lorang) Turkana men customarily have several wives.
- the terms *ethnocentrism* and *cultural relativism* used in the video program.

Learning Objectives

When you have completed all assignments in this lesson, you should be able to:

1. Describe several significant ways in which anthropology is a scientific study of humankind. TEXTBOOK PAGES 6–10, 20–25; VIDEO PROGRAM

2. List some other fields of study with which cultural anthropology shares subject matter. TEXTBOOK PAGES 7–10, 25–26

3. Identify the focus of the field of physical anthropology. TEXTBOOK PAGE 8; VIDEO PROGRAM

4. Define *cultural anthropology* and the subareas of *archaeology, linguistic anthropology,* and *ethnology.* TEXTBOOK PAGES 8–14, 18–20; VIDEO PROGRAM

5. Define *ethnography, participant observation,* and *holistic perspective.* TEXTBOOK PAGES 13–14

6. Define the terms *hypothesis* and *theory.* TEXTBOOK PAGE 21

7. Identify some of the ways the study of cultural anthropology is relevant to today's world. TEXTBOOK PAGES 12, 26–27; VIDEO PROGRAM

Study Activities

Vocabulary Check

Check your understanding of terms by writing the letter of the appropriate definition in the space next to the corresponding term. Check your choices with the Answer Key at the end of the lesson.

_____	1. physical anthropology	_____	5. ethnography
_____	2. cultural anthropology	_____	6. hypothesis
_____	3. archaeology	_____	7. theory
_____	4. ethnology		

a. the study of cultures from a comparative or historical point of view
b. the study of material remains, usually from the past, to describe and explain human behavior
c. systematic study of humans as biological organisms
d. systematic description of a culture based on firsthand observation
e. a set of validated hypotheses that systematically explains phenomena
f. scientific study of all aspects of language
g. focuses on the patterns of life in a society
h. a tentative explanation of the relationship between certain phenomena

Completion

Fill each blank with the most appropriate term from the list immediately following that paragraph.

1. One example of the use of the scientific approach in anthropology is the work of the ethnographer, who gathers extensive _____ about a culture before attempting to describe cultural patterns. Ethnological theories in anthropology usually are the result of careful _____ comparisons. Ethnography is the _____ of a culture, based on firsthand observation, that is used by ethnologists in making useful generalizations about humans and their behavior.

analysis	data	hypothetical
cross-cultural	description	theory

2. According to the video program, "our vision must be wide and clear" if we are to understand a culture different from our own. The _____ attempts to learn how all parts of the culture fit together in a complete _____. Such an approach is called a holistic _____.

analysis	method	perspective
ethnographer	observation	system

3. One subdivision of cultural anthropology that is concerned with the study of material remains is known as _____. The branch of anthropology that focuses on cultures of the present is known as _____, and the branch that studies human languages is known as _____ anthropology.

archaeology	forensic
ethnology	linguistic

Self-Test

Objective Questions

Select the one best answer.

1. One of the major problems facing anthropologists doing research is
   a. identifying a culture different from their own.
   b. forming an objective hypothesis that is not culture-bound about phenomena in another culture.
   c. formulating a theory before beginning to study a culture.
   d. constructing a satisfactory questionnaire before interviewing members of a society.

2. The subject matter of cultural anthropology is closely related to that of the
   a. social sciences.
   b. natural sciences.
   c. biological sciences.
   d. physical sciences.

3.   The humanistic side of anthropology is most evident in the discipline's concern with

   a. a culture's values and achievements in the arts and literature.
   b. the evolution of humankind.
   c. human behavior.
   d. scientific methodology.

4.   A major concern of physical anthropology is

   a. social interactions of humans.
   b. humans as biological organisms.
   c. conflict between human cultures.
   d. artifacts left by ancient cultures.

5.   The primary focus of interest of cultural anthropology is

   a. humans as biological organisms.
   b. human activity as revealed by material remains.
   c. the scientific study of language.
   d. patterns of human behavior in societies.

6.   Ethnography is the

   a. technique of learning a people's culture through participation.
   b. viewing of a culture in the broadest possible perspective.
   c. systematic description of a culture based on firsthand observation.
   d. study of a people's language.

7.   A *theory* is a

   a. system of validated hypotheses.
   b. summary of data from other theories.
   c. description of material objects.
   d. tentative conclusion.

8.   A *hypothesis* is a

   a. well-supported body of knowledge.
   b. collection of observed facts.
   c. tentative explanation of the relationship between certain phenomena.
   d. statement that is usually beyond challenge.

9. The "Garbage Project" of the University of Arizona suggests that

   a. techniques of anthropology are best employed in studying isolated societies.
   b. techniques of archaeology may be employed to study contemporary North American culture.
   c. the questionnaire is always a valid research tool.
   d. ethnographic studies are best accomplished in a present-day industrial environment.

10. According to the textbook, the most important contribution anthropology can make to present-day North American society is to

    a. preserve a record of cultures that no longer exist.
    b. prove the superiority of Western culture over other societies.
    c. identify serious weaknesses in our own society.
    d. promote clearer understanding of other peoples and cultures.

Short-Answer Essay Questions

1. Summarize the events that occurred when the British established a colony on land previously inhabited only by the Tasmanian aborigines.
2. How does anthropology differ from other social sciences in its approach to studying people?
3. List and briefly describe the three specializations within the field of cultural anthropology.
4. Give at least one reason anthropological research is important in today's world.

Suggested Activities

1. Do library research on the Tasmanians, the destruction of their people and culture, and the opinion of English-speaking scientists of the Tasmanians in the nineteenth century.

2. Use the *Readers' Guide to Periodical Literature* to locate recent articles on ethnography, archaeology, and linguistic anthropology. Read at least two of these articles and write a brief summary of each. In your own mind, consider the scope of cultural anthropology as reflected by the range of articles you discovered.

3. Set up a "garbage study" in your household to test ideas about your lifestyle and values. Design your study, deciding what you will look for and what your findings might indicate. Write a report describing your findings and conclusions.

Answer Key

STUDY ACTIVITIES

Vocabulary Check

1.	c	5.	d
2.	g	6.	h
3.	b	7.	e
4.	a		

Completion

1. data, cross-cultural, description
2. ethnographer, system, perspective
3. archaeology, ethnology, linguistic

SELF-TEST

Objective Questions

Page numbers refer to the textbook.

1. b (Objective 1; pages 8–9, 21–25)
2. a (Objective 2; page 8)
3. a (Objective 2; page 25)
4. b (Objective 3; page 8; video program)
5. d (Objective 4; pages 8–10; video program)
6. c (Objective 5; page 13)
7. a (Objective 6; page 21)
8. c (Objective 6; page 21)
9. b (Objective 7; page 12)
10. d (Objective 7; pages 26–27; video program)

Short-Answer Essay Questions

1. Summarize the events that occurred when the British established a colony on land previously inhabited only by the Tasmanian aborigines.

   Your answer should include:

   - Diseases introduced by the British killed large numbers of the existing population.

   - Many Tasmanians were abused by members of the "superior" culture.

   - The introduction of sheep grazing on a wide scale rendered the region unsuitable for hunting as traditionally practiced by the Tasmanians.

   - As a result of severe disruption of their culture, the people died out in just a few years.

2. How does anthropology differ from other social sciences in its approach to studying people?

   Your answer should include:

   - Anthropologists are generalists who look at the broad bases of human behavior rather than at any one aspect.

- Anthropology is unique among the social sciences because it is based on the study of human behavior and biology in all known societies—both present and past—rather than on the study of recent European and North American societies.

3. List and briefly describe the three specializations within the field of cultural anthropology.

   Your answer should include:

   - Archaeology, which usually focuses on ancient cultures, studies material remains to learn about past lifestyles and cultural patterns.

   - Linguistic anthropology studies languages by developing accurate descriptions of words and how they are used, and by carefully constructing the history of individual languages.

   - Ethnology is based on historical and contemporary studies of specific cultures; it concentrates on studying human behavior and makes comparisons between cultures to arrive at more general principles about human behavior and culture.

4. Give at least one reason anthropological research is important in today's world.

   Your answer should include some of the following:

   - North Americans now live in a global community in which all people are interdependent. A knowledge of other people and their cultures is essential if we are to make intelligent decisions and act wisely in our business, political, and social relationships with them. Therefore, such understanding of other peoples and cultures is a basic survival skill for daily interactions of worldwide communication and travel.

   - Rapid changes occurring in our own and other societies require better understanding of the principles underlying the behavior of people in their cultures and societies.

   - Changes occurring in relatively isolated traditional societies may cause many such societies to disappear as they adopt Western lifestyles. The disappearance of any culture (such as the Tasmanians in the nineteenth century) is an irreplaceable loss.

The Nature of Culture 2

Assignments

Before viewing the video program	• Read the Overview and the Learning Objectives for this lesson. Use the Learning Objectives to guide your reading, viewing, and thinking. • Read textbook Chapter 2, "The Nature of Culture," pages 30–53. • Read Background Notes 2A, "Aspects of Culture and Society"; 2B, "The Txukarrame of Brazil"; and 2C, "The Boran," in this study-guide lesson.

View video program 2, "The Nature of Culture"

After viewing the video program	• Review the terms used in this lesson. In addition to those terms in the Learning Objectives, you should be familiar with these:

        adaptation   pluralistic societies
        enculturation   social structure
        gender   subculture

• Review the reading assignments for this lesson.
• Complete each of the Study Activities and the Self-Test in this study-guide lesson; check your answers with the Answer Key at the end of this lesson.
• According to your instructor's assignment or your own interests, complete one or more of the Suggested Activities. You also may be interested in the readings listed at the end of Chapter 2 in the textbook.

Overview

Every field of knowledge possesses certain key concepts or understandings that are crucial to its full appreciation. For example, the concept of "number" is essential to understanding mathematics, "element" to chemistry, and "force" to physics. Anthropology is no exception. As a branch of the social sciences that attempts to understand and explain human behavior, anthropology, too, has basic ideas crucial to any study of the discipline.

Two especially important concepts you should understand from the beginning of your study of anthropology are *culture* and *society*. Although those terms are already familiar to you, you probably don't use them in the same sense that they are used by anthropologists.

Before you begin your study of this lesson, you might find it helpful to think about the popular meanings of *culture* and *society* and be aware that these two words will take on more complex dimensions for you throughout the rest of this course. *Culture* means much more than manners and the arts; *society* involves more than a select and highly publicized status group. You should note also that *culture* and *society* have distinct meanings. The two words are not, strictly speaking, interchangeable. However, they *are* related, because culture cannot exist without society, and every human society has a culture.

This lesson will introduce you to the anthropological definitions of culture and society and to some of the many varieties of cultures throughout the world. You will also learn some universal characteristics of cultures and how culture profoundly influences every significant aspect of life in all societies.

By the end of this lesson, you probably will realize that you truly are a "person of culture," if not in the popular sense, at least in the anthropologist's view. But, then, so is every other human on Earth today.

Video Program: The ever-shrinking world is a backdrop for this study of the diversity of cultures that have evolved, flourished, and, in some instances, died in ages past and present. The learning of behavior, beliefs, attitudes, and skills is illustrated by scenes of !Kung hunters. Human beings are shown to be dependent upon culture's customs and patterns, not only for physical survival, but for order and tranquillity. The program also illustrates how symbols, such as the wooden posts and body painting of the Txukarrame and other Indians of the Amazon River basin, play an important role in each specific culture. Film of traditional and modern Boran of Kenya shows that cultures are always changing. The need to understand how differing values and beliefs meet the needs of specific cultures is seen in contrasting examples from other cultures. The program concludes by showing the devastating results of one culture's inability to adapt, prompting us to realize that the loss affects us all.

As you view the video program, look for:

- the universal needs fulfilled by all cultures.

- examples of how culture is "learned" and symbolic.

- an example of ethnocentrism from one of the first European contacts with the New World.

- the culture of the Indians of the Xingu River region of Brazil. In particular, note the symbolism of the *kuarupe* ceremony and the purposes of the ceremony.

- the Boran culture and how it illustrates that cultures are integrated and change.

- scenes showing the great variety of human cultures, as revealed in clothing, ceremonies and rituals, ways of finding and eating food, and ways of organizing members of societies into families and work groups.

- the crisis faced by Indian groups in Brazil.

Learning Objectives

When you have completed all assignments in this lesson, you should be able to:

1. Compare Tylor's definition of culture with a modern definition of the term. TEXTBOOK PAGE 32; BACKGROUND NOTES 2A

2. Explain what anthropologists mean when they say that culture is "shared." TEXTBOOK PAGES 32–37; BACKGROUND NOTES 2A

3. Define society and explain its relationship to culture. TEXTBOOK PAGES 32–37; BACKGROUND NOTES 2A

4. Explain what anthropologists mean when they say culture is "learned" and based on symbols. TEXTBOOK PAGES 37–39; VIDEO PROGRAM; BACKGROUND NOTES 2A

5. Define integration as a characteristic of culture and recognize that cultures can tolerate some internal inconsistencies. TEXTBOOK PAGES 39–41; VIDEO PROGRAM; BACKGROUND NOTES 2A

6. Explain how adaptation is an important aspect of human culture. TEXTBOOK PAGES 46–47; VIDEO PROGRAM; BACKGROUND NOTES 2A

7. Recognize that all cultures change over time. TEXTBOOK PAGE 47; VIDEO PROGRAM; BACKGROUND NOTES 2C

8. Explain how culture must balance the needs of both individuals and groups if a society is to survive. TEXTBOOK PAGES 48–49

9. Contrast ethnocentrism and cultural relativism. TEXTBOOK PAGES 49–51; VIDEO PROGRAM

10. Describe a standard for evaluating the success of a culture that avoids the extremes of ethnocentrism and cultural relativism. TEXTBOOK PAGES 49–51; BACKGROUND NOTES 2A

ASPECTS OF CULTURE AND SOCIETY

We are all bearers of culture. We carry with us an intricate set of rules for appropriate behavior, as well as instructions on how to survive in our social and physical environment. We can use and manufacture tools. We also have coherent and unified explanations for how the world came to be the way it is and for our place in it. We can communicate our understanding of the world with others like us. These are all aspects of culture. Anthropologists sometimes speak of culture as "patterns" for behavior, meaning that a *culture* consists of all one needs to know to behave as a member of a particular society is expected to behave.

We acquire this knowledge as members of society. We are *enculturated* as members of social groups. Culture is not invented anew by each new baby that is born. It is accumulated and transmitted to each new member of the group. This process is not always a conscious one, and sometimes the individual is not aware of the extent to which culture influences his or her behavior.

A *society* is a group of people sharing a common culture and locality. Every society has institutions for enculturating its members. Individuals first learn about their cultural traditions as members of a family. Later, they may learn by observing people outside the family or through specially established institutions, such as apprenticeships or schools.

Anthropologists sometimes also use the term *culture* to refer to a specific cultural system, as when William A. Haviland, author of the textbook for this course, refers to the culture of the Kapauku Papuans (pages 39–41). However, it is sometimes difficult to understand the difference between society and culture when culture is used to describe specific societies. It is simplest to think of culture as the total pattern of human behavior, and society as a group of people who behave according to a set of cultural assumptions. One anthropologist has suggested that culture is like a musical composition and society is like the orchestra that performs it.

It is not quite that simple, of course, since not all social groups are societies. Students in a classroom are a social group behaving according to a set of cultural assumptions. They are members of a society, but they do not constitute a society, according to most anthropological definitions. A society is generally defined as a group that has all of the institutions necessary to sustain itself through time, including ways of obtaining food, protecting its members from environmental extremes and other hazards, reproducing itself, and passing on cultural traditions to new members.

Cultural knowledge underlies all areas of our lives, from getting and preparing food to gaining favor with influential elders in the community. It guides our behavior in economic, political, and other spheres. Within a given cultural tradition, different aspects are likely to form a coherent system; that is, they are *integrated*. In North American society, for example, the predominance of nuclear families may be related to geography and to social mobility, which in turn is related to industrialization.

In this course, there will be many other examples of integration among different institutions within a society or cultural system. However, there is *variability* within any culture, more than many early anthropologists expected or believed.

Intracultural variability is especially marked in complex societies such as in the United States. For example, not everyone in U.S. society lives the same way. The life of an inner-city family will not be the same as that of a farm family, and neither will duplicate the experience of a wealthy jet-setter. Religious institutions in the United States range from the simple practices of the Quakers (Friends), who have no formal creed or other ecclesiastical forms, to the Roman Catholic church, with its hierarchical character and long tradition of emphasis upon ritual and symbol. Yet, geography, economic status, and religion notwithstanding, most of the people in the United States share common cultural assumptions. They agree that mashed potatoes should be eaten with a fork instead of hands. They drive cars on the right side of the road and recognize that a red light means "stop," while a green light means "go."

They even generalize this very useful cultural information by understanding that when people speak of having the "green light," they can go ahead with a project or an action they have been considering.

When there is much diversity, as in U.S. society, it is appropriate to speak of *subcultural variation*, a term used to refer to groups that have an identity that distinguishes them from others in the society but that still partake of a common cultural heritage and participate in some of the society's overarching institutions. For example, Vietnamese who have immigrated to the United States may retain their way of preparing food, maintaining a household, and observing religious beliefs, but they are subject to the same federal, state, and local laws and systems of taxation as everyone else in the United States.

Even in small-scale societies, which anthropologists once thought of as uniform, there is a degree of variation. Young people do not have access to the esoteric knowledge of elders, and men and women may have different roles and associated cultural knowledge. Also, any cultural system contains and can tolerate, up to a point, inherent inconsistencies and conflicts. Folk wisdom in U.S. society advises both that "a penny saved is a penny earned" and that "you can't take it with you." These inconsistencies usually do not cause great difficulty for members of U.S. society, since they can apply whichever rule is compatible with their goals. They learned how and when to apply the rules at the same time they learned the rules.

Most anthropologists consider the environment to be an important influence on culture and a factor in culture change and adaptation. When anthropologists go into the field, they note the physical environment, as well as the customs and social institutions of the people they are studying. However, the physical environment is not the only influence on the development of specific cultures. The influence of other factors on culture is demonstrated by the fact that different groups have different solutions for problems posed by the same environment.

The video program describes in some detail the cultural practices of two groups, the Txukarrame of Brazil (and similar Indian groups in the same region) and the Boran of Ethiopia and Kenya.

The Txukarrame and the Boran cultures represent different adaptations to two vastly different types of environment. In the following descriptions, note the role of the environment in these cultures.

Background Notes 2B

THE TXUKARRAME OF BRAZIL

Several closely related Indian groups live near the Xingu River of Brazil, a river that runs into the Amazon. One group, the Txukarrame, typifies the cultural practices of these Indians. They use slash-and-burn techniques for growing food. First, they cut down trees in the forest to form a garden plot, then plant it with manioc, a bitter tuber that provides nutritious starch. They plant season after season, until the land begins to lose its fertility. Then they clear a new plot of land, allowing the forest to reclaim the older one. This form of agriculture is well suited to the forest environment, because it does not deplete the soil and forest resources as much as more intensive forms of agriculture. Large-scale agriculture using commercial fertilizer and heavy equipment destroys delicate forest soils. Slash-and-burn agriculture allows the Txukarrame to live close to the forest, where they can hunt for monkeys and other small animals and gather honey from wild bees. The Txukarrame also fish with bows and arrows from dugout canoes.

Although the Txukarrame life may appear simple, carving a living out of the forest requires many skills and a large stock of cultural knowledge. Young males must learn to hunt and fish. Girls must learn to prepare manioc, which is poisonous if not properly processed.

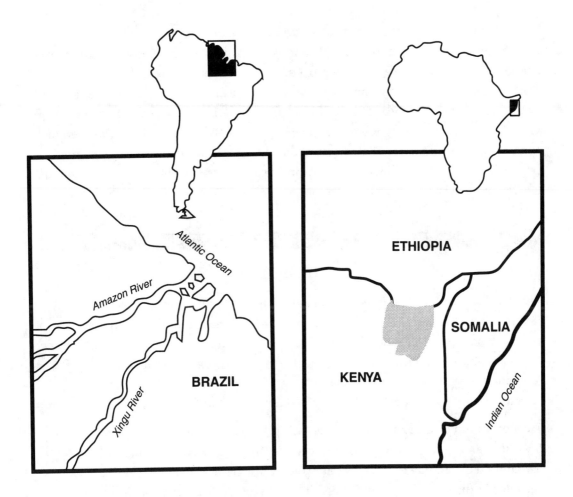

Figures 2.1 and 2.2: The Txukarrame of Brazil's Amazon River Basin and the Boran of Kenya are societies whose cultures reflect different environmental conditions.

Young boys and girls of the Txukarrame society learn the cultural knowledge they must have by watching their parents and other adults, but their training becomes more formal at adolescence. At this time, they go into a period of seclusion that marks their passage from childhood to adulthood, and they learn their place in society. The *kuarupe* ceremony symbolizes the permanence of Txukarrame society and the link of present-day members with their ancestors. Young women coming out of seclusion during the *kuarupe* ceremony symbolically take the place of members of the village who have died. This ceremony perpetuates cultural knowledge by providing a context for teaching all that people must know and do as members of Txukarrame society.

Background Notes 2C

THE BORAN

The Boran live in southern Ethiopia and northern Kenya, an environment entirely different from the forests of Brazil. They are pastoral nomads, meaning that they are herders who move from place to place. The Boran live in a sparse environment, to which they have adapted culturally. Anthropologist Asmarom Legesse writes, "Their entire sociopolitical system is so flexible that it allows them to circumvent all but the most extreme droughts and to rehabilitate their communities and herds after every disaster."

The Boran herd cattle, and cow's milk is their principal source of food. They use their few sheep and goats primarily for meat and sometimes buy grains from neighboring agricultural communities. But they value their cattle more than any other livestock. As noted in the video program, the Boran believe that humans and their cattle were created at the same time, whereas other animals were created later. They can trace the pedigrees of their cattle, and no important ceremony can be conducted without cattle sacrifice.

Sharing and openness are pervasive aspects of Boran society. Their dwellings have no doors, they willingly share their food, and they readily answer questions, even when asked by strangers. The social organization is very flexible. Local communities consist of a few families that come together for a single season. Each camp has a leader whose primary responsibility is to call together meetings of elders whose advice governs the leader's ability to keep order in the camp. The camp leader is chosen on the basis of seniority, but seniority is determined by lineage or kinship, not by age.

The Boran live in huts that are easily carried from place to place, since they are built of branches covered with skins. The entire possessions of a household can be loaded onto a single camel.

Every year, Boran herdsmen return to their ancestral wells, when temporary watering places dry up. These wells, not their huts, are considered home. Wells are owned by lineages and controlled by the senior male member of the lineage. Wells are a kind of gathering place where kin can exchange information. The wells are important sources of water in an area that is plagued by recurring drought, but they are also centers of social activity.

There is division of labor by sex among the Boran. Women construct houses, process dairy products, and manufacture leather goods. Woodcarving, care of cattle, performance of ritual, and political and military activities are carried out by men. Training of boys and girls is informal and emphasizes practical aspects of Boran life. Girls learn how to thatch a roof and milk cows, tend a hearth, and care for children. All children must learn how to manage cattle, how to find water, and how to live through a drought. Additionally, boys are taught tribal lore and religious beliefs, as well as an understanding of relationships with neighboring tribes.

The video program shows how Boran beliefs about cattle and herding practices are integrated with other social institutions and how all members work to help the group survive in a hostile environment. However, the Boran way of life is threatened by modernization: pressures to settle in one place, give up traditional ways of training and send their children to schools, pay taxes, and fit into either the Kenyan or Ethiopian systems of government.

The way in which the Boran adapt to these pressures will be determined, in part, by their cultural assumptions. A change in one part of a cultural system has implications for the rest. Whether the Boran can retain a cultural identity and viability as a society in the face of changes being forced upon them remains to be seen.

Study Activities

Vocabulary Check

Check your understanding of terms by writing the letter of the appropriate definition in the space next to the corresponding term. Check your choices with the Answer Key at the end of the lesson.

_____	1. Edward Burnett Tylor	_____	8. integration
_____	2. society	_____	9. adaptation
_____	3. social structure	_____	10. ethnocentrism
_____	4. culture	_____	11. cultural relativism
_____	5. subculture	_____	12. gender
_____	6. enculturation	_____	13. pluralistic societies
_____	7. language		

a. societies with a diversity of cultural patterns

b. a set of rules or standards that, when acted upon by the members, produces behaviors within the range of variation the group considers proper and acceptable

c. the most important symbolic aspect of culture

d. wrote the first comprehensive definition of culture

e. the belief that one's own culture is superior to all others

f. term used both for the process and the results of a process by which organisms (or cultures) achieve a beneficial adjustment to their environment

g. a group of people occupying a specific locality who are dependent upon each other for survival and who share a common culture

h. the relationships of groups within a society that hold it together

i. a basis for scientific evaluation of a culture

j. the concept that a culture can be evaluated only according to its own standards and values

k. the process by which culture is transmitted from one generation to the next

l. the tendency for all aspects of a culture to function as an interrelated whole

m. a distinctive set of standards and behavior patterns by which a group operates within a larger society

n. meanings assigned by cultures to the biological differentiation of the sexes

o. outlined three levels of needs that every culture must resolve

Completion

Fill each blank with the most appropriate term from the list immediately following that paragraph.

1.   When members of a society share a common _____, they can usually _____ the actions of others in a particular set of circumstances. Although a society may have a common _____ tradition, not all members have _____ roles.

cultural	different	social
culture	language	uniform
control	predict	

2.   Culture is accumulated and _____ to each new generation. The chief means by which culture is thus shared is _____. Although all aspects of the culture are _____, their "harmony" need not be perfect. There is usually room for individual _____ in a culture; thus, there is always potential for _____.

change	integrated	related
differences	language	transmitted

3.   Animals that have survived environmental changes over many generations have done so by developing _____ characteristics that result in a _____ adjustment. Humans, however, depend primarily on cultural _____ for survival.

adaptation	integration
beneficial	physical

4.   The viewpoint that "anything is permissible" is an extreme form of cultural _____ . A more moderate view, suggested by Goldschmidt, suggests that the success of a culture can be judged by how well it satisfies the physical and psychological _____ of its members. The culture should ensure that the society _____ in a way that is reasonably _____ for its members.

ethnocentrism	needs	relativism
fulfilling	pluralism	survives

Self-Test

Objective Questions

Select the one best answer.

1. A key part of Edward Burnett Tylor's classic definition of culture is that culture is
    a. a group of people who occupy a specific locality and depend upon each other for survival.
    b. a set of rules or standards that, when acted upon by members of a society, produces behavior members consider proper and acceptable.
    c. a complex whole that includes knowledge, belief, art, law, morals, custom, and any other capabilities and habits.
    d. the observable behaviors that reveal the relationships between various groups within the larger society.

2. A key part of William Haviland's definition of culture is that culture is
    a. a group of people who occupy a specific locality and depend upon each other for survival.
    b. a set of rules or standards that, when acted upon by the members of a society, produces behavior members consider proper and acceptable.
    c. a complex whole that includes knowledge, belief, art, law, morals, custom, and any other capabilities and habits.
    d. the observable behaviors that reveal the relationships between various groups within the larger society.

3. A culture is "shared" in the sense that
    a. elements of a culture are frequently passed on to societies in other areas.
    b. people in the same locality learn to work together.
    c. some members of the group will try to teach their beliefs to others.
    d. members of the group generally hold the same ideals, values, and standards.

4. "A group of people who occupy a specific locality and who share common cultural traditions" is Haviland's definition of

   a. society.
   b. subculture.
   c. culture.
   d. social structure.

5. In the process called *enculturation,*

   a. the individual flees from the influence of culture.
   b. one learns the culturally appropriate ways of satisfying one's needs.
   c. one can select any of the available subcultural variations.
   d. the major traits of the culture are inherited biologically.

6. Language is the most important

   a. ethnocentric aspect of a culture.
   b. social aspect of a culture.
   c. adaptive aspect of a culture.
   d. symbolic aspect of a culture.

7. Anthropologists have found that the parts of a culture tend to function as an interrelated whole. This phenomenon is called

   a. enculturation.
   b. harmony.
   c. integration.
   d. pluralism.

8. Cultural adaptation, as defined in the textbook, includes all of the following aspects EXCEPT

   a. the process by which organisms make a beneficial adjustment to an available environment.
   b. the results achieved through changes in biological or physical structure over many generations.
   c. possession of characteristics that enable organisms to overcome hazards and secure needed resources.
   d. the results of the process by which the adjustment was made.

9. The human species is unique among animals in its adaptations because humans

    a. have not needed to adapt to varying environments.
    b. have usually made cultural adaptations.
    c. depend primarily on biological adaptation.
    d. make adaptive adjustments only to changes in the natural environment.

10. Of the following factors, the one that has forced cultural changes in Boran society is

    a. introduction of metal tools.
    b. physical changes in the environment.
    c. new patterns of education for youth.
    d. a breakup of kinship and lineage patterns.

11. The example in the textbook describing the plight of nomadic tribes in the region south of the Sahara illustrates that

    a. modernization is usually beneficial if introduced quickly.
    b. enforced cultural change may threaten a society's survival.
    c. introducing a market economy into a society can overcome environmental problems.
    d. enculturation cannot take place in a nomadic society.

12. If the culture emphasizes the needs of the society at the expense of individual needs and interests, the danger

    a. is comparatively little, because survival of the society is assured.
    b. of social upset is great, because a culture is usually unable to affect the values and standards of large numbers of people.
    c. is slight, because people within a society do not recognize that their own activities are restricted.
    d. from excessive stress and alienation experienced by many individuals is great.

13. In general, the most important incentive for members of the society who adhere to its cultural standards is

    a. economic advantage.
    b. greater freedom of action.
    c. social approval and acceptance.
    d. leadership positions.

14. The belief that one's own culture is superior to any other in all ways is called

    a. ethnocentrism.
    b. cultural relativism.
    c. cultural materialism.
    d. maladaptation.

15. The view that individual cultures should be evaluated only according to their own standards

    a. is generally not held today, although nineteenth-century observers favored it.
    b. was introduced as a reaction against cultural relativism.
    c. was introduced as a reaction against ethnocentrism.
    d. is impossible in light of subcultural variation.

16. Walter Goldschmidt's approach to evaluating cultures is concerned mainly with how the culture

    a. promotes technological advancement.
    b. satisfies physical and psychological needs.
    c. uses environmental resources.
    d. encourages literacy and education.

Short-Answer Essay Questions

1. Briefly contrast Sir Edward Burnett Tylor's definition of *culture* with that suggested by Haviland in the textbook. What is the most significant difference between the two definitions?

2. Summarize the characteristics of culture that have been observed by anthropologists to be common to all cultures.

3. According to Haviland, what are the dangers of an excessive tendency to meet only the needs of the society or only the needs of the individual?

4. Contrast the type of environments to which the Txukarrame and Boran societies have adapted, indicating how they have adapted, and briefly summarize the cultural threat that each society faces today.

Suggested Activities

1. Write an essay contrasting the popular uses of the terms *society* and *culture* with their meanings in anthropology.

2. Try to recall and describe in a list your initial reactions to the societies you viewed in the video program for this lesson, and for those you read about in Chapter 2 of the textbook and the Background Notes. Examine your reactions for any evidence of ethnocentric attitudes—judging these societies by the norms and values you have learned in your own society. Conversely, are you bending over backward to achieve the kind of cultural-relativism attitude that Haviland describes as "anything goes"?

   Write a brief summary of this exercise, and describe any steps you can take now to better understand a society by applying Walter Goldschmidt's standard (described in the textbook, pages 50–51).

3. In addition to Tylor's and Haviland's definitions of culture, anthropologists have suggested many other definitions. Using library resources, find at least five other definitions of culture and write a brief paper comparing the definitions. Comment on why you feel it has been difficult to develop one definition that is generally accepted.

Answer Key

STUDY ACTIVITIES

Vocabulary Check

1. d	5. m	8. l	11. j
2. g	6. k	9. f	12. n
3. h	7. c	10. e	13. a
4. b			

Completion

1. culture, predict, cultural, uniform
2. transmitted, language, integrated, differences, change
3. physical, beneficial, adaptation
4. relativism, needs, survives, fulfilling

SELF-TEST

Objective Questions

(Page numbers refer to the textbook.)

1. c (Objective 1; page 32)
2. b (Objective 1; page 32)
3. d (Objective 2; page 32)
4. a (Objective 3; page 33)
5. b (Objective 4; pages 37–38; video program)
6. d (Objective 4; page 39; video program)
7. c (Objective 5; page 39; video program; Background Notes 2A)
8. b (Objective 6; page 46)
9. b (Objective 6; page 46; video program)
10. c (Objective 7; video program; Background Notes 2C)
11. b (Objective 7; page 47)
12. d (Objective 8; page 49)

13. c (Objective 8; page 48)
14. a (Objective 9; page 49; video program)
15. c (Objective 9; page 50; video program)
16. b (Objective 10; pages 50–51)

Short-Answer Essay Questions

1. Briefly contrast Sir Edward Burnett Tylor's definition of *culture* with that suggested by Haviland in the textbook. What is the most significant difference between the two definitions?

    Your answer should include:

    - Tylor's definition: "That complex whole which includes knowledge, belief, art, law, morals, custom and any other capabilities and habits acquired by man as a member of society."

    - Haviland's definition: "A set of rules or standards that, when acted upon by the members of a society, produce behavior that falls within a range of variance the members consider proper and acceptable."

    - Haviland's definition reflects the emphasis upon values and beliefs, rather than on observable behavior, as the essential aspect of culture.

2. Summarize the characteristics of culture that have been observed by anthropologists to be common to all cultures.

    Your answer should include:

    - Culture is shared by all the members of the society.

    - Culture is learned as a person grows up in the culture.

    - Culture is based on symbols and transmitted from one generation to the next, primarily through symbols; language is the most important symbolic aspect of culture.

    - Culture is integrated. Although some individual differences are permitted, all parts of the culture must be more or less harmonious with each other.

    - Culture changes over time.

3. According to Haviland, what are the dangers of an excessive tendency to meet only the needs of the society or only the needs of the individual?

Your answer should include:

- If society's needs are met at too great an expense of individual needs, the individual is placed under excessive stress, which may lead to antisocial behavior and eventually a loss of social cohesion.

- If individual needs are met at too great an expense of society's needs, the result can be social breakdown and violent change.

4. Contrast the type of environments to which the Txukarrame and Boran societies have adapted, indicating how they have adapted, and briefly summarize the cultural threat that each society faces today.

Your answer should include:

- The Txukarrame have adapted to the forest lands of Brazil, becoming horticulturists, or farmers, but they also hunt and fish.

- The Txukarrame and the other Indian cultures of the region are being pushed away from their forest lands and even hunted and killed by people seeking to claim the land for other purposes.

- The Boran live in a sparse environment in Kenya and Ethiopia that periodically suffers drought. They are nomadic, primarily herding cattle, although they also raise a few sheep and goats.

- The Boran are under strong pressure from Ethiopian and Kenyan governments to give up their nomadic patterns to settle and establish villages. Among other requirements of the governments are formal education for the children in government-run schools. These requirements are in conflict with the social structure and values of the Boran and would weaken or replace the practices by which their young are enculturated.

How Cultures 3
Are Studied

Assignments

Before viewing the video program	• Read the Overview and the Learning Objectives for this lesson. Use the Learning Objectives to guide your reading, viewing, and thinking. • Review Chapters 1 and 2 in the textbook, particularly pages 11–26, 41–46, and 49–51. • Read Background Notes 3A, "Studying the Yanomamo"; 3B, "Coping with Ethical Problems"; and 3C, "Overcoming Limits and Responding to Change," in this study-guide lesson.

View video program 3, *"How Cultures Are Studied"*

After viewing the video program	• Review the terms used in this lesson. In addition to those terms in the Learning Objectives, you should be familiar with these:

> cross-cultural comparison   holistic perspective
> cultural relativism   participant observation
> ethnographic present

• Review the reading assignments for this lesson.
• Complete each of the Study Activities and the Self-Test in this study-guide lesson; check your answers with the Answer Key at the end of this lesson.
• According to your instructor's assignment or your own interests, complete one or more of the Suggested Activities. You also may be interested in the readings listed at the end of Chapters 1 and 2 in the textbook.

Overview

The first two lessons introduced you to anthropologists such as Franz Boas, Margaret Mead, and Bronislaw Malinowski, whose contributions to this discipline are respected deeply by all workers in the field. You also read in the textbook brief firsthand accounts from ethnologists Mac Marshall and Annette B. Weiner of their fieldwork experiences. In addition, Chapter 1 of the textbook described the ideal of scientific objectivity and scientific method that all of these (and virtually all other) anthropologists seek to maintain and stated that, at best, applying the methods of science to present-day cultures is difficult. At the same time, such study must be exciting and rewarding for those who seek it out.

In this lesson, the video program concentrates on the anthropologist as ethnographer in the field. Napoleon Chagnon spent nearly two years living with, and learning about, a society whose people call themselves the Yanomamo. He recorded his experiences and findings in a book and a sampling of his activities on film. His film provides glimpses of how the anthropologist must gather, record, and, finally, understand or interpret thousands of details. The process is painstaking, time consuming, and laborious, and, as you will see, it can be frustrating and even dangerous for the ethnographer. Forming a hypothesis and testing it may demand all of the ethnographer's skills and energy for months or even years.

Chagnon was both an observer and a participant in Yanomamo society, adopting some of their customs so that he would be accepted and trusted by them. He faced up to the thorny problems that confront the researcher who works and lives in a society that is comparatively untouched by other cultures. Chagnon's participation required a "give-and-take" type of trading. There was danger that he could introduce new elements into the lives of the Yanomamo that could ultimately lead to serious disruptions. This lesson asks you to consider some of the ethical, philosophical, and personal dilemmas faced by ethnographers as they study in the field.

Most of the other lessons in this course will describe societies, cultures, and cross-cultural patterns found in the human family. Your interest will be increased when you recall that nearly all the descriptions, accounts, photos, films, and videos brought together in the materials for this course were gathered by researchers, such as Napoleon Chagnon, who overcame innumerable difficulties to make new contributions to our understanding.

Video Program: Anthropologist Napoleon Chagnon describes his apprehension as he canoes up the Orinoco River for an ethnographic study of the Yanomamo Indians of Venezuela. Chagnon tells how he traded goods for information, always following the customs dictated for visitors. He describes the major research he pursued for years and shows how the ethnographer must put aside prejudices and actively participate in a society to gather the most comprehensive picture of the culture. Film shows Chagnon sleeping, eating, and sharing hallucinogenic drugs with the Yanomamo tribesmen; making friends and enemies; and, ultimately, being accepted by the tribe. Finally, Chagnon emphasizes the importance of appreciating the value of other cultures. The program also considers ethical issues inherent in participant-observation research.

As you view the program, look for:

- Chagnon's description of fieldwork and participant observation.
- these unfamiliar names: Mishimishimabowei-Teri (the village); Nanokawa, Dedeheiwa, Rerebawa, Moawa (villagers), *hekura* (spirits).
- the importance of generosity and reciprocity to the Yanomamo.
- cultural practices that Napoleon Chagnon adopted to make the villagers accept and trust him.
- the techniques used to develop records of kinship and social organization.
- examples of the fierce and combative behavior of the Yanomamo.
- Chagnon's statements about the importance of cultural relativism.

Learning Objectives

When you have completed all assignments in this lesson, you should be able to:

1. Contrast *ethnology* and *archaeology*. TEXTBOOK PAGES 11–14, 18–20

2. Identify the difference between ethnology and ethnography. TEXTBOOK PAGES 13–14, 18–20; VIDEO PROGRAM

3. Describe the anthropologist's commitment to a scientific approach to studying culture. TEXTBOOK PAGES 20–25, 49–51; BACKGROUND NOTES 3B AND 3C

4. Explain how ethnographic studies are important to the understanding of cultures. TEXTBOOK PAGES 13–14, 18–20; VIDEO PROGRAM

5. Put in the correct order and define *theory, hypothesis,* and *hypothesis testing*. TEXTBOOK PAGES 20–21

6. Describe ways fieldworkers attempt to deal with the problems of cultural bias and subjectivity. TEXTBOOK PAGES 20–25, 41–46, 49–51; VIDEO PROGRAM; BACKGROUND NOTES 3A, 3B, AND 3C

7. List aspects of the Yanomamo culture studied by Napoleon Chagnon. VIDEO PROGRAM; BACKGROUND NOTES 3A AND 3B

8. Discuss the ethical questions raised by studying a traditional group where the fieldworker could be a source of change and modernization. TEXTBOOK PAGE 26; VIDEO PROGRAM; BACKGROUND NOTES 3B.

STUDYING THE YANOMAMO

Reports of fieldwork among "primitive" people in exotic lands are part of anthropology's appeal for fledgling anthropologists and the public alike. But the reality of doing fieldwork is often more harsh than glamorous. In his book, *Yanomamo: The Fierce People* (New York: Holt, Rinehart and Winston, 1977), Napoleon Chagnon describes his first meeting with the Yanomamo, the people he was to live among and study:

> I looked up and gasped when I saw a dozen burly, naked, filthy, hideous men staring at us down the shafts of their drawn arrows! Immense wads of green tobacco were stuck between their lower teeth and lips, making them look even more hideous, and strands of dark-green slime dripped or hung from their noses. . . . My next discovery was that there were a dozen or so vicious, underfed dogs snapping at my legs, circling me as if I were going to be their next meal. I just stood there, holding my notebook, helpless and pathetic. Then the stench of the decaying vegetation and filth struck me and I almost got sick. I was horrified. What sort of welcome was this for the person who came here to live with you and learn your way of life, to become friends with you? (p. 5)

Chagnon stayed among the Yanomamo for 19 months, learning to understand their way of life and eventually to view some of them as friends. He also returned to the field many times to conduct detailed studies. As a result of his research, Chagnon came to view the Yanomamo way of life as being a coherent, internally consistent way of coping with the Yanomamo people's tropical forest environment and their experience of the world.

The Yanomamo live in a forest area of southern Venezuela and adjacent portions of northern Brazil in widely scattered villages of about 80 people. Their territory is hilly terrain that is difficult to cross on foot. During the wet season, in summer, many trails between villages are covered with water, and rivers in the area become impassable torrents. Even in the dry season, the dense forest forms a canopy that keeps the sun from reaching the ground. Thorns, snakes, and small biting insects also make travel through the region uncomfortable or hazardous.

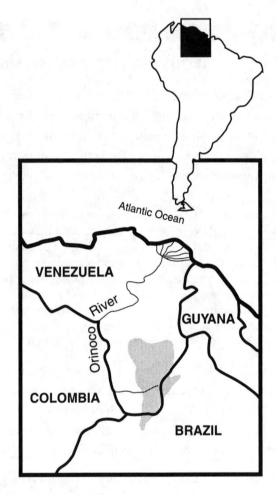

Figure 3.1: Anthropologist Napoleon Chagnon studied the Yanomamo, isolated tribal peoples living in the forest headwaters of the Orinoco River.

Yanomamo tools are simple. They hunt with bows and arrows tipped with *curare*, a poison obtained from a jungle vine. They make fire with wood drills and fashion knives from the incisor teeth of a large rodent, the *agouti*. They also make crude, poorly fired clay pots, which break very easily. Women, who are considered to be very clumsy, are rarely allowed to handle them. Consequently, men do the cooking that requires use of the clay pots.

The Yanomamo live in circular houses constructed from poles, vines, and leaves. They make simple, temporary canoes from the bark of a tree.

The forest furnishes many varieties of plants and animals that the Yanomamo use for food. They hunt monkeys, wild turkeys and pigs, armadillos, anteaters, tapirs, deer, a small species of alligator, small rodents, and several species of small birds. They also gather palm fruits, Brazil nuts, and edible roots. In addition, they eat wild honey and several species of grubs, which are the fat, white larvae of certain kinds of insects.

Most food comes from simple farming. The Yanomamo clear a section of forest, plant a garden, then continue to plant crops there until the soil begins to lose its fertility. When this happens, they clear a new garden spot. In these gardens, the Yanomamo plant bananas and plantain, a starchy fruit similar to the banana. Important root crops are manioc, taro, and sweet potatoes that are boiled or roasted over coals. They also cultivate corn, tobacco, and cotton from which they make yarn fibers for hammocks.

Chagnon suggests that aggression is an important part of Yanomamo culture. Incidents of aggression described by Chagnon include wife beating, chest-pounding duels (in which two men hit each other in the chest with their fists), and fights with clubs and axes. In an axe fight, the men usually hit each other with the flat side of an axe, but this often causes serious injury. Warfare takes the form of raids, in which the object is to enter an enemy village, kill one or more of the men living there, and flee without being discovered. If members of the raided village do not retaliate in kind, they are considered cowardly. Chagnon reports that one village in the area he studied was raided twenty-five times in the 19 months he spent doing his fieldwork.

The Yanomamo believe it is in the "nature of man" to fight, because men were born "in the blood of the Moon." According to Yanomamo myth, Moon used to steal remains of the dead, so the original Yanomamo tribesmen shot him with arrows. When Moon's blood flowed over the earth, it became men who were warlike and fierce.

The Yanomamo spirit world is also potentially hostile, and Yanomamo shamans, who are healers and workers of magic, spend much of their time trying to bring these spirits under control. The men blow into their noses a hallucinogenic drug in the form of a dark green powder. Much of it, mixed with mucus, drips back out again. This mixture was the green slime that so startled Chagnon when he saw it hanging from the men's noses on his first visit to the Yanomamo. The drug is produced from the bark of a particular tree, the *ebene*, and, according to the Yanomamo, the drug produces colored visions and allows the user to get in touch with his *hekura*, miniature demons that live on rocks and mountains. As the drug begins to take effect, the men begin to chant to the *hekura*, inviting them to come and live in their chests. When a man can control a number of *hekura*, by luring them into his chest, he can become a shaman and heal the sick or work magic against the enemies of his people. Shamans send their *hekura* to capture the souls of enemy children and use magic to ward off the *hekura* of their enemies. When a Yanomamo child becomes ill, the illness is often thought to be caused by soul loss, brought about by *hekura* sent by an enemy.

Chagnon argues that these beliefs are consistent with the Yanomamo view of people as being fierce, living in a world dominated by warfare. He writes, "The . . . relationship between man and spirit is largely one of hostility" (p. 52).

He notes that this view permits the Yanomamo to deal with their forest environment and their experience of the world as a potentially hostile place, and he adds ". . . each individual Yanomamo enters the world with the physical, social, and ideological traditions at his disposal that will permit him to confront and adjust to the jungle [forest], his neighbors, and the demons that cause sickness" (p. 53).

The Yanomamo have changed considerably since Chagnon began studying them in 1964, largely because of missionary activity and the 1987 gold rush in Brazil. The anthropologist calls the gold rush "the most dramatic and devastating single event in recent Yanomamo history." Gold miners use hydraulic pumps that suck river bottoms bearing gold ore and pass the mud through troughs where toxic mercury compounds extract the gold from the mud. The poisoned residue is then allowed to flow back into the rivers, where it constitutes a hazard for both human and animal life.

More than a thousand Yanomamo in Brazil have died from diseases introduced through contact with gold miners, and others have been killed in direct confrontations. Air strips have been gouged out of the rain forests, and many Yanomamo have become dependent on handouts from the miners, so they no longer practice their traditional means of subsistence.

Yanomamo in Venezuela, where Chagnon studied, have been protected from gold miners by the government. However, missionaries in both Venezuela and Brazil pose a threat by distributing shotguns, which escalate the level of violence among males and radically alter traditional lines of authority.

Background Notes 3B

COPING WITH ETHICAL PROBLEMS

Chagnon was able to overcome his initial repugnance for the Yanomamo and conduct extensive fieldwork among them. But the problems in doing fieldwork do not end there. An anthropologist studying a group of people who are little known to outsiders collects information that may be harmful to the people under study if it is not treated carefully. Therefore, the anthropologist must abide by a professional standard of ethics designed to minimize potentially harmful effects of fieldwork.

In the video program, Chagnon says that he exchanged machetes and other goods for information, but adds that he is concerned about the impact of these exchanges on the Yanomamo culture. Each new implement introduced into a culture like that of the Yanomamo can have a major impact on the environment and disrupt traditional social relationships. For this reason, Chagnon tried to limit the amount and kinds of goods he offered the Yanomamo for exchange. In his book *Yanomamo*, Chagnon explains that tribesmen who live close to missions try to borrow shotguns from the missionaries, claiming to need them for hunting game. But the shotguns are often used in fights, giving one group an advantage over the other and escalating the violence. Even if the shotguns were used only for hunting, that might upset the Yanomamo people's adaptation to their environment.

The Yanomamo are limited in the amount of game they can take because of their reliance on the bow and arrow. Even though they are skilled hunters, they kill only enough game to meet their needs. With shotguns, they would be more efficient killers and, perhaps, deplete the forest of its game resources. If the Yanomamo overtaxed the forest's capacity to support life, they might be faced with starvation or the need for drastic change in their way of life. In the anthropological literature, there are many examples of people who have upset their delicate balance with the natural environment and subsequently faced population crises or famine.

Another ethical dilemma arises from the fact that anthropologists may have information, medicines, and other artifacts that could improve the health of the people being observed. Yet the anthropologists are not trained to diagnose illness or administer medications and do not have the financial resources to solve major health problems of people being studied.

Introducing new technology can also upset established social ties and alliances. If a missionary or anthropologist gives an axe or a steel knife to a young boy or outsider who, unknown to the anthropologist, is in the group only temporarily, he gives that person the means and prestige to challenge traditional authority. At the same time, customs for keeping the peace and ensuring the security of the group will be overthrown and hostilities may be escalated. Thus, a "generous" gesture can cause unintended harm.

Sometimes the mere presence of anthropologists can exert a disruptive influence upon the group. Chagnon mentions in the video program that each group wanted him to remain with them because they desired a monopoly on his trade goods. Having an anthropologist in the village can also bring prestige to its inhabitants, giving them power over their neighbors.

Anthropologists must always be aware of their potential for changing the groups they are studying and make every attempt to minimize harmful effects of their fieldwork. At the same time, anthropologists must avoid taking a proprietary attitude toward "their" people, resisting all change in an attempt to preserve their "laboratory."

All people change, of course. Change is a natural process that occurs within all human groups. Even people who seem to us to be "primitive" have undergone a long evolutionary history. Groups split apart and join with others. Climatic variations introduce new types of plants and animals into their environment and eliminate others, requiring new types of adaptations. The anthropologist cannot put a glass jar over a people to keep them "unchanged."

The term *ethnographic present* is used to convey the idea that an ethnography is a slice of history, a description of a particular group at a particular time. The group may change considerably when it is contacted by others after the anthropologist leaves the group. But ethnographic books and films are written in the present tense because they represent the "present" at the time the anthropologist conducted the study. Thus, cultures can be compared across barriers of time and space, and ethnographies can form the basis for ethnology. Their usefulness for cross-cultural comparison is limited only by the accuracy and thoroughness of the ethnographer.

Ethnographic fieldwork techniques can also be used for studying complex societies. Anthropologist William Pilcher made a widely acclaimed study of Portland longshoremen. James Spradley studied urban transients, and Hortense Powdermaker studied the Hollywood film industry in the 1940s. Today, studies are underway among such diverse populations as ethnic minorities, policemen, and professional athletes.

Anthropological fieldwork is an intensive research strategy producing information that would be missed by the sole use of questionnaires and other survey methods. For all of its hazards, frustrations, and discomforts, ethnographic fieldwork is considered the best way to find out how people really live.

Background Notes 3C

OVERCOMING LIMITS AND RESPONDING TO CHANGE

Although anthropologists try to be as free of cultural bias as possible, they are still products of their own culture. Anthropology as a discipline is a product of the Western tradition of scientific inquiry and, therefore, reflects our cultural assumption that research into human social interaction is both important and necessary.

As the field develops, theoretical assumptions underlying anthropological fieldwork change. Early in this century, anthropologists were very concerned with the question of defining "race," eventually identifying the term as a cultural concept, rather than as a biological one. More recently, they have become interested in the relationship of economics to other social institutions, and the degree of variability within cultures.

Anthropology itself changes in response to new developments within our society. Since the 1960s, recognition of the importance of women's contribution to society has increased decisively, and modern field studies are designed to get a more balanced overall picture of individual cultures. This change represents a significant shift in anthropological theory. Not only do women make up one half of society numerically, but they control important activities, such as birth and death rituals, and the economic contribution of women provides the material basis for other social expressions. For example, among many foragers, women contribute the major portion of the diet through gathering plant materials and, in most New Guinea groups, women grow the yams and pigs that are central to male displays of status. Even the sex or temperament of anthropologists can affect access to data. Men wouldn't be allowed to witness childbirth practices or women's rituals in many or most societies, and women may be barred from men's secret rituals.

Anthropologists must recognize that some limitations on the ability to collect data are beyond their control. All scientific research is limited in opportunities to observe naturally occurring phenomena. However, anthropologists try to overcome limitations by being as systematic and thorough as possible in collecting data.

Study Activities

Vocabulary Check

Check your understanding of terms by writing the letter of the appropriate definition in the space next to the corresponding term. Check your choices with the Answer Key at the end of the lesson.

_____ 1. ethnology
_____ 2. archaeology
_____ 3. ethnography
_____ 4. hypothesis
_____ 5. theory

_____ 6. holistic perspective
_____ 7. cultural relativism
_____ 8. *hekura*
_____ 9. ethnographic present

a. study of material objects from both the past and present, to describe and explain human behavior and culture
b. a view that may generally be accepted as true but is not beyond challenge
c. a series of tests or trials designed to prove or disprove a supposition
d. systematic description of a culture based on extensive firsthand observation
e. a view stating that a culture can be evaluated only according to its own standards and values
f. the anthropological principle that all cultural institutions must be viewed in the broadest possible context
g. the study of culture from a comparative or historical point of view
h. one of the ancient myths of the Yanomamo that explains the origins of man
i. a description of a particular group at a particular time
j. a tentative explanation of the relationship between certain phenomena
k. in Yanomamo mythology, little spirits that are believed to live in rocks and mountains

Completion

Fill each blank with the most appropriate term from the list immediately following that paragraph.

1. Although it is true that scientists begin a study by forming a _____, ethnographers usually immerse themselves totally in their studies until previously unseen _____ become clear. Such an approach requires closest observation of the tiniest details and is time consuming; however, this approach best assures an objective approach and protects against cultural _____.

bias	patterns	theory
hypothesis	relativism	

2. Anthropologists attempt to be as objective as possible in their studies of other cultures. They try to avoid judging other cultures on the basis of their own cultural standards. In its extreme form, judgment of other social groups by one's own cultural standards is known as _____. However, gaining an objective view is not easy; it requires studying another culture while _____ in it. For example, Napoleon Chagnon learned the language and customs of the Yanomamo to study settlement patterns. Only after gathering extensive data did he develop a hypothesis regarding _____ growth and breakup.

cultural relativism	family village
ethnocentrism	participating

3. Chagnon obtained much of his knowledge of the Yanomamo from _____, like Dedeheiwa, who related information about the society and its culture. In addition to learning about customs and traditions, Chagnon developed records of _____ ties and created maps showing villages and _____.

gardens	kinship
informants	missions

4. The Yanomamo are a _____ people. Chagnon found that as many as 30 percent of the males in one village _____ as a result of _____ between villages, usually carried out in early morning _____.

combative	raids
died	warfare

Self-Test

Objective Questions

Select the one best answer.

1. Archaeology is defined as the study of
    a. material remains.
    b. ancient ruins.
    c. food production techniques.
    d. behavior by firsthand observation.

2. Of the following social scientists, the one who is most likely to make cross-cultural comparisons is the
    a. linguist.
    b. ethnologist.
    c. ethnographer.
    d. sociologist.

3. During his stay with the Yanomamo, Napoleon Chagnon was engaged in
    a. archaeology.
    b. ethnology.
    c. ethnography.
    d. sociology.

4. *Ethnocentrism* is best defined as the
    a. belief that one's own culture is superior to others.
    b. study of individuals in isolated societies.
    c. belief that each society must be judged according to its own values.
    d. study of material remains to describe and explain human behavior.

5. The scientific approach is best described as the

    a. rejection of theories on the basis of logic.
    b. development of imaginative explanations for observed phenomena.
    c. development of testable explanations for observed phenomena.
    d. development of sufficient proof of an explanation to ensure that it
        cannot be challenged.

6. The most important reason for ethnographic fieldwork is that it

    a. provides an opportunity to make a photographic record of a society.
    b. eliminates the need for a more rigid scientific approach.
    c. is a means of becoming familiar with the traits of primitive cultures.
    d. provides an opportunity to discover previously unknown patterns in culture.

7. The most desired result of participant observation by the ethnographer is

    a. a wide variety of factual data from which others can make generalizations.
    b. a recorded history based on the traditions of the people studied.
    c. sufficient facts to judge whether the society studied is superior to others.
    d. an explanation of how the society's practices and traditions fit into
        a meaningful whole.

8. All the following statements about hypothesis testing are true except

    a. alternative hypotheses should be disproven.
    b. the hypothesis begins as a tentative explanation.
    c. one item of supporting data will verify a hypothesis.
    d. a hypothesis must be testable.

9. Science defines the term *theory* as

    a. a set of validated hypotheses that systematically explains phenomena.
    b. a tentative supposition about how certain phenomena are related.
    c. a proven explanation of phenomena that should remain accepted despite any
        further discoveries.
    d. an explanation generally accepted as true, although it cannot be verified.

10. Napoleon Chagnon states that anthropology must communicate the concept of cultural relativism because he believes that

a. the Yanomamo are in danger of losing their culture in the near future.
b. modern technology and practices must be taught quickly to primitive cultures.
c. people should appreciate that all cultures have developed unique and workable ways of solving the problems of living.
d. the customs and traditions of many primitive peoples are superior to Western culture.

11. According to the video program for Lesson 3, one of the aspects of Yanomamo culture that Chagnon studied in considerable detail was

a. courtship customs.
b. communication between villages.
c. marriage ceremonies.
d. combativeness.

12. Chagnon took extensive photographs of individuals during his fieldwork with the Yanomamo to

a. learn kinship ties.
b. determine total population.
c. help remember names.
d. record effects of aging.

13. Chagnon was especially careful about the items he traded with Yanomamo villagers because

a. the items traded could become too expensive during extended field study.
b. many normal trade items are taboo to Yanomamo.
c. new technology can cause unexpected harm to a traditional culture.
d. government regulations prohibit the trade of many items.

14. Of the following statements, the one that is closest to an ethical standard for ethnologists who are in contact with an isolated society is that ethnologists should

    a. make every effort to prevent any change in societies being studied.
    b. be aware that their contact with an isolated society could cause harm to that culture.
    c. avoid any participation in societies under study.
    d. introduce improved technology as rapidly as possible, except for weapons.

Short-Answer Essay Questions

1. Briefly describe the general procedure followed by scientists as they attempt to understand and explain natural phenomena.

2. Explain how ethnographers attempt to avoid preconceptions that might bias their studies.

3. What were some of the aspects of the life of the Yanomamo that Napoleon Chagnon studied extensively?

4. What are some adverse effects that an ethnographer or others who come in contact with an isolated society may unwittingly have on a society?

Suggested Activities

1. Imagine that you will construct a time capsule to let a future generation know what North American culture was like during the last years of the twentieth century. You have only a limited space in a protected vault. What material items could you select (excluding books and photographs) that would best reflect the *nonmaterial* parts of your culture that seem most important to you? Write a brief essay justifying your selection of artifacts for such a time capsule.

2. The term "culture shock" is frequently used to describe the reactions of persons (especially those who are not prepared) who suddenly find themselves in a society markedly different from their own. You might wish to consult Philip Bock's book *Culture Shock: A Reader in Modern Cultural Anthropology* (Lanham, Md .: University Press of America, 1981). You might also locate one or more periodical articles on this subject and read guidebooks published by the government or private sources to aid people in the armed forces, Peace Corps volunteers, employees, and other persons preparing for duty involving contact with cultures other than their own. Try to make a list of situations and behaviors that might cause culture shock.

3. Develop a suggested "code of ethics" to apply to ethnographers and others who come into contact with previously isolated societies such as the Yanomamo. You should recognize a reality of today's world: Modern means of travel and communication make it inevitable that all humans will be affected by technological change. For example, the frontiers of Venezuela and Brazil are being pushed back, just as the North American frontier receded in the nineteenth century, and the forest-dwelling Yanomamo will have more and more contact with other cultures.

4. Because this lesson introduces you to Napoleon Chagnon, as well as to participant observation as the chief methodology of the ethnographer, you may be interested in reading and writing a report on Chagnon's vivid and comprehensive book *Yanomamo: The Fierce People* (Fort Worth: Harcourt Brace, 4th ed., 1992).

Answer Key

STUDY ACTIVITIES

Vocabulary Check

1. g	3. d	5. b	7. e	9. i
2. a	4. j	6. f	8. k	

Completion

1. hypothesis, patterns, bias
2. ethnocentrism, participating, village
3. informants, kinship, gardens
4. combative, died, warfare, raids

SELF-TEST

Objective Questions

(Page numbers refer to the textbook.)

1. a (Objective 1; page 11)
2. b (Objective 2; page 20)
3. c (Objective 2; video program)
4. a (Objective 3; page 49)
5. c (Objective 3; pages 20–25; Background Notes 3B and 3C)
6. d (Objective 4; pages 13–14, 18–20; video program)
7. d (Objective 4; page 13; video program)
8. c (Objective 5; page 21)
9. a (Objective 5; page 21)
10. c (Objective 6; video program)
11. d (Objective 7; video program)
12. a (Objective 7; video program)
13. c (Objective 8; video program; Background Notes 3B)
14. b (Objective 8; page 26; video program; Background Notes 3B)

Short-Answer Essay Questions

1. Briefly describe the general procedure followed by scientists as they attempt to understand and explain natural phenomena.

   Your answer should include:

   - The scientific approach requires both imagination and skepticism.

   - A scientist first forms a hypothesis, or a tentative explanation, about the relationship between certain phenomena.

   - A hypothesis is tested by gathering data that support it and that disprove alternative hypotheses.

   - A system of proven hypotheses may constitute a theory, or a "most probable truth." However, theories are subject to later challenge and revision.

2. Explain how ethnographers attempt to avoid preconceptions that might bias their studies.

   Your answer should include:

   - Ethnographers attempt to be as objective as possible by gathering and studying data extensively, using the participant-observer method as their major data-collecting technique.

   - They try to find patterns that were not previously known before starting to frame hypotheses.

   - They try to avoid ethnocentrism; that is, they do not judge the culture studied by the standards of their own culture.

3. What were some of the aspects of the life of the Yanomamo people that Napoleon Chagnon studied extensively?

   Your answer should include at least three or four of the following:

   - Social organization of the Yanomamo—including kinship ties, genealogy, dwelling patterns, and movement from village to village.

   - Village patterns—organization and layout of villages, location of present and former villages, and village breakups.

   - The Yanomamo language.

   - Myths, traditions, beliefs, and practices concerning magic and spirits.

   - The fierce combative behaviors of the Yanomamo.

4. What are some adverse effects that an ethnographer or others who come in contact with an isolated society may unwittingly have on a society?

   Your answer should include:

   - Fieldworkers and others in contact with a relatively isolated society could introduce new technologies that might alter cultural practices.

   - Since a culture is an integrated whole, any change in the culture might have disastrous effects on the culture's ability to survive and the society's ability to adapt to new conditions.

   - Both new tools and the very presence of a fieldworker might upset established social relationships and alliances. For example, shotguns among the Yanomamo gave some villages great advantage over others in their battles. It is also possible that such weapons could lead to depletion of game in the forests. Napoleon Chagnon was aware that his presence in a village gave that village added status and prestige.

Language and Communication 4

Assignments

Before viewing the video program	• Read the Overview and the Learning Objectives for this lesson. Use the Learning Objectives to guide your reading, viewing, and thinking. • Read the Introduction to Part II of the textbook, pages 88–89, and Chapter 4, "Language and Communication," pages 90–119. Also read the Original Study in Chapter 3, "The Intellectual Abilities of Chimpanzees," pages 64–66. • Review the definition of gender and the discussion of gender as a cultural trait in Chapter 2, pages 33–34.

View video program 4, "Language and Communication"

After viewing the video program	• Review the terms used in this lesson. In addition to those terms in the Learning Objectives, you should be familiar with these:

American sign language	gender
displacement	Indo-European
ethnolinguistics	Sapir-Whorf hypothesis

• Review the reading assignments for this lesson.
• Complete each of the Study Activities and the Self-Test in this study-guide lesson; check your answers with the Answer Key at the end of this lesson.
• According to your instructor's assignment or your own interests, complete one or more of the Suggested Activities. You also may be interested in the readings listed at the end of Chapter 4 in the textbook.

Overview

You probably have seen motion pictures or television programs that reveal how wild animals communicate anger or pleasure through sounds and physical movement. Scientists have solved the mystery of how honeybees inform their hive mates about the location of a good food source. You may have had a pet who responded to your call, particularly if it had to do with food; and your pet probably developed distinctive signals to gain your attention. For a moment, though, pause and reflect how extremely limited your life would be if your communications were limited only to emotions or a few basic wants, like food and water. For example, the lack of language would eliminate most kinds of education (including telecourses), except rather simple demonstrations. The ability to communicate complex information through sounds generally is regarded as a uniquely human trait.

A very limited range of communication and a restricted capacity for learning new skills, such as simple toolmaking, were probably the beginnings of language in the earliest humans. Some physical changes evolved as well to make possible the exchange of information that must have taken place among people long before written history began.

From these beginnings, humans today speak between 3,000 and 5,000 different languages and have developed many more in the course of human history. All these languages are based on a limited number of sounds, which all human beings are capable of making. Even the simplest of these languages is remarkably complex and sophisticated—so much so that the scientific study of language is a well-established discipline of its own, with numerous subdisciplines, and is called *linguistics*.

Why should scientists—or you, for that matter—study language? First of all, language is the central means by which every society expresses its cultural values and ideas. Second, all human culture depends upon our capacity to learn and to share our information, beliefs, and experience with the generations that succeed us; unless we can communicate what we learn, human culture would not be preserved beyond our own generation. Culture is based on symbols, and symbols include sounds or gestures to which we have assigned common meanings agreed upon by the group as a whole. Symbols make it possible to communicate, and language, which is the oral and written expression of symbols, is the *primary* tool of human communication. Thus, language is indispensable to human culture.

In the video program for Lesson 3, you saw Napoleon Chagnon add to his Yanomamo vocabulary as his informant slowly and carefully spoke words one syllable at a time. In this lesson, you will learn something of the techniques that linguistic scientists have developed for learning and recording languages that, until now, have never been written. These and related techniques have been developed to the point that we now know something about ancient, unwritten languages from which present-day ones evolved. It is possible to trace, for example, the probable "family tree" of our language.

Video program: As this program shows vividly, the feelings and aspirations of every culture are expressed in the sounds and movements that constitute language, the primary means of human communication. The program contrasts closed (animal) communication with open (human) communication. Linguist Keith Kernan discusses the structure of language, and the intricacy of language is illustrated with segments showing children wrestling with syntax and sentence structure. The use of body language as a means of communication is illustrated by a taxi driver, who explains how he identifies fares as he drives the streets of Manhattan. Claudia Kernan's discussion with students examines the dialect of "black" English. The concluding segment examines the relationship between language and thought, with illustrative examples from the languages of the Hopi and the Nuer.

As you view the program, look for:

- a contrast of closed (animal) communication versus open (human) communication.

- Keith Kernan's examples of phonemes, morphemes, and syntax.

- an explanation of language acquisition.

- several vivid demonstrations of the importance of kinesic messages in communication.

- Claudia Kernan in a discussion about "black" English with black students and other examples of "black" English usage in its social context.

- how the Kwakiutl are working to preserve their language.

- discussion of the questions: How does language influence thought, and in what ways does thought influence language? Information comes from the languages of the Hopi and the Nuer.

- the importance of language in presenting and transmitting culture.

Learning Objectives

When you have completed all assignments in this lesson, you should be able to:

1. Explain the difference between symbols and signals, and discuss how human language is symbolic, has meaning, and follows a set of rules. TEXTBOOK PAGES 92–97; VIDEO PROGRAM

2. Discuss the implications of teaching symbolic communications to chimpanzees and gorillas. TEXTBOOK PAGES 64–66, 113–116

3. Define *linguistics* and distinguish between descriptive and historical linguistics. TEXTBOOK PAGES 94, 97, 102–104; VIDEO PROGRAM

4. Define the following terms found in the field of descriptive linguistics: *phonology, phonetics, phonemes, morphemes, syntax, grammar*. TEXTBOOK PAGES 94–97; VIDEO PROGRAM

5. Describe and give examples of *kinesic messages* and *paralanguage*. TEXTBOOK PAGES 97–101; VIDEO PROGRAM

6. Define the following terms found in the field of historical linguistics: *language family, linguistic divergence, glottochronology, core vocabulary*. TEXTBOOK PAGES 102–104

7. Describe the hypothesis developed by Benjamin Lee Whorf about the relationship between language and thought, and recognize the differing points of view of other linguists. TEXTBOOK PAGES 104, 106–107; VIDEO PROGRAM

8. Define and give examples of *sociolinguistics, dialects*, and *code switching*. TEXTBOOK PAGES 112–113; VIDEO PROGRAM

9. Recognize that all known languages are complex, sophisticated, and able to express infinite meanings. TEXTBOOK PAGES 92–94, 117; VIDEO PROGRAM

Study Activities

Vocabulary Check

Check your understanding of terms by writing the letter of the appropriate definition in the space next to the corresponding term. Check your choices with the Answer Key at the end of the lesson.

_____ 1. signal
_____ 2. linguistics
_____ 3. descriptive linguistics
_____ 4. phonetics
_____ 5. phonemes
_____ 6. morphemes
_____ 7. syntax
_____ 8. grammar

_____ 9. paralanguage
_____ 10. kinesics
_____ 11. Indo-European
_____ 12. glottochronology
_____ 13. core vocabulary
_____ 14. code switching
_____ 15. dialects
_____ 16. displacement

a. the ability to refer to things and events removed in time and space
b. smallest units of sound that carry a meaning
c. changing from one level of language to another
d. registers and explains all the features of a language at one point in time
e. varying forms of a language, similar enough to be mutually intelligible to the various users
f. includes English as one of this language family
g. extra-linguistic noises that accompany language
h. sound or gesture that has a natural or self-evident meaning
i. formal structure of a language consisting of all observations about morphemes and syntax
j. a method of dating divergence in language branches
k. includes lower numbers and names for natural objects
l. study of how speech sounds are produced, transmitted, and received
m. scientific study of language
n. smallest classes of sound that make a difference in meaning
o. analysis of body language
p. the rules or principles of making phrases and sentences
q. study of the relationship between language and culture

Completion

Fill each blank with the most appropriate term from the list immediately following that paragraph.

1. Language is a system of communication that uses combinations of sounds as _____ for all kinds of information. For communication to take place, there must be general agreement about the _____ of the sounds and the _____ that guide the way the language is expressed. All present societies use language so complex that even the simplest cannot be called "primitive." Cultural patterns and cultural knowledge are so rich and complex that language is essential, not only for transmitting the culture to new generations, but for exchanging information and experiences between members of the culture day-to-day.

meanings	signals
rules	symbols

2. The modern scientific study of all aspects of language is _____. A branch of this science that studies how languages have developed a long time is known as _____. Studies have found that English is one branch of a language family descended from a single ancestral language called proto _____.

descriptive linguistics	Indo-European	Romanic
historical linguistics	linguistics	

3. Attempts to teach gorillas and chimpanzees to speak like humans have not been successful because of key differences in their nervous systems and sound-producing mechanisms. However, there have been dramatic examples of success in teaching language to these primates using various kinds of _____ languages. It is possible that these animals have the ability to use symbolism and language similar to that of young human beings. Some primates have demonstrated the ability to communicate about something not present in space and time, a characteristic known as _____. Such experiments also suggest that language may have originated in meaningful _____.

displacement	phonemes
gestures	sign

4. The study of the structure and use of language in relation to its social setting is known as _____. A major area of interest in this discipline is the study of language uses that reflect particular regions or classes; these forms are called _____. A related concern is whether or not differences in speech among peoples in the same area also reflect other cultural differences.

descriptive linguistics   morphemes   phonemes

dialects   morphology   sociolinguistics

Self-Test

Objective Questions

Select the one best answer.

1. From the standpoint of linguistics, a symbol is

    a. a sound or gesture that has a natural or evident meaning.
    b. the smallest unit of sound that conveys meaning.
    c. a gesture or sign used as a substitute for a word.
    d. a sound or gesture that has an agreed-on meaning.

2. The rules a language follows in phrase and sentence construction constitute the language's

    a. morphology.
    b. syntax.
    c. glottochronology.
    d. grammar.

3. Experiments with chimpanzees and gorillas such as Washoe and Lana seem to show that these primates have some language ability. The findings seem to indicate that Washoe and Lana have

    a. the ability to vocalize words.
    b. the ability to understand and form sentences.
    c. language ability nearly equal to that of adult humans.
    d. no ability to think of events separated from them in space and time.

4. Which of the following subjects would LEAST likely fall within the field of linguistics?
   a. history of languages
   b. toolmaking techniques
   c. gesture communications
   d. glottochronology

5. Of the following divisions, the one that is most concerned with the relationships of older languages to modern ones is
   a. descriptive linguistics.
   b. theoretical linguistics.
   c. historical linguistics.
   d. sociolinguistics.

6. Of the following divisions, the one that is most concerned with studying the complete system of a single language at one point in time is
   a. descriptive linguistics.
   b. theoretical linguistics.
   c. historical linguistics.
   d. sociolinguistics.

7. A *phoneme* is
   a. the smallest unit of sound that carries meaning.
   b. a combination of sounds in a language.
   c. the smallest class of sounds that may make a difference in meaning.
   d. a chart that lists all written symbols for the sounds produced in a language.

8. In linguistics, *syntax* refers to the
   a. principles governing the production, transmission, and receiving of speech sounds.
   b. rules governing the making of phrases, clauses, and sentences.
   c. rules governing the formation of words and construction of sentences.
   d. study of sounds in combination.

9. An example of a kinesic message is

    a. a change in voice quality.
    b. a hand or arm gesture.
    c. a word that imitates a natural sound.
    d. the smallest unit of sound that conveys meaning.

10. Studies of core vocabulary are important in glottochronology because

    a. the rate at which common words change is helpful in determining the date that one language branched off from another.
    b. the number of words in common everyday use is a rough measure of the total vocabulary now used in a language.
    c. it is thought that the names of body parts, low numbers, and similar words change very little over time.
    d. the knowledge of various dialects reveals the comparative social status of different groups that speak the same language.

11. Of the following viewpoints, the one that is OPPOSITE that of the hypothesis developed by Benjamin Lee Whorf is that

    a. language limits the kinds of sensations that engage the attention of the mind.
    b. language predisposes a person to see the world in a certain way.
    c. language reflects reality and will change as that reality changes.
    d. a language will have more words describing those conditions that are very important to the society.

12. In the hypothesis developed by Benjamin Lee Whorf, the phrase "grooves of expression" means that

    a. a language is a shaping force that predisposes people to see the world in a certain way and that guides their thinking and behavior.
    b. a language reflects reality and changes in reality.
    c. all languages have certain common ways of expressing concepts.
    d. one part of human communication involves sounds that do not necessarily form words.

13. Of the following fields of study, the one that is most concerned with the dialects of a particular language is
   a. descriptive linguistics.
   b. theoretical linguistics.
   c. historical linguistics.
   d. sociolinguistics.

14. The black students in the video program describe how they could change from one level of English to another called "black" English. The students were demonstrating
   a. the use of paralanguage.
   b. code switching.
   c. the use of kernel sentences.
   d. changes in syntax.

15. In studying the languages of various isolated societies, anthropologists have found
   a. all languages are able to convey complex and subtle messages.
   b. some small-scale societies have primitive languages involving few sounds and gestures.
   c. all known languages developed from the same primitive language.
   d. most unwritten languages are restricted to words and gestures that have natural or biological meanings.

Short-Answer Essay Questions

1. Describe the techniques used by the fieldworker who is gathering information for descriptive linguistics.

2. Explain the terms *kinesic messages* and *paralanguage,* and give two examples of each.

3. Briefly explain and provide examples of the various points of view concerning the influence of language upon perception and perception upon language.

4. What evidence suggests that language might have originated in gestures?

Suggested Activities

1. Consult the *Readers' Guide to Periodical Literature* for articles on attempts to teach chimpanzees, gorillas, and other apes to communicate. Select and read several articles and write a brief summary of your reading. In particular, comment on what the articles suggest concerning primate ability to think in symbols and to demonstrate displacement in thought.

2. A portion of the video program shows Claudia Kernan and several students in serious discussion of "black" English, and textbook Chapter 4 (pages 112–113) reports conversations between American inner-city blacks. Try to answer these questions:

   a. What are some of the ways that "black" English differs from white middle-class or "college-accepted" English?

   b. What reasons might there be for black Americans to wish to preserve their own usage of English?

   c. What are some reasons anthropologists would wish to record and preserve this dialect?

   d. What problems in communication might occur between persons who speak different dialects of the same language?

3. Most people migrating to the United States have to learn to speak and read English. Discuss how the difficulties of learning a "second" language illustrate the close relationship of language and culture and language and thought.

4. Consult *The Oxford Dictionary of English Etymology* (Oxford, England: Oxford University Press, 1966) for etymologies of certain categories of words (such as textiles, fruits and vegetables, body parts) and trace their origins and histories. How much selective borrowing from other languages is involved?

Answer Key

Vocabulary Check

1. h	5. n	9. g	13. k
2. m	6. b	10. o	14. c
3. d	7. p	11. f	15. e
4. l	8. i	12. j	16. a

Completion

1. symbols, meanings, rules
2. linguistics, historical linguistics, Indo-European
3. sign, displacement, gestures
4. sociolinguistics, dialects

SELF-TEST

Objective Questions

(Page numbers refer to the textbook.)

1. d (Objective 1; page 92)
2. b (Objective 1; page 96)
3. b (Objective 2; page 115)
4. b (Objective 3; pages 94, 97, 103)
5. c (Objective 3; page 102)
6. a (Objective 3; page 102)
7. c (Objective 4; page 95; video program)
8. b (Objective 4; page 96; video program)
9. b (Objective 5; page 98)
10. a (Objective 6; page 103)
11. c (Objective 7; page 106; video program)
12. a (Objective 7; page 106; video program)

13. d (Objective 8; page 112)
14. b (Objective 8; pages 112–113; video program)
15. a (Objective 9; pages 92–94, 117; video program)

Short-Answer Essay Questions

1. Describe the techniques used by the fieldworker who is gathering information for descriptive linguistics.

    Your answer should include:

    *   The fieldworker gathers all the spoken sounds, or phonemes, that may make a difference to meaning. Usually, one needs special training in phonetics to distinguish sounds accurately.

    *   Fieldworkers also collect and list morphemes, the smallest units of sounds that carry meaning. Many of these might be words, but some sounds that carry meaning, such as prefixes and suffixes, might be less than words.

    *   The fieldworker must determine the syntax, or the rules for forming phrases and sentences.

    *   A complete grammar of the language is a major goal of the descriptive linguist, including all of the rules governing the use of morphemes and syntax.

2. Describe *kinesic messages* and *paralanguage,* and give two examples of each.

    Your answer should include:

    *   Kinesic messages are communications through postures, facial expressions, and body motions.

    *   Examples of kinesic messages include facial expressions such as smiling, nodding in agreement, or biting one's lip to express doubt.

    *   Paralanguage refers to vocal noises that are extralinguistic. It is less developed as a communication system than is language.

    *   Examples of paralanguage include voice qualities, such as pitch range or articulation control; vocalizations, such as laughing or crying; or a vocal qualifier, such as a rapid change in pitch.

3. Briefly explain and provide examples of the various points of view concerning the influence of language upon perception and perception upon language.

Your answer should include:

- Benjamin Lee Whorf developed a theory that language is a force that guides thought and behavior; by using habitual "grooves of expression," people become predisposed to view the world in a certain way.

- An opposing point of view is that language reflects reality, rather than affecting the way people perceive it.

- A third point of view, somewhere between these extremes, was expressed by Peter Woolfson, who suggested that language provides a kind of "filtering system" that selects the sensations to which people will pay attention. The textbook states that a people's language does not stop them from thinking in new and novel ways.

4. What evidence suggests that language might have originated in gestures?

Your answer should include:

- Language has been an essential part of human culture for an extremely long time. Some anthropologists believe that the culture developed by *Homo erectus*, an early probable ancestor of our own species, implied some level of spoken communication.

- The ability of primates, such as Washoe and Loulis, to communicate using sign language suggests that the earliest humanlike creatures could have communicated quite a bit of information by gestures. As cultures became more complex, imitating sounds from nature might have helped free hands for other tasks (such as toolmaking) and set the stage for transfer from a gesture-based to a vocal-based language.

Psychological Anthropology 5

Assignments

Before viewing the video program	• Read the Overview and the Learning Objectives for this lesson. Use the Learning Objectives to guide your reading, viewing, and thinking. • Read textbook Chapter 5, "Growing Up Human," pages 120–149. • Read Background Notes 5A, "Psychological Anthropology and Personality," in this study-guide lesson.

View video program 5, "Psychological Anthropology"

After viewing the video program	• Review the terms used in this lesson. In addition to those terms in the Learning Objectives, you should be familiar with these:

> behavioral environment   patterns of affect
> core values   psychological anthropology
> dependence training   self-awareness
> independence training

• Review the reading assignments for this lesson.
• Complete each of the Study Activities and the Self-Test in this study-guide lesson; check your answers with the Answer Key at the end of this lesson.
• According to your instructor's assignment or your own interests, complete one or more of the Suggested Activities. You also may be interested in the readings listed at the end of Chapter 5 in the textbook.

Overview

What makes you think of someone as having a pleasing personality? Almost certainly, it is some quality or combination of qualities you have observed in that person's behavior, which is the outward manifestation of personality. Personality itself is defined as those specific physical, mental, and emotional qualities that are characteristic of an individual. Virtually everything we can possibly know about a person comes from our observations of behavior or the observations of others. How do you know, for example, that your friend is kind, or inquisitive, or humorous? Probably because you have seen acts of kindness, watched expressions of curiosity, or heard your friend tell a funny story or laugh at appropriate times.

In this lesson, you will look beyond behavior to thought and emotion, because a person's outward behaviors are determined mostly by the way that individual thinks and feels. The anthropologist is interested in the influence of the culture on individual thinking, feeling, and behavior. You have already learned that culture is transmitted from one generation to the next through language and other symbols. Since a person's thoughts are expressed in the words of a language, you can understand that the culture has a strong influence on how people view themselves and everything else in the environment.

Much of our information on the relationship between personality and culture comes from cross-cultural studies of child-rearing methods. The manner in which a child is cared for and trained reflects the cultural values of the responsible adults, and it also affects the developing personality of the child.

A second focus of study for this lesson is that of "typical" personalities in a society. Some studies have yielded interesting results concerning the "typical" or "average" personality in some societies, but the studies and their findings are still considered controversial. In recent years, anthropologists have examined varying concepts of "normal" from one culture to another and have studied the means by which shamans (healers) in non-Western societies treat illness or behavior considered deviant in their society. As examples in the video program demonstrate, traditional healers typically view illness as due to social factors—usually the failure to live up to social responsibilities. In the process of conducting healing rituals, shamans call on the gods or spirits to help restore health and harmonious relationships. However, patients must also agree to fulfill their responsibilities to the gods and to other family members. Thus, traditional healing systems emphasize the importance of social relationships in both the cause and treatment of disease.

Lesson 6 continues this exploration of psychological anthropology through a close examination of deviance and healing from a cross-cultural perspective.

Video Program: Beginning with a definition of enculturation, the program describes Margaret Mead's attempt to document the influence of culture on individual personality by studying the various patterns of child rearing in several cultures, including Samoa. The program next explores the link between personality and culture and the concept of national character. Early national character studies during the 1940s are described, along with the criticisms of these efforts. The program also examines how societies have ways of treating individuals who deviate from accepted norms, because of physical illness or emotional disorders. Shamans in several societies are shown, including one from the Melemchi in Nepal, from Bali, and from the Yanomamo in Brazil. The narrator describes how, through their treatments and rituals, shamans address the social ills of the group as a whole.

As you view the program, look for:

- the enculturation process as illustrated by the experiences of two young boys in different cultures.

- the filmed scenes of Margaret Mead as she studied child-rearing practices in the Samoan and other cultures.

- descriptions of "national character" studies during World War II, with historical film from those times; and the contrasts with studies made after the war.

- the way in which traditional healing systems define illness as a social problem.

- how shamans from various cultures treat illnesses

Learning Objectives

When you have completed all assignments in this lesson, you should be able to:

1. Define *personality*. TEXTBOOK PAGE 127; BACKGROUND NOTES 5A.

2. Define *enculturation* and give several examples of how it occurs. TEXTBOOK PAGES 122–137; BACKGROUND NOTES 5A; VIDEO PROGRAM.

3. Recognize that the environment is interpreted (perceived) and organized through a person's culture, especially language. TEXTBOOK PAGES 123–126; VIDEO PROGRAM

4. Explain what anthropologists have learned about the relationship between culture and personality from their cross-cultural studies of child-rearing techniques. TEXTBOOK PAGES 127–137; VIDEO PROGRAM

5. Cite examples of different cultural perceptions regarding time, space, objects, values, ideas, and standards. TEXTBOOK PAGES 124–126, 133–135; VIDEO PROGRAM

6. Define *modal personality* and describe several difficulties involved in assessing it. TEXTBOOK PAGES 138–139

7. Describe "national character" studies and describe several objections to these studies. TEXTBOOK PAGES 139–141; VIDEO PROGRAM

8. Explain why abnormal personality is a relative concept and describe several healing systems developed by traditional societies to respond to abnormal personalities TEXTBOOK PAGES 141–147; BACKGROUND NOTES 5A; VIDEO PROGRAM

PSYCHOLOGICAL ANTHROPOLOGY AND PERSONALITY

The term *psychological anthropology* may at first seem a bit unwieldy. Indeed, it may sound like a contradiction in terms, since the one tends to focus on the individual and the other emphasizes society and culture. Neither field is really so limited, perhaps because humans are themselves so complex. The field of anthropology quickly evolved in the direction of comprehensive assessment of human behavior. In the formative years of anthropology in the United States, for example, Franz Boas and others undertook studies in which psychology and anthropology were clearly associated. This interest continued with the work of pioneers such as Mead and Benedict, whom you met in earlier lessons. In the past, psychological anthropology focused on two general issues: (l) enculturation, or how an individual acquires information about and becomes a functioning member of his or her culture, and (2) "cultural personality types," or variations in personality from one culture to another.

These early studies, which came to be generally classified under the heading of "culture and personality," were based on the assumption that personality is a product of one's cultural environment and that, consequently, individual variation within a culture will be minimal. There was a great deal of interest in determining personality types for use in classifying individuals and cultures. Personality, in this context, is generally understood as the set of traits that distinguish an individual and characterize his or her interactions with others.

In the case of Ruth Benedict, the concept of personality was generalized to apply to whole cultures. Even when not carried to this extreme, there were attempts to explain cultural differences in terms of personality traits.

Margaret Mead sought to tie variations in child-rearing practices to cultural values. Essentially, she tried to show that certain personality traits are encouraged or inhibited through child-rearing practices that vary from one society to another.

In recent years, interest has shifted to studies of intracultural variation, as well as to analyses of cross-cultural differences. These studies have added a new dimension to psychological anthropology because they allow researchers to consider the range of variation within a culture and to reexamine the concept of abnormal behavior.

As a social science, anthropology traditionally has focused on normative beliefs and behaviors—beliefs and behaviors shared by most members of the group. But this approach overlooks the range and diversity found in any human group.

All groups have norms, or generally accepted standards of behavior. We are able to live in social groups because we know what to expect from the people with whom we interact. Norms enable us to predict behavior of other people and make it clear what is expected of us as members of social groups. We dress, speak, and make exchanges based on our understanding of norms.

Within these guidelines, however, is a range of acceptable behaviors. Behavior expected of a young, unmarried woman is not the same as that expected of a grandmother. Norms vary according to the setting. People behave differently when entertaining business associates at a restaurant than when they are having a family picnic at the beach. Our ability to detect subtle differences in expectations and react appropriately affects our acceptance into our social community.

However, not all people conform to social norms at all times. In fact, most people deviate from the norm at one time or another. Norms are idealized concepts; actual behavior is always subject to negotiation.

In any society, some people consistently deviate from the norm and others occasionally go far beyond acceptable standards. Deviant behavior, if extreme and unchecked, threatens the underlying assumptions on which society is based. But even deviance conforms to normative standards, according to the psychological anthropologist Robert B. Edgerton. Gang members in U.S. urban areas violate norms of the larger society, but they conform to rigid standards of behavior within their own social groups.

What might be deviant behavior in one society might not be considered deviant in others. Among the Gururumba of Papua New Guinea, a form of greeting is for one man to grab the genitals of the other. This custom would be considered deviant in our society, but is well within normative standards of behavior among the Gururumba. However, some types of behavior are considered deviant in all societies. The Haviland textbook mentions the appearance of schizophrenia in its various manifestations throughout the world. Although it appears in slightly different forms in different cultures, is recognizable as schizophrenia and is considered deviant in all societies—even if explanations and forms of treatment for it differ.

Deviant behavior is generally defined in two ways: (1) as an intentional violation of the social code (such as criminality) and (2) as a result of circumstances beyond a person's control. In most societies, psychological disturbances are viewed as being beyond a person's control. In North American society, these are classified as neuroses (involving a slight degree of disturbance) or psychoses (involving a high degree of disturbance interrupting the person's ability to function in society).

In other societies, a psychological disturbance may be attributed to witchcraft or to possession by supernatural beings. However, in all cases, including North American society, people are diagnosed as "ill" or disturbed on the basis of their ability to perform the social duties expected of them.

All societies have methods for treating these disturbances, and the treatment is related to the diagnosis. In modern psychiatry, the patient may be treated with drugs, psychodrama, catharsis, and other techniques considered effective in treating psychological disturbances. In cultures that explain psychological disturbance as being due to spirit possession, the patient may be treated with various forms of exorcism. However, anthropologists specializing in cross-cultural psychology have noted that exorcism rituals often use many of the techniques considered effective in modern psychiatry, including psychodrama, catharsis, and drugs.

Study Activities

Vocabulary Check

Check your understanding of terms by writing the letter of the appropriate definition in the space next to the corresponding term. Check your choices with the Answer Key at the end of the lesson.

_____ 1. personality

_____ 2. enculturation

_____ 3. self-awareness

_____ 4. psychological anthropology

_____ 5. independence training

_____ 6. dependence training

_____ 7. modal personality

_____ 8. core values

a. a personality typical of a society as indicated by the central tendency of a defined frequency distribution

b. explores the interaction of personality and culture

c. the process by which culture is transmitted from one generation to the next

d. encourages compliance

e. encourages self-reliance and personal achievement

f. involves behavior, thought, and feelings

g. includes the ability to identify oneself as a distinct object

h. emphasizes personal achievement

i. objects and other features organized by the culture into a "cognitive map"

j. values especially promoted by an individual culture

Completion

Fill each blank with the most appropriate term from the list immediately following that paragraph.

1. Enculturation is a term used for the process by which the culture is _____ from one generation to the next. Enculturation begins with the development of _____. The individual also becomes aware of the world around him or her; however, the culture defines those parts that are especially significant, and it provides values, ideals, and standards by which the individual will act. The environment as perceived by the individual is therefore termed the _____ environment. This environment also includes spatial and temporal orientation, or an understanding of _____.

    behavioral   time and space   self-awareness

    cultural personality   transmitted

2. Studies have indicated that the interrelationship between culture and personality is _____. In particular, there seems to be a relationship between _____ and the personalities of adults. However, how cause and effect are involved is not certain.

    child-rearing patterns   heredity

    nonrandom   random

3. Dependence training of children is found more often in _____ families. In this type of situation, children learn to subordinate their own desires to those of the group. Independence training is usually found in societies with _____ families. In contrast with societies that teach dependence, the children are given less attention and indulgence while young. They are taught to be _____ and self-reliant.

    competitive   cooperative   nuclear

    compliant   extended

4. "Modal personality" is a statistical concept that supposes there is a hypothetical personality, composed of the personality traits that appear most frequently (the "central tendency") in a large group. Unlike some other approaches to identifying group personality, this approach recognizes that there will be considerable _____ in the personalities of group members. Gathering valid data to define modal personality usually involves _____ of a representative sampling of the population, the cooperation of the people being tested, and a minimum of such problems as language barriers or personal conflict between the investigators and the population.

      psychological testing   variation

      similarity

5. Critics of studies that supposedly reveal "national character" point out that social phenomena are complex. It is dangerous to make too many _____ about the qualities of a nation based on limited data. In any society, there are countless individuals who vary from the "typical," even if it exists. Such studies have ignored the influence on personality of other factors besides country of origin, such as social status and _____.

      generalizations

      occupation

Self-Test

Objective Questions

Select the one best answer.

1. The definition of personality in the textbook includes all of the following elements EXCEPT

    a. behavior.
    b. thoughts.
    c. feelings.
    d. values.

2. In Western industrialized societies, child-rearing is

    a. the sole responsibility of the parents.
    b. includes professionals as part of the process.
    c. discontinued as early as possible.
    d. based almost entirely on the child's wishes.

3. The behavioral environment is

    a. organized and perceived through the culture.
    b. identical to the objective environment.
    c. different for the child than for the adult.
    d. similar in all cultures.

4. Anthropologists study child-rearing techniques because those practices

    a. reveal inherited personality traits.
    b. show parenting practices are basically the same everywhere.
    c. have a significant effect on the personality of adults.
    d. prove Freud's personality theories are universal.

5. The children of Ju/'hoansi (!Kung) food foragers, in contrast to children of Ju/'hoansi sedentary villagers,

   a. begin working at more difficult tasks at a younger age.
   b. are subjected to stricter discipline.
   c. are exposed more-or-less equally to adults of both sexes.
   d. tend to have fewer relationships with adult males.

6. Margaret Mead's studies in Samoa

   a. revealed child-rearing practices are similar in all societies.
   b. provided evidence that adolescence is not always accompanied by some degree of stress and conflict.
   c. revealed the Oedipus complex theory is not valid in all societies.
   d. demonstrated that Western child-rearing techniques are superior.

7. The type of society in which parents typically spend the least amount of time with their children is probably

   a. an industrial society.
   b. a subsistence farming society.
   c. an extended society.
   d. a hunting-gathering society.

8. The seventeenth-century Penobscot Indians tended to view nature as

   a. essentially friendly and a valuable resource.
   b. inhabited by a variety of beings, natural and supernatural.
   c. an inconvenient limitation to their ambitions.
   d. controlled by a stern but benevolent god.

9. Among the Mbuti, the children light the hunting fire because the task

   a. is a dirty one.
   b. gives training important to hunting skills.
   c. is unimportant and left to unskilled persons.
   d. must be done by uncontaminated persons.

10. A self-concept that included a physical body and "vital self" was found in

    a. the seventeenth-century Penobscot Indians.
    b. seventeenth-century British settlers in North America.
    c. both seventeenth-century Penobscot Indians and British settlers.
    d. neither of these groups.

11. One difficulty in determining modal personality is that

    a. the concept does not recognize variations of personality within a culture.
    b. studies that tested for modal personality could not be duplicated by other researchers.
    c. the measurement techniques for this research are difficult to carry out in the field.
    d. the studies cannot be applied to most societies.

12. A frequent criticism of "national character" studies is that they

    a. give too much attention to occupation and social status.
    b. fail to consider most child-rearing practices.
    c. ignore modal personality studies.
    d. do not sufficiently recognize countless individuals who vary from the generalization.

13. The core value that North Americans of European descent hold in highest esteem is

    a. individualism.
    b. ferocity.
    c. compliance.
    d. cooperation.

14. Of the following behaviors, the one that was thought to be associated with great spiritual powers in some American Plains Indian tribes was

    a. obsession with cannibalism.
    b. demon possession.
    c. a man's assuming the dress of a woman.
    d. depression.

15. Anthropological studies seem to indicate that culture influences the
    a. form a mental illness will take.
    b. diagnosis of a mental condition.
    c. treatment of a mental condition.
    d. all of the above.

Short-Answer Essay Questions

1. Explain the contribution of Margaret Mead's studies of Samoan society to (a) the understanding of adolescence and (b) the acceptance of anthropology in the United States.

2. Briefly describe concepts of self, space, values, and ideas held by the Penobscot Indians in the seventeenth century.

3. Contrast the core values of the cultures of the Chinese and of North Americans of European descent.

4. Describe several ethnic psychoses and traditional systems of treating illness and deviant behavior.

Suggested Activities

1. Margaret Mead's *Coming of Age in Samoa* (New York: Morrow, 1928) is a pioneering work in psychological anthropology that is well worth reading, even today. Obtain the book from your library or bookstore for an interesting reading adventure. After reading it, you may wish to read reviews and comments that appeared in the December, 1983, *American Anthropologist* concerning Mead's work and criticism that has been leveled against it (85:904ff). Write a brief discussion on the importance of Mead's work as you understand it after these readings.

2. Read a current article on the subject of raising children, or select a few chapters from a current book on the subject. Do you find elements or suggestions that are consistent with independence training? Do you find any that seem to oppose independence training, or even promote dependence training? Write a brief summary of what you have found.

3. Have you ever observed an example of dependence training among the families you know? If possible, do a bit of anthropological fieldwork by interviewing either the parents or the children in such a family. What values and behaviors have been taught to the children? Describe the kind of parent-child contact in this family, the types of duties assigned to children in their early years, and the adult roles that the parents and children believe the children will assume when grown.

Answer Key

STUDY ACTIVITIES

Vocabulary Check

1. f   5. h
2. c   6. d
3. g   7. a
4. b   8. j

Completion

1. transmitted, self-awareness, behavioral, time and space
2. nonrandom, child-rearing patterns
3. extended, nuclear, competitive
4. variation, psychological testing
5. generalizations, occupation

SELF-TEST

Objective Questions

(Page numbers refer to the textbook.)

1. d (Objective 1; page 127)
2. b (Objective 2; page 124; video program)
3. a (Objective 3; page 124; video program)
4. c (Objective 4; pages 127–132, 136–137; video program)
5. c (Objective 4; pages 128–129)
6. b (Objective 4; page 127; video program)
7. a (Objective 4; page 131)
8. b (Objective 5; page 126)
9. d (Objective 5; page 134)
10. a (Objective 5; page 125)
11. c (Objective 6; page 139)
12. d (Objective 7; page 140; video program)
13. a (Objective 7; page 141; video program)
14. c (Objective 8; pages 141–142)
15. d (Objective 8; Background Notes 5A; video program)

Short-Answer Essay Questions

1. Explain the contribution of Margaret Mead's studies of Samoan society to (a) the understanding of adolescence and (b) the acceptance of anthropology in the United States.

   Your answer should include:

   • Mead found that adolescents in Samoa did not go through the stresses that similar-age youth experience in Western societies. Her study served as a test of a psychological hypothesis that had generally been accepted to that time.

   • When Mead's book on Samoa became well known in the United States, it encouraged interest in anthropology as a science, and made the public aware that much could be learned from the study of other societies.

2. Briefly describe concepts of self, space, values, and ideas held by the Penobscot Indians in the seventeenth century.

   Your answer should include:

   - The Penobscot Indians of the 1600s viewed themselves as consisting of both body and "vital self"; the latter was able to leave the body, perform acts, and interact with other "selves." If the self did not return to the body, the person became sick and died.

   - They viewed their space as a flat world, surrounded by saltwater, and centered upon the Penobscot River.

   - Some values and ideas held by the Penobscot are closely related to their self-awareness. They were a secretive people, protecting themselves from attacks (especially on the vital self) by distrusting strangers and being cautious in their dealings with living things in the forest (which also were believed to have vital selves).

3. Contrast the core values of the cultures of the Chinese and of North Americans of European descent.

   Your answer should include:

   - The core values of the Chinese culture are kin ties and cooperation. Compliance and subordination of the individual to the family and its needs are thus of utmost importance.

   - North Americans of European descent have "rugged individualism" as a core value. They believe that individuals, working alone and hard enough, will achieve what they want for themselves. Their obligations to others are limited and subject to change. For example, marriage can be ended by divorce, and parents are no longer responsible for children when the latter reach adulthood.

4. Describe several ethnic psychoses and traditional systems of treating illness and deviant behavior.

    Your answer should include:

    •   Ethnic psychoses are mental disorders characteristic of a particular group. One example is Windigo psychosis, a disorder found among the northern Algonkian Indian groups, such as the Chippewa, Cree, and Ojibwa. Individuals afflicted by the psychosis developed the delusion that they were transformed into Windigos, beings with a craving for human flesh. Afflicted individuals also developed the delusion of seeing people around them as animals that the Algonkian hunted as game.

    •   Shamans in traditional healing systems use rituals—which may include altered states of consciousness—to diagnose the cause of illness and deviant behavior by calling upon gods or spirits. The cause of illness is typically viewed as due to some breakdown in social relationships. For example, the Balinese shaman Jero determined that her patient had neglected his duties to his dead mother. The Yanomamo shaman Marshuh Dome attributes new diseases brought by gold miners to sorcery worked by the miners.

Alejandro Mamani: A Case Study in Psychological Anthropology 6

Assignments

Before viewing the video program	• Read the Overview and the Learning Objectives for this lesson. Use the Learning Objectives to guide your reading, viewing, and thinking. • Read Background Notes 6A, "A Case Study of Abnormality," in this study-guide lesson. Note the location of the Aymara on the map included with the Background Notes. • Review textbook Chapter 5, "Growing Up Human," pages 120–149, paying particular attention to "Normal and Abnormal Personality," pages 141–147. • Also review Background Notes 5A, "Psychological Anthropology and Personality."

View video program 6, "Alejandro Mamani: A Case Study in Psychological Anthropology"

After viewing the video program	• Review the reading assignments for this lesson. • Complete each of the Study Activities and the Self-Test in this study-guide lesson; check your answers with the Answer Key at the end of this lesson. • According to your instructor's assignment or your own interests, complete one or more of the Suggested Activities.

Overview

As you approach this lesson, remember that culture defines appropriate behavior, shapes ideas and values, and orders relationships between individuals. It should not be surprising, then, that culture also defines abnormal behavior. Besides defining what is normal or abnormal, the culture may even generate problems that lead to emotional stress and, perhaps, mental illness for its members. For example, as you learned in the previous lesson, some child-rearing practices in present-day North America tend to make it difficult for children to meet or accept the socially approved norms for sex-role behavior. In other words, some cultural traditions actually create pitfalls and obstacles to achieving culturally sanctioned goals.

The story in the video program, however, deals with problems probably caused as much by the rhythm of life itself as with the culture. The case study concerns an Aymara man with a mental illness. Anthropologists have gathered evidence indicating that the specific form a mental illness takes is culturally determined. Even if the illness is one that appears in most societies (as the condition suffered by Alejandro Mamani may well be), the Aymara culture strongly affects the way that the illness is manifested. Most North Americans, for example, do not expect to meet a person who is afflicted by evil spirits, as Mamani appears to be. But despondency and despair in old age or at approaching death are not unique to the Aymara.

The culture also defines and names mental illnesses and determines treatments with which to "cure" the sufferer. One society may class as "honored behavior" what another condemns as "abnormal," and treatment or support may be administered or withheld accordingly.

Your challenge in this lesson, particularly while viewing the video program, is to understand the complex system of beliefs and values that underlie the illness of one man. If you can describe the relationship between that culture and the illness, the attempts at cures, and the final resolution of the problem, you will have gained an important anthropological insight into one aspect of mental health and mental illness. You may also gain insight into your own culture's treatment of mental problems and the elderly.

Video Program: Alejandro Mamani, an elderly Aymara Indian, is the subject of this ethnographic study of mental illness and approaching death. Mamani, a village leader, believes he has been invaded by evil spirits and despairs of losing his faculties. Various Aymara cures are attempted, but the "possession" recurs. Mamani's family discusses the problem, weighing the cost of medical treatment against the slim chance of cure, and reluctantly decides against further treatment. An especially interesting segment shows the ethnographic filmmakers' dilemma and decision to step across the line between observation and participation as they offer limited help to the suffering man. The program offers insights into the treatment of mental problems and of the elderly in all cultures, mental illness, and the social consequences of mental disturbances.

As you view the program, look for:

- Alejandro Mamani's description of the different spirits tormenting him.

- reaction of the community and his family to Mamani's illness; and, later, the reaction of his family to the costs of the illness.

- the kind of diagnosis made, and the various cures that are attempted. Note how both are based in important Aymara beliefs.

- the manner in which Alejandro Mamani resolves two difficult problems for himself: division of his property and a final solution to his illness.

Learning Objectives

When you have completed all assignments in this lesson, you should be able to:

1. Describe the types and roles of "spirits" in the Aymara culture and Mamani's interpretation of the spirits that have possessed him. VIDEO PROGRAM; BACKGROUND NOTES 6A

2. Describe the variety of reactions of members of Mamani's family and community to his illness. VIDEO PROGRAM; BACKGROUND NOTES 6A

3. Describe the various "cures" tried by Mamani and explain the cultural interpretation of how they work. VIDEO PROGRAM; BACKGROUND NOTES 6A

4. Discuss in what ways Mamani's behavior can be seen as a preparation for dying. VIDEO PROGRAM; BACKGROUND NOTES 6A

A Case Study of Abnormality

The video program for this lesson describes a case of psychological disturbance among the Aymara Indians of the Bolivian Andes. In some ways, the illness of Alejandro Mamani is similar to that of people experiencing psychological disturbances in North American culture. But its diagnosis and treatment and the circumstances surrounding the illness are rooted in the cultural experiences of the Aymara. Alejandro Mamani is an old man living in Vitocota, a small village near Lake Titicaca 12,000 feet above sea level. Like his neighbors, he is a peasant farmer relying on his land, where he plants primarily potatoes and raises chickens, goats, and sheep.

Until the Bolivian revolution of 1952, most Aymara worked as tenant farmers on land owned by the *mestizos*, the Spanish-speaking middle class. After the revolution, the large landholdings were broken up and distributed to the peasants who worked the land. But the land is not very fertile, and harsh weather is a continual threat to survival.

By Aymara standards, Alejandro Mamani is a wealthy man. Not only did he have enough land and animals to make a living, but he secured title to his land for his children despite bureaucratic obstruction. He also earned respect by serving in many religious and secular offices and by helping to finance costly religious festivals.

The Aymara commonly get drunk at ceremonies and religious festivals, and this custom provided the occasion for Alejandro Mamani's illness. On the way home from a funeral where he became drunk, Mamani went to sleep at a well-known place where evil spirits dwell. While he was asleep, several spirits took possession of his body. Since then, according to the video program, Mamani cannot sleep at night, and, when he dozes off, he has nightmares in which the spirits appear as men and women, dancing, talking, and arguing with him. As he becomes increasingly ill, the spirits begin to appear in the daytime as well. One of the spirits appears to be his dead wife. He is attracted to this spirit, because the Aymara believe the spirit of a recently dead person tries to pull others

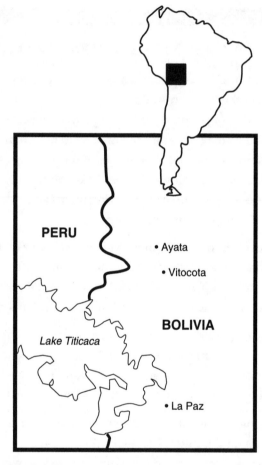

Figure 6.1: The Aymara Indians live and farm in a mountainous region in northern Bolivia bordered by Peru and Lake Titicaca.

after it. The Aymara also consider dreams as omens and consider them significant both for the person who experiences them and for the community as a whole.

Mamani says the spirits who are possessing him are not Aymara peasants but *mestizos*. Nevertheless, he undergoes a "divination" ceremony to determine the identity of the spirits. Divination is a ritual means of diagnosis conducted by specially trained diviners. In Mamani's case, curers propose to treat him by transferring his illness into several animals. The curers spend the night with Mamani and the animals—a dog, a rooster, lizards, a piglet, and a chick. At dawn, they take the animals to the place where Mamani became afflicted and set them free. The hope is that the spirits will have entered the body of one of the animals and be unable to find their way back to Mamani. In another treatment, Mamani fumigates a spirit with sulfur. The spirit leaves him temporarily, but demands tribute to stay away. Mamani and his family also consider seeing a medical doctor for a cure, but they have little faith in his ability. They say the medical doctor cures physical illness, but cannot help with spirit possession. When his family tires of having to pay for his cures, Mamani calls them together and transfers his property to them before committing suicide. Although suicide is disapproved of in Aymara culture, Mamani is remembered with respect, and his action is considered logical in view of his afflictions.

Mamani's illness illustrates several general themes in psychological anthropology. The diagnosis of his illness, explanations about how it occurred, and treatment for it are consistent with the values of Aymara culture. However, the symptoms are recognizable to us and fit within the explanatory framework of modern psychiatry. All societies have normative standards for behavior. Implicit in these standards are definitions of deviance and limits of acceptable behavior. When individuals fail to conform to these standards, societies have systems for reintegrating individuals into their social group. Divination and other diagnostic methods may serve to uncover social relationships between the patient and other members of his or her family. When an individual is unable to be reintegrated into the society, his or her social role will be redefined to definitively exclude him or her from the group.

Study Activities

Vocabulary Check

Check your understanding of terms by writing the letter of the appropriate definition in the space next to the corresponding term. Check your choices with the Answer Key at the end of the lesson.

_____ 1. ethnic psychosis   _____ 4. divination
_____ 2. Windigo   _____ 5. spirit possession
_____ 3. psychosis

a. a mild degree of mental disturbance
b. a behavior pattern in which a man takes the dress and manners of a woman
c. any mental disorder peculiar to a particular ethnic group
d. a mental experience among the Aymara considered abnormal when occurring frequently and intensely
e. a means of diagnosis and treatment used to cure Mamani
f. a psychosis associated with fear of cannibalism
g. a mental disturbance that severely affects the individual's functioning

Completion

Fill each blank with the most appropriate term from the list immediately following that paragraph.

1. The definition for "abnormal behavior" seems to depend on the _____ in which it occurs. Some behaviors that are deviant in one society would be considered normal in others. Other conditions, such as schizophrenia, would be recognized universally as abnormal. However, the specific _____ that the mental illness takes may depend on the culture. Also determined by the culture are _____ and _____.

         culture   form   treatment

         diagnosis   individual

2. Alejandro Mamani's belief in spirits is not considered abnormal in Aymara society. The Aymara religion is a combination of traditional Indian beliefs and _____; both traditions contribute to the idea that much of life is animated by spirits. But the frequency and severity of spirit _____ in the case of Alejandro Mamani are taken as indicators of illness, and attempts are made to cure Mamani, using various attempts at divination and driving the spirits away. Mamani's family grows resentful of the mounting _____ associated with his illness.

> costs   Roman Catholicism
>
> possession

Self-Test

Objective Questions

Select the one best answer.

1. Belief in spirits among the Aymara is

   a. widespread and a part of their religion.
   b. taken as a sign of severe abnormality.
   c. common only among children and the elderly.
   d. unusual, but tolerated by the community.

2. Mamani's condition first became apparent when it began disturbing his

   a. sleep.
   b. vision.
   c. coordination.
   d. hearing.

3. Mamani's family and friends reacted to his illness in all of the following ways EXCEPT with

   a. sympathy.
   b. belief that a cure should be attempted in the community.
   c. disbelief.
   d. embarrassment.

4. After Mamani's abnormal behavior has gone on for some time, his family reacts by

    a. trying to seek more effective cures.
    b. coming to accept it as normal.
    c. resenting the gossip of the villagers.
    d. resenting the cost of attempted cures.

5. Mamani was placed with animals for a night to

    a. attempt a transfer of spirits from him to them.
    b. shame Mamani for his behavior.
    c. bring him back to reason through contact with familiar things.
    d. give him a feeling that something useful was being done.

6. The purpose of the "divination" ceremony that was performed for Mamani was to

    a. identify the spirits troubling him.
    b. rid him of his belief that he was possessed.
    c. protect him from evil spirits.
    d. protect him from witchcraft.

7. When Mamani decided to will the last of his property, his family

    a. tried to dissuade him from giving in to his illness.
    b. felt he was no longer responsible for his actions.
    c. seemed to consider it appropriate.
    d. was fearful that such action would bring bad luck.

8. Mamani may have been motivated to discontinue seeking cures because

    a. he felt that if he ignored spirits they would go away.
    b. he felt that too much money had been spent.
    c. his children felt that too much money had been spent.
    d. the villagers disapproved of the attempted cures.

Short-Answer Essay Questions

1. Describe some of the types of spirits that the Aymara believe in. What types of spirits have attacked Alejandro Mamani?

2. Describe the assumptions inherent in the cures attempted for Mamani's illness.

3. In what ways does Mamani's behavior seem to be a preparation for his own death?

Suggested Activities

1. Conduct a survey about beliefs in spirits in your community. Check newspaper advertisements (especially the "personals" column) for "psychic readers." Determine whether there are laws restricting these kinds of practices in your community or state. Write a brief summary of your findings, and defend your opinion as to whether such beliefs should be considered "abnormal" in this society.

2. Do some investigation, including scanning current "self-help" books and talking with at least one professional, to gather evidence on whether a "midlife crisis" (such as male menopause) is a culturally induced phenomenon. In other words, is it a cultural neurosis or an ethnic psychosis? Or is it a universal response to aging? Speculate on factors in North Amercan society that might induce such crises.

3. Read and prepare a brief review of *The Bolivian Aymara*, by Hans C. Buechler and Judith Maria Buechler (Holt, Rinehart and Winston, 1971).

Answer Key

STUDY ACTIVITIES

Vocabulary Check

1. c   4. e
2. f   5. d
3. g

Completion

1. culture, form, diagnosis, treatment
2. Roman Catholicism, possession, costs

SELF-TEST

Objective Questions

(Page numbers refer to the textbook.)

1. a (Objective 1; video program; Background Notes 6A)
2. a (Objective 1; video program; Background Notes 6A)
3. c (Objective 2; video program; Background Notes 6A)
4. d (Objective 2; video program; Background Notes 6A)
5. a (Objective 3; video program; Background Notes 6A)
6. a (Objective 3; video program; Background Notes 6A)
7. c (Objective 4; video program; Background Notes 6A)
8. c (Objective 4; video program; Background Notes 6A)

Short-Answer Essay Questions

1. Describe some of the types of spirits that the Aymara believe in. What types of spirits have attacked Alejandro Mamani?

   Your answer should include:

   - The Aymara believe in spirits associated with specific places or animals, other spirits associated with natural forces, and some demon spirits, as well as spirits of the dead.

   - Mamani believes that several types of spirits have attacked him, including demons and spirits of the dead such as his wife.

   - The spirit of a dead person may come to a member of the community to lure or entice that person to join the spirit world. Some of the latter include spirits from the *mestizos*, or middle class of his country.

2. Describe the assumptions inherent in the cures attempted for Mamani's illness.

   Your answer should include:

   - The forms of cures tried on Mamani differed, but all assumed the presence of spirits of various types.

   - The purpose of attempted cures was to either drive the spirits and demons away or transfer them to the bodies of animals. The cures also assumed that a person with knowledge or special powers could bring about such cures.

3. In what ways does Mamani's behavior seem to be a preparation for his own death?

   Your answer should include:

   - In the video program for this lesson, Mamani seems preoccupied with death and speaks of suicide as a way out of his problems.

   - One of the spirits troubling him is that of his dead wife, who, according to tradition, may be trying to pull his soul after hers.

   - In a formal and ceremonial division of property, he finally distributes the last of his possessions to his children and another woman whom he raised from childhood. In Mamani's mind, this leaves him free to end his life.

Patterns of Subsistence: 7
Food Foragers and Pastoralists

Assignments

Before viewing the video program	• Read the Overview and the Learning Objectives for this lesson. Use the Learning Objectives to guide your reading, viewing, and thinking. • Read textbook Chapter 6, "Patterns of Subsistence," pages 150–167 and 174–177. (The remaining pages in this chapter will be assigned in the next lesson.) • Read Background Notes 7A, "The Egalitarian Society," and 7B, "Subsistence Patterns of the Netsilik, the Nuer, and the Basseri," in this study-guide lesson.

View video program 7, "Patterns of Subsistence: Food Foragers and Pastoralists"

After viewing the video program	• Review the terms used in this lesson. In addition to those terms in the Learning Objectives, you should be familiar with these:

carrying capacity
convergent evolution
cultural ecology
cultural preadaptation
culture core

ecosystem
horticulture
parallel evolution
pastoralist
subsistence pattern

• Review the reading assignments for this lesson.
• Complete each of the Study Activities and the Self-Test in this study-guide lesson; check your answers with the Answer Key at the end of this lesson.
• According to your instructor's assignment or your own interests, complete one or more of the Suggested Activities. You also may be interested in the readings listed at the end of Chapter 6 in the textbook.

Overview

When did you last track a wild animal through the forest? Or eat wild berries you gathered from a vine? For most people in North America, these are elusive pleasures, providing a much needed escape from the routines of everyday life. Yet, in this lesson, you will discover that humankind, for much of its existence, found its food where it grew and flourished naturally. People lived together in groups small enough that the abundance of wild plant and animal life provided them with ample diets. This first subsistence pattern is called **food foraging** or **hunting and gathering**. It refers to a lifestyle organized around hunting, fishing, and the gathering of edible plants.

People in foraging societies needed many sophisticated skills to convert the natural resources of their environment to their own use. Most groups traveled from place to place, building simple shelters in temporary camps. They had the technology to make tools like bow-and-arrows. They stalked game and killed it, using stone knives they fashioned themselves. Women, who provided most of the food through gathering, knew how to identify edible plants, distinguishing them from similar plants that could be poisonous.

Foraging people developed methods to distribute food throughout the group so that everyone shared in the abundance of nature. They developed a division of labor based on age and gender. They solved problems of social organization that allowed them to maintain order within the group and make decisions about where to hunt. They provided a context in which dependent children could grow to maturity.

Raising animals and plants in a systematic fashion is a comparatively recent innovation. About 10,000 years ago, major changes in subsistence patterns began to appear. In parts of the world, humans began to produce food instead of hunting or gathering it from the environment. In **pastoralist** societies, people began to domesticate animals, collecting sheep, goats, and pigs, and, still later, other animals into herds to provide food and other needs. Such a change is not as simple as, for example, leaving one trade to take up another. The shift from foraging to pastoralism resulted in an entirely different way of life, one organized around the important job of caring for animals. Since domesticated animals, unlike wild animals, could be "owned," social customs organized around rights to animals developed.

Food-foraging and pastoralist societies still exist today, following the ways of their ancestors. Scenes in the video program show dramatic moments in the lives of food-foraging and pastoralist societies. Their lives are neither drab nor lacking in adventure and satisfaction.

Even in North American society, segments of the population gather food from nature, but these subsistence activities have been dramatically altered by increases in population resulting from a more settled way of life. Indeed, commercial fishing, whaling, and seal hunting may threaten the survival of some species, so that environmentally oriented groups campaign vigorously to eliminate or control the killing of whales, seals, porpoises, and other creatures.

The next lesson will describe two other patterns of subsistence: horticulture and intensive agriculture. Both types of food production result in lifestyles that are radically different from those of food foragers and pastoralists.

Video Program: This first of two programs on subsistence patterns, from food foraging to food producing, explores ancient patterns, some of which are still followed today. The program describes several of the earliest forms of subsistence and how people adapted to their environments. The African !Kung woman's role as gatherer of nuts, fruit, berries, and roots is shown, as is the meat-hunting task of Mbuti pygmy men. Another segment shows how the Netsilik Eskimos have adapted to their harsh environment, which precludes any agriculture, by hunting seals. Other segments include the Nepali Sherpas and their herding of zomo, a hybrid of a yak and a milk cow; the Iranian Basseri and their unending search for fertile grazing land for sheep and goats; a modern forager among the discards of an urban area in the northeastern United States; and the Kwakiutl and their use of technology in fishing. Throughout the program, the relationship of subsistence patterns to cultural patterns and lifestyles is explored.

As you view the program, look for:

- the importance of the woman's role in food-foraging cultures.

- the technology and skill used in hunting by the Netsilik and the division of labor between the sexes.

- examples of social patterns among food foragers.

- two examples of pastoral peoples, the Nuer and the Basseri. These scenes emphasize the striking differences between the environments for each and challenges that each group must meet to survive.

- the role of foraging in modern societies.

- the impact of technology and government regulation on the Kwakiutl.

Learning Objectives

When you have completed all assignments in this lesson, you should be able to:

1. Understand that culture is the mechanism by which humans meet their basic survival needs. TEXTBOOK PAGES 151–159; BACKGROUND NOTES 7B

2. Define *adaptation* and describe evolutionary adaptation. TEXTBOOK PAGES 152–156

3. Describe the concept of culture area. TEXTBOOK PAGES 156–158

4. Describe the importance of and the characteristics of the food-foraging subsistence pattern and cite examples of this kind of society. TEXTBOOK PAGES 159–167; VIDEO PROGRAM; BACKGROUND NOTES 7A AND 7B

5. Identify elements of human social organization that developed as a result of the food-foraging subsistence pattern. TEXTBOOK PAGES 163–167; VIDEO PROGRAM; BACKGROUND NOTES 7A

6. Define *egalitarianism* and explain why the food-foraging subsistence pattern promotes egalitarianism among its members. TEXTBOOK PAGES 166–167; VIDEO PROGRAM; BACKGROUND NOTES 7A

7. Describe the characteristics of the pastoral subsistence pattern and cite examples of pastoral cultures. TEXTBOOK PAGES 174–176; VIDEO PROGRAM; BACKGROUND NOTES 7B

THE EGALITARIAN SOCIETY

There probably never has been an egalitarian society in the sense that all individuals have equal access to resources and prestige and perform identical tasks. Age and sex are universal bases for social distinction. A newborn baby does not have the same rights and responsibilities as a venerable elder and, in all societies, women don't do the same work as men or have the same social position.

Although these differences are rooted in biology—a baby cannot do the work of an adult man or woman, and the childbearing role of women is protected in all societies—the precise nature of the differences is culturally determined. Babies are treated differently from culture to culture, and the work of women may vary from raising pigs or growing yams in New Guinea to gathering Mongongo nuts among the !Kung of the African Kalahari Desert.

Among the Tsembaga of New Guinea, women raise pigs and men cook the pigs. In the United States, men traditionally cared for livestock and women did the cooking. Still, one pattern seems to hold true cross-culturally: Men operate in the public realm and women's work is typically defined as domestic. This difference is accentuated in industrialized societies, where the workplace is separated from the home.

It sometimes confuses students that anthropologists speak of egalitarianism when all societies make status distinctions on the basis of age and sex. In fact, individuals rarely have equal access to resources, nor do they make equal contributions to subsistence. But individuals are part of a social group, the family. In an egalitarian society, families are equal in status. No family unit is singled out for preferential access to resources and prestige, nor is it released from an obligation to provide labor for subsistence activities. Thus, in an egalitarian society, individuals have rights and obligations conferred on them by virtue of membership in a kin group, and all kin groups have equal access to resources.

Anthropologists distinguish egalitarian societies from stratified societies, which are characterized by rank, specialization of labor, and unequal access to resources. Status differences occur when individuals or families accumulate more wealth or privilege than others, whether through their own efforts or through inheritance. In an egalitarian society, no individual or family group may rise above others by inheritance, accumulation of wealth, or specialized knowledge. (The characteristics of stratification will be described in more detail in Lessons 16 and 17.)

Background Notes 7B

SUBSISTENCE PATTERNS OF THE NETSILIK, THE NUER, AND THE BASSERI

Producing food and allocating resources such as water or hunting rights are subsistence activities. All groups everywhere must have ways of caring for the survival needs of their members. People must feed themselves and shelter themselves from extremes of cold and heat, but the means for doing so vary from group to group, depending on environment and custom.

Obviously, resources available in the environment limit the types of foods people eat and the materials available to construct shelter and clothing. But resources are defined by the people who use them, and not all people exploit their environment in the same way. Some things defined as food by one group of people may be considered repulsive by others. For example, some South American Indians eat grubs, which are fat worms. Guinea pigs are raised for food in Peru. But neither would be considered food for humans in North American society.

When anthropologists analyze subsistence patterns, they must consider three variables: biological needs for food and shelter, environmental resources, and social adaptations for converting environmental resources into forms that can be used by people to meet their survival needs. These are the basis for an anthropological definition of subsistence: a cultural means for making environmental resources available for human consumption.

The three peoples presented in some depth in the video program—the Netsilik, the Nuer, and the Basseri—live in widely varying environments. They represent two subsistence modes, food foraging and pastoralism. Foragers typically range over a territory, hunting animals and gathering plants and other materials. They do not cultivate crops or keep domestic animals. Pastoralists, on the other hand, live by herding. They may also move from place to place, but their migrations are determined by grazing lands and other resources needed by their animals.

THE NETSILIK

The Netsilik live along the Arctic coast northwest of Hudson Bay. The region is treeless, and plant life consists primarily of lichen, mosses, and various grasslike plants. The Netsilik are almost exclusively hunters, since there is little to gather in their environment.

Yet the Netsilik must use the limited resources available to them to feed, house, and clothe themselves. Asen Balikci, an anthropologist who has studied them extensively, wrote, "The Netsilik, living in one of the harshest areas of the inhabited North, were able to survive in this cold desert environment because of their efficient and remarkably adapted technology" (*Netsilik Eskimo*. New York: Natural History Press, 1971, p. 3). They build houses out of snow and ice and make children's toys of ice. Caribou and sealskins are used for making clothes (including waterproof boots), sleeping bags, and kayaks. Because wood is scarce, most tools are made of bone. Lamps and pots are made of soapstone.

Like many other food foragers, the Netsilik migrate seasonally. Their lives are organized around two seasons, which present radically different environments and different resources to be exploited and which give rise to different social interactions. Winter, the long season, lasts from late September to July. During this time, the sea is covered with

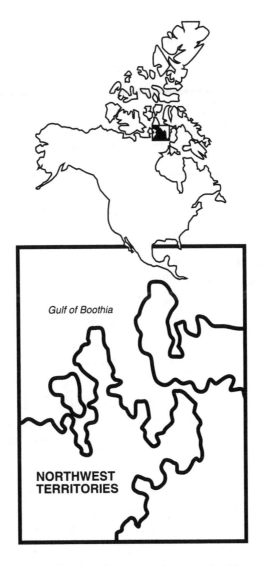

Figure 7.1: The Netsilik, native people of northern Canada, are a food-foraging culture. Like many food foragers, the Netsilik migrate seasonally.

ice and temperatures may drop as low as 20 to 40 degrees below zero Fahrenheit. July and August make up summer, the short season.

In summer, temperatures average about 50 degrees Fahrenheit in the daytime, the sea ice melts, and the Netsilik migrate inland to fish and hunt caribou. Food is relatively plentiful, more varied, and easier to obtain in the summer than in the winter. The Netsilik construct sealskin tents on the marshy tundra near fishing places, where they have built permanent stone weirs, or dams. They trap and spear salmon in the weirs and harpoon trout in the lakes.

In late summer, the Netsilik hunt caribou with bows and arrows, but they are not very good archers. They are more effective in hunting from their kayaks, which are outfitted with two long spears. Men in kayaks spear the caribou at lake crossings.

When food is plentiful in summer, each man hunts and fishes for himself and his extended family. But by January, the Netsilik gather in large winter camps of 50 to 100 people for seal hunting. Seal hunting is the primary subsistence activity for the Netsilik from January until the end of May. Seals are air-breathing animals, so they must have breathing holes in the ice. The hunter waits at a breathing hole and harpoons the seal as it comes to the surface to breathe. Because seals roam over a wide area, they use a number of breathing holes. A single Netsilik, hunting for his own family, could not hope to keep guard at all the holes or predict which hole the seal will use. It would be difficult for a single hunter to catch a seal, since he could not possibly watch all the breathing holes. Cooperation among a group of hunters increases the probability that one, or several, will get a seal.

Cooperation in the large winter hunting camps is encouraged by "sharing partnerships." In addition to providing seal meat for members of their extended families, Netsilik men give meat to their partners according to a rigid set of rules. Ideally, a man should have twelve partners, each of whom is entitled to receive a specific part of the seal. If a man is absent from the camp and cannot take part in division of the seal, one of his relatives takes his place. These sharing partnerships form a permanent set of alliances that extend loyalties beyond the hunter's family and give the sealing camp social cohesion.

Summer camps are smaller and are held together by kinship ties, but winter camps draw together hunters who are not bound together by kinship. The sharing partnerships extend the "kinship" tie and stabilize social networks in the winter camps. In the sharing of resources, the lack of systems of social stratification, and the specialization of roles, the Netsilik exemplify the egalitarian qualities of food-foraging cultures.

THE NUER

In French detective lore, the good inspector says *cherchez la femme* if you want to solve the crime. Anthropologist E. E. Evans-Pritchard says *cherchez la vache* (look for the cow) if you want to understand the Nuer (*The Nuer: A Description of the Modes of Livelihood and Political Institutions of a Nilotic People*. London: Oxford University Press, 1968). The Nuer are pastoralists who live in the Sudan, near the headwaters of the Nile.

They raise cattle for milk and other subsistence needs, figure their wealth in cattle, and use them as links in social relationships. Evans-Pritchard writes, "Cattle are their dearest possession and they gladly risk their lives to defend their herds or pillage those of their neighbors."

The area in which the Nuer live is extremely flat and covered with tall grasses. During the rainy season, which peaks in July and August, the area is flooded by the many rivers that cross the region, and the Nuer move their cattle to villages on sandy ridges. When the rains stop in December and January, water supplies near the villages are soon exhausted and the Nuer begin to move near lakes, marshes, and rivers. In late November or early December, the young people take the cattle to camps near watering places, leaving the older people to harvest grain and repair huts and cattle shelters. As water becomes scarcer, the young people are joined at their camps by married people and the camps grow to contain as many as several hundred people.

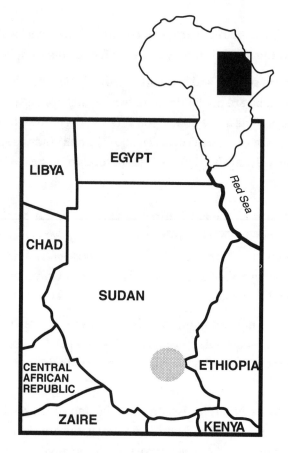

Figure 7.2: The Nuer, who live in flat, grassy lands in central Africa, are pastoralists whose subsistence and social and economic lives revolve around cattle. Each household owns its own food and provides independently for the needs of its members, although much food sharing takes place.

When the rains begin in May, the older people return to the village to prepare the ground for planting millet and corn. The young people bring the cattle back to the village by June. After about ten years, a village site is farmed out or grazed out and the Nuer move on to a new location.

The cattle are chiefly used for milk, and milking is done by women and children. The Nuer drink fresh milk, eat it soured, and make cheese from it. They do not slaughter their cattle for food, but they eat cows that die of natural causes. They also sacrifice cattle during ritual observances and eat their meat.

The area does not have either iron or stone, two materials traditionally used in tool-making. Wood is also scarce, but their cattle provide many subsistence needs for the Nuer other than food. Bedding, thongs, and various utensils are made from the skin, bones, and horns. The Nuer use dung to plaster walls and floors and burn it for fuel. In an area with little wood, dung is a useful fuel for cooking. The ashes of burnt dung are used for dyeing and straightening hair, tooth powder, and mouthwash. Cow's urine is used in making cheese, tanning leather, and for bathing one's face and hands. The Nuer bleed their cows frequently, boiling the blood for drinking or allowing it to coagulate and then cooking it.

Generally, the Nuer consume fish during the dry season and grain and meat during the wet season. Milk is a staple year round. The Nuer are never able to achieve a food surplus, and famine is always a threat. Their mobility is, in fact, an adaptation to their environment that helps to ensure a steady food supply. In the Nuer pastoral culture, each household owns its own food and provides independently for the needs of its members, but much food sharing takes place formally and informally at the village level. When cattle are sacrificed, the food is widely distributed, and members of the group are expected to share when food is scarce. Food sharing and the cattle economy allow the Nuer to survive in an area with little plant resources and where there are seasonal fluctuations in availability of water.

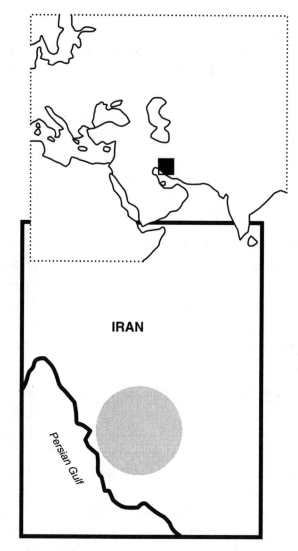

Figure 7.3: The Basseri, who live in southern and western Iran, are pastoralists who migrate seasonally. Tent dwellers, the Basseri do not own land, but they grow wheat, trade for other agricultural foods, and herd animals in a mountainous region.

THE BASSERI

Like the Nuer, the Basseri of southern Iran and the Bakhtiari of western Iran (described in the textbook, pages 174–176) are pastoralists. But the Iranian environment presents an entirely different set of challenges from that of the Nuer. The Basseri are tent-dwellers who migrate seasonally through a mountainous area.

In winter, when the mountains are covered with snow, the Basseri pasture their large herds of sheep and goats on the plains and foothills. During the spring, the herds graze on a well-watered plateau near the center of the territory. By summer, most of the lower-lying pastures have dried up and the Basseri move their herds to the mountains, nearly 6,000 feet above sea level.

The Basseri get milk, meat, wool, and hides from their herds, but their primary foods are sour milk and cheese. During summer, when pastures are rich, they can settle temporarily and build up food surpluses to help them through the leaner winter months. The Basseri also eat agricultural products, most of which are obtained by trade, but they also grow wheat at their summer camps. They do little hunting or gathering.

The Basseri trade wool and hides, and they are skilled weavers. The women weave saddlebags, carpets, and sleeping rugs from homespun wool and hair. Goat hair is woven to make tents. Woven goat hair is especially useful for the Basseri. In the winter, it retains heat and repels water; in the summer, it insulates against heat and permits free circulation of air. Donkeys and camels are used for pulling or carrying loads, and some of the more wealthy men have horses for riding.

Basseri social life and traditions are organized around migration. They do not own land, and individuals do not own property. But family groups, known as "tents," hold full rights over possessions, such as bedding, cooking equipment, a herd of sheep and goats (usually numbering about a hundred), and from six to twelve donkeys. In winter, the Basseri live in groups of two to five tents, but they gather in larger camps of ten to forty tents the rest of the year.

The tribe has rights over migration routes, which are recognized by local populations and authorities. Thus, though the Basseri do not own the land, they have access to it on a seasonal basis. The "tribal road," or *il-rab*, is regarded as the property of the tribe.

Like the Nuer, the Basseri live by their herds and use their products for shelter as well as for food. Both groups have sexual division of labor, but women and children do the cattle herding among the Nuer and Basseri men herd the sheep and goats. The Nuer occupy a relatively flat area, threatened only by mosquitos and other pests, but the Basseri must drive their herds along steep mountain trails. Women's work usually does not involve great danger, because their reproductive role is too important to the survival of the group and must be safeguarded. However, their work is no less important. Among such groups as the Nuer and the Basseri, all able-bodied individuals must make a major contribution to subsistence, but the nature of that contribution is determined by survival needs of the community.

Study Activities

Vocabulary Check

Check your understanding of terms by writing the letter of the appropriate definition in the space next to the corresponding term. Check your choices with the Answer Key at the end of the lesson.

_____ 1. adaptation
_____ 2. ecosystem
_____ 3. convergent evolution
_____ 4. culture area
_____ 5. culture core

_____ 6. cultural ecology
_____ 7. carrying capacity
_____ 8. egalitarian
_____ 9. pastoralist
_____ 10. subsistence pattern

a. the study of the interaction of specific human cultures with their environment
b. a member of a society in which animal husbandry is viewed as the ideal way of making a living and in which movement of all or part of the society is considered a normal and natural way of life
c. comprises the physical environment and the organisms living within it
d. in cultural evolution, the development of similar adaptations to similar environmental conditions by peoples of quite different cultural backgrounds
e. the number of people who can be supported by the available resources at a given level of technology
f. societies in which family groups are equal in status and have equal access to resources
g. the features of a culture that play a part in the society's way of making a living
h. a group's means for obtaining and allocating resources to care for the survival needs of its members
i. a two-way adjustment of those changes made by an organism on its environment and those induced by the environment on the organism.
j. a geographic region in which a number of different societies follow similar patterns of life
k. in cultural evolution, the development of similar adaptations to similar environmental conditions by people with similar cultural backgrounds

Completion

Fill each blank with the most appropriate term from the list immediately following that paragraph.

1. The ways in which a society uses its resources to meet basic human needs are studied as patterns of _____ by anthropologists. The specific ways employed by a society are determined by those shared skills and standards called its *culture*. Unlike other animals, humans can _____ to the environment, by making changes in the environment and by modifying their own _____. For example, the Comanche and the Cheyenne, who came from different backgrounds to the Great Plains, made similar _____ to the area, a phenomenon called _____ evolution.

adapt	customs	react
adaptations	divergent	subsistence
convergent	parallel	

2. It is likely that the majority of food-foraging societies have lived in environments that provide relatively plentiful amounts of food. Because they do not raise crops or animals, it is necessary for such societies to _____ from place to place in search of food resources. A typical group of food foragers probably has no more than _____ members. Membership in the group does not remain static, however. There are moves from one group to another by individuals or families for the purpose of visiting, _____, or seeking a more congenial setting. In food-foraging cultures, men have been the _____, while women generally have been the _____ . Although the hunting may or may not be cooperative, _____ within the group is customary.

100	affluent	hunters
200	food sharing	marriage
300	gatherers	move

3.   Pastoral cultures are so named because they raise _____ animals. These are _____ peoples, moving in response to the seasons. The Nuer move to villages on _____ in the summers to avoid lowland floods, while the Bakhtiari and Basseri move to _____ during the summer months. The lands on which the pastoralist societies dwell contrast strongly with those of food foragers, who are found today only in inaccessible forests and marginal areas, such as _____ and _____. Pastoralists are found in areas that do not lend themselves to agriculture, such as deserts, _____, and _____.

arctic tundra	grasslands	sandy ridges
deserts	mountains	wild
domestic	nomadic	

Self-Test

Objective Questions

Select the one best answer.

1.   The way in which a society meets its need for subsistence is determined by a society's
   a. heredity.
   b. environment.
   c. culture.
   d. intelligence.

2.   The attitudes, beliefs, labor patterns, and other factors that help determine how a society will subsist are called its
   a. cultural ecology.
   b. culture area.
   c. culture core.
   d. ethnology.

3. The concept of adaptation is best described as

    a. the invention of new tools or modifying materials for new uses.
    b. the application of previously learned skills to new situations.
    c. a two-way interaction between living things and the environment.
    d. the physical changes that increase the likelihood of survival.

4. An example of maladaptation is provided by the

    a. presence of sickle-cell anemia in nonmalaria regions.
    b. pastoralism of the Basseri.
    c. Nuer in the Sudan environment.
    d. drinking of blood by the Nuer.

5. A culture area can best be described as a

    a. set of similar cultural adaptations by widely separated societies.
    b. geographic region in which several cultures follow a similar life pattern.
    c. limited geographic region in which various societies have widely
        varying cultures.
    d. specific trait or behavior that is found in many cultures.

6. The food-foraging subsistence pattern

    a. persisted for approximately the past 100 years.
    b. involved all peoples from very early human societies to about 10,000 years ago.
    c. lasted from about 10,000 years ago to recent times.
    d. was never a universal subsistence pattern.

7. The food-sharing practices of food-foraging societies are

    a. similar to those of other primates.
    b. used only when game and wild vegetation are plentiful.
    c. rare and are used only as part of religious ceremonies.
    d. common.

8. An example of a food-foraging society still in existence is the

   a. Basseri.
   b. Netsilik.
   c. Bakhtiari.
   d. Nuer.

9. Features of social organization associated with food-foraging cultures include

   a. sexual division of labor, accumulation of wealth, importance of the camp as a semipermanent center of social activity.
   b. regular sharing of food, inherited social status, importance of the camp as a semipermanent center of social activity.
   c. sexual division of labor, stratified social organization, regular sharing of food.
   d. sexual division of labor, regular sharing of food, importance of the camp as a semipermanent center of social activity.

10. According to the textbook and video program, sexual division of labor in food-foraging societies probably arose in part from

    a. the importance of animal hunts, which provided most of the diet.
    b. biological differences between men and women.
    c. the need to keep the camp under guard and protected at all times.
    d. an urge to accumulate additional material wealth.

11. In a food-foraging culture, women generally

    a. provide the larger share of the diet from their gathering activities.
    b. undergo greater risk in obtaining food than men.
    c. travel great distances to obtain food supplies.
    d. hold the accumulated wealth of a family.

12. The term *egalitarian* implies

    a. equality.
    b. primitive.
    c. wealthy.
    d. civilized.

13. Which of the following is NOT an egalitarian aspect of food-foraging cultures?

    a. Families share food.
    b. Group membership is changed easily.
    c. A pattern of giving rather than receiving is practiced.
    d. Women share the same tasks and equal responsibilities with men.

14. Two words that best describe pastoralist cultures are

    a. nomadic and herders.
    b. gatherers and urban dwellers.
    c. farmers and nomadic.
    d. animal herders and urban.

15. Pastoralists move from one location to another in order to

    a. obtain fertile land for growing crops.
    b. find ample wild game for the group.
    c. have adequate water and grazing lands.
    d. avoid conflict with other families in the group.

Short-Answer Essay Questions

1. List several important characteristics of food-foraging cultures.

2. Suggest several reasons that make study of food-foraging cultures important to understanding both early human beings and modern industrial societies.

3. Briefly describe the concept of an egalitarian society from an anthropological perspective and identify the characteristics of food-foraging cultures that illustrate egalitarianism.

Suggested Activities

1. Before the coming of Europeans to the New World, most parts of North America were inhabited by one or more Indian groups. Seek information at your local library about the lifestyle and customs of one of these groups as they existed before European influence arrived. Which subsistence pattern did this group seem to follow? Write a brief report or summary of the information you find. In particular, try to include in your report any seasonal migratory patterns, information on the exact division of labor, and information on the kinds of social status or stratification that existed within the group.

2. Write a short paper on how your life would change if you had to live without basic items of technology such as television, telephones, refrigerators, hot and cold running water, and automobiles.

3. Cultural adaptation has enabled humans to survive and expand in a variety of environments. As an exercise in helping you understand how you have adapted to your sociopolitical environment either at home, at college, at work, or in some other environment, keep a detailed one-week log of your travel in and out of your community and the ways in which you deal with the contingencies of daily life.

4. Write a brief essay identifying food-foraging activities in present-day North America. Suggest what needs these activities fulfill.

Answer Key

STUDY ACTIVITIES

Vocabulary Check

1.	i	6.	a
2.	c	7.	e
3.	d	8.	f
4.	j	9.	b
5.	g	10.	h

Completion

1. subsistence, adapt, customs, adaptations, convergent
2. move, 100, marriage, hunters, gatherers, food sharing
3. domestic, nomadic, sandy ridges, mountains, arctic tundra, deserts, grasslands, mountains

SELF-TEST

Objective Questions

(Page numbers refer to the textbook.)

1. c (Objective 1; pages 152–156)
2. c (Objective 1; pages 158–159)
3. c (Objective 2; page 152)
4. a (Objective 2; page 153)
5. b (Objective 3; page 156)
6. b (Objective 4; page 159; video program)
7. d (Objective 4; pages 165–166; video program)
8. b (Objective 4; video program; Background Notes 7B)
9. d (Objective 5; pages 163–167)
10. b (Objective 5; pages 163–165; Background Notes 7A)
11. a (Objective 5; pages 163–165; video program)

12. a (Objective 6; pages 166–167; Background Notes 7A)
13. d (Objective 6; pages 166–167; video program; Background Notes 7A)
14. a (Objective 7; pages 174–176; video program; Background Notes 7B)
15. c (Objective 7; pages 174–176; video program; Background Notes 7B)

Short-Answer Essay Questions

1. List several important characteristics of food-foraging cultures.

   Your answer should include:

   • wide-ranging movement within a territory

   • small-sized groups, usually no larger than 100 members

   • sexual division of labor

   • food sharing

   • importance of the camp as a somewhat permanent area and center of social activity

   • egalitarian society

2. Suggest several reasons that make study of food-foraging cultures important to understanding both early human beings and modern industrial societies.

   Your answer should include:

   • Although only a small fraction of Earth's population today belongs to food-foraging cultures, more than 90 percent of all humans who ever lived were food foragers.

   • Food foraging is the oldest and longest-lasting adaptation humans have made to their environment.

   • Many of the ways that individuals, communities, and nations relate to each other today had their beginnings in the patterns of food-foraging cultures.

   • Basic concepts and practices that can be traced to food-foraging cultures include sexual division of labor, the development of camp as a semipermanent center of social activity, a profound respect for nature, sharing (especially of food) within the community, and egalitarianism.

3. Briefly describe the concept of an egalitarian society from an anthropological perspective and identify the characteristics of food-foraging cultures that illustrate egalitarianism.

Your answer should include:

- Egalitarianism implies the ideal of equality of all people. In an egalitarian society, all members ideally would have equal access to resources and prestige, and all would have equal abilities to perform the work.

- In practice, the egalitarianism of food-foraging peoples includes the organization of labor within the family. Though an individual's activities are determined largely by age and sex, the tasks of men and women are equally important to the group.

- Food foragers and their families share equally with other family groups in their larger group. Each food forager shares equal responsibility for obtaining food.

- Food foragers do not accumulate property or other forms of wealth. Thus, distinctions based on wealth do not occur in such societies.

- Group composition changes frequently in food-foraging cultures, because of needs for ensuring reproduction, marriage, avoiding conflict, or adapting to changing seasons.

Patterns of Subsistence: 8
The Food Producers

Assignments

Before viewing the video program	• Read the Overview and the Learning Objectives for this lesson. Use the Learning Objectives to guide your reading, viewing, and thinking. • Read textbook Chapter 6, "Patterns of Subsistence," pages 167–174 and 176–182. • Read Background Notes 8A, "The Change from Food Foraging to Food Production"; Background Notes 8B, "Afghanistan Wheat Farming"; and Background Notes 8C, "Taiwanese Rice Farming," in this study-guide lesson.

View video program 8, "Patterns of Subsistence: The Food Producers"

After viewing the video program	• Review the terms used in this lesson. In addition to those terms in the Learning Objectives, you should be familiar with these:

> nonindustrial cities stratified social order
> seasonal (dry) uplands swidden farming
> slash-and-burn horticulture tropical wetlands
> specialization of labor

- Review the reading assignments for this lesson.
- Complete each of the Study Activities and the Self-Test in this lesson; check your answers with the Answer Key at the end of this lesson.
- According to your instructor's assignment or your own interests, complete one or more of the Suggested Activities. You may also be interested in the readings listed at the end of Chapter 6 in the textbook.

Overview

It is obvious, from the preceding lesson, that cultures neither change at the same rate nor necessarily in the same direction. In Lesson 7, did it appear that a logical progression would be from food foraging to pastoral, then to agricultural subsistence patterns? In fact, changes in subsistence patterns have not necessarily occurred in such order. Food-foraging and pastoral societies still exist, successfully retaining much of the culture of their ancestors. In this lesson, which investigates two food-production subsistence patterns (horticulture and intensive agriculture), you will again meet examples of cultures that use the same technology and skills as their ancestors. You will also learn how intensive agricultural practices have been altered by technology resulting from industrialization.

It is not certain what caused some societies to change from food gathering to food producing. Perhaps a settled agrarian life appears more attractive than migratory food hunting, but there is evidence that such a change may not have always improved life. And some societies have changed from food-producing to food-foraging patterns.

Another important change in subsistence patterns is the shift from relatively simple agricultural practices, or horticulture, to intensive farming. Again, the evidence does not show conclusively what caused the change. Intensive agriculture, however, did set the stage for other developments, including the accumulation of substantial surpluses, the development of cities, and the emergence of more complex political and social patterns designed to meet new social problems.

A full appreciation of horticulture and intensive agriculture requires more than merely understanding the social changes that resulted from them.

The textbook and video program portray examples of horticultural and agricultural life, in the context of both daily work and seasonal cycle. Taking time to learn details of rice farming or the growing of a "prestige garden" seems particularly important to a study of anthropology, especially if you come from an urban industrial environment.

Appreciation also involves the many institutions and social practices, still a part of our culture today, that arose together with (and often because of) changes in agricultural methods. The village and the city are only two of many important cultural patterns that developed as human beings adapted to the new ways of food production.

Video Program: This program examines several methods of food production and various features of food-producing societies. The Yucatec Maya are shown employing the slash-and-burn technique of soil preparation. Rituals associated with food production are illustrated with film of Melanesian farmers practicing the hazardous land-diving ritual originally intended to ensure a good yam harvest. The program also looks at examples of intensive agriculture, including that practiced by the Khmer in Angkor and by North Americans on the Great Plains. Other societies featured are the Taiwanese and wet rice cultivation, and the Balinese, who have a complex social order that regulates the agricultural cycle of rice growing, using irrigation systems, draft animals, and fertilizer. The program emphasizes the influence of intensive agriculture on social order, including specialization of labor, social stratification, and the rise of government organizations.

As you view the video program, look for:

- the practice of slash-and-burn horticulture among the Maya of the Yucatán in Mexico.

- intensive agriculture, seen in Taiwan, Afghanistan, Bali, and Western industrial societies. Note the description of social conditions and social problems growing out of substantial changes in agricultural patterns.

- the crucial relationship of modern civilization to the technology used in agriculture.

Learning Objectives

When you have completed all assignments in this lesson, you should be able to:

1. Describe the significance of the transition from a food-foraging to a food-producing way of life and identify when this transition first occurred. TEXTBOOK PAGES 167–169, 173; VIDEO PROGRAM; BACKGROUND NOTES 8A

2. Describe the characteristics of the horticultural pattern of subsistence and cite examples of horticultural societies. TEXTBOOK PAGES 152–153, 167–169, 173–174; VIDEO PROGRAM; BACKGROUND NOTES 8A

3. Describe the natural environments in which food-producing ways of life are found. TEXTBOOK PAGE 173; VIDEO PROGRAM; BACKGROUND NOTES 8B AND 8C

4. Describe intensive agriculture and its relationship to the rise of cities. TEXTBOOK PAGES 176–181; VIDEO PROGRAM; BACKGROUND NOTES 8A

5. Briefly describe the characteristics of life in nonindustrial cities. TEXTBOOK PAGES 176–182; VIDEO PROGRAM; BACKGROUND NOTES 8A AND 8C

THE CHANGE FROM FOOD FORAGING TO FOOD PRODUCING

Popular writers sometimes make it sound as if the transition from food foraging to food producing occurred overnight, when people learned for the first time that planting a seed will allow it to grow into a plant or learned how to domesticate a wild animal. This concept is misleading because it implies that the development of agriculture is based entirely on acquisition of knowledge and that food production is always "better" than food foraging.

Food foragers possess sophisticated knowledge about the plants (and plant reproduction) and animals in the territories they occupy. Their survival depends on being able to identify edible plants, know the seasonal developmental cycles of plants, and distinguish them from poisonous varieties that may appear very similar. Foragers acquire sophisticated information about biological processes by observing animal behavior and butchering the animals they kill for food. Their cultural heritage includes all the information that members of a food-foraging society need to know to survive in their environment.

Individuals reared in a modern city would face a bewildering array of survival choices if set down in the middle of an African savannah or in a tropical rain forest. Even farmers would starve before their knowledge of agriculture could bear fruit. Clearly, both food foraging and food production require specialized knowledge and skills, but the expertise in one is not transferable to the other.

Another misconception about subsistence patterns is that a switch to agriculture frees people from working long, monotonous hours and ensures a secure food supply. On the contrary, ethnographic studies have shown that food foragers spend fewer hours in subsistence activities than do agriculturalists. The modern factory worker works longer hours than either food foragers or small-scale agriculturalists. Also, people relying on domesticated plants and animals are more susceptible to weather variations and disease than food foragers, who use a wider range of natural resources and can readily move to another area for more abundant game and vegetation.

Agriculture is not necessarily a "better" way of life for all people. However, the ability to produce and store food has profound implications for social organization.

The change from food foraging to farming implies a shift from nomadism to a more sedentary way of life. People who grow food tend to stay in one place instead of traveling from place to place in search of food. They live in more-or-less permanent dwellings, which means they devote more time and energy to the construction of their buildings. They accumulate more and heavier material goods, especially household goods. Pottery is an inconvenience to a food forager, who is better served by containers made of light-weight materials such as bark or animal skins.

Food foragers have no need to individually "own" their territories. However, a horticulturist, who invests time and resources in planting seeds, must be assured access to the plants when they mature and to the plot of land on which they are growing. With the accumulation of material goods and the need for year-round access to a particular plot of land, property rights and inheritance become more important.

Large-scale agricultural projects, such as irrigation systems, require coordination of labor. Conversely, innovations in agriculture may allow production of a surplus. Grain crops, which mature only at certain times, must be stored to ensure a continuing supply of staples such as corn and wheat. Producing a storable food surplus can free some members of a society from subsistence activities. At the same time, storing food resources requires management and allocation.

Freeing individuals in a society from direct involvement in subsistence activities allows development of skilled artisans, specialists, and managers, with the authority to control labor and settle disputes involving property.

The authority to command the labor of others makes it possible to construct monumental architecture and develop urban centers. Specialization of labor and development of an authority structure provide a foundation for different classes, or social inequality, and different access to resources. Thus, the development of a complex, stratified society is directly dependent on the ability to produce large food surpluses, which in turn is dependent on intensive agriculture.

Because of this interdependence, anthropologists maintain that social organization is directly tied to subsistence. (Anthropologists usually distinguish between horticulturists, who grow only enough for subsistence while using a relatively simple technology, and intensive agriculturalists.) Small-scale horticulturists do not, as a rule, develop large cities and highly stratified social systems, as is possible with an intensive agricultural pattern.

The following examples on wheat farming in Afghanistan and rice farming in Taiwan illustrate the relationship between agriculture and political systems.

Background Notes 8B

AFGHANISTAN WHEAT FARMING

Aq Kupruk is a settlement in Afghanistan near the border below Turkmenistan, Uzbekistan, and Tajikistan. The people of Aq Kupruk have farmed wheat since prehistoric times. Of the adult males, 70 percent own land and the rest work as tenant farmers. In April, wheat is planted in the high fields near the town. The fields are plowed with a pair of oxen and a wooden-frame plow with an iron plowshare or point. At harvest time, usually in July, the men move to temporary quarters near the fields. If additional help is needed for the harvesting, hired laborers are brought in. The wheat is cut with small, curved hand sickles that are much more efficient than large scythes for use on the hillsides. Teams of oxen are walked over the wheat to separate the grain from the chaff, and the farmers toss the wheat into the air with pitchforks to let the wind blow the lighter

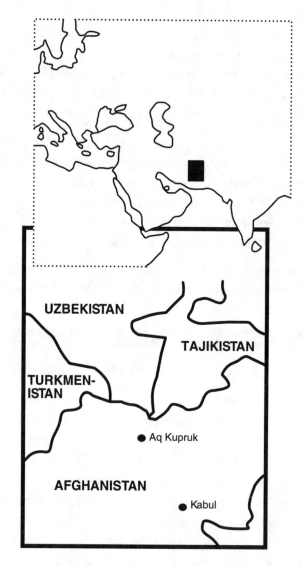

Figure 8.1: The characteristics of an intensive agricultural subsistence pattern are exhibited by wheat farmers in Afghanistan. They plow fields, plant vegetable and fruit gardens, herd livestock, fish, and hunt birds.

chaff away from the heavier grain. Finally, the wheat is taken to the mills to be ground into flour. The village mills are powered by water from a canal, which also irrigates produce gardens in the village. Every summer, the canal must be dredged and the mill rebuilt. Everyone who uses the mill or benefits from the irrigation is expected to help.

Most of the irrigated gardens are planted in corn, turnips, carrots, millet (a cereal grass), lentils, chickpeas, onions, potatoes, cucumbers, tomatoes, eggplant, sesame, linseed, spinach, coriander, cumin seed, and squash. Melons are grown on a small scale and many fruit and nut trees are also grown. Some cotton is grown, but it is almost exclusively for personal use. Sheep and goats are herded. The people also fish and hunt birds, such as pigeons, doves, and partridges.

Traditionally, sons inherit full shares of land from their fathers, while daughters receive half shares, which become part of their dowries. To prevent dividing the land into smaller shares, one son may inherit all the land, with cash shares going to the other children.

The village of Aq Kupruk comprises two linguistic groups: Tajik and Uzbek. The Tajik outnumber the Uzbek by about two to one, and the most affluent residents of Aq Kupruk are a subgroup of Tajik. The village is the political and economic center of the farming area around it. Its market bazaar is an especially important part of the local economy.

No formalized association exists among the shop owners of the bazaar, but a chief of merchants is informally chosen among the resident shop owners. The chief serves as a mediator between the bazaar merchants and the district governor. Tradesmen and shop owners sell rugs, household goods, and items from Kabul, the capital of Afghanistan. Farmers bring produce to sell in the open market. Most transactions are on a cash-and-carry basis. However, some shop owners lend money at high interest rates. In some cases, the money is not meant to be repaid. However, the borrower is expected to support the lender in factional disputes.

TAIWANESE RICE FARMING

Among Taiwanese rice farmers, agriculture provides the basis for a strong, centralized, bureaucratic government.

Rice is the primary crop in Taiwan. When the Japanese governed the island, from 1895 until the end of World War II, they wanted Taiwan to serve as a rice-producing area, so they built a number of large-scale irrigation systems to encourage wet rice production.

Most of Taiwan's approximately 20 million people are Chinese. When Chiang Kai-shek's Nationalist Chinese government was defeated by the Chinese Communists, he fled to the island with about a million of his followers. The Nationalist Chinese leader planned to use the island as a base to regain the mainland. Aided by the United States, the Nationalist government began to develop the agricultural and industrial resources of the island.

Growing rice is demanding work. In Taiwan, spring rice is planted early, vegetables are grown in the summer, and a second rice crop is planted early in the fall. The first job before planting is to clear the straw from the earlier rice harvest. Straw may be hauled off to use as cattle forage or burned to add fertility to the soil.

Rice fields are flooded a week before plowing to soften the soil. Plowing is done with a water buffalo or, more recently, with a power tiller. After the field has been thoroughly plowed, the soil is broken up further with a harrow, a pronged framework that is dragged over the ground. The soil is then treated with chemical fertilizer, which is sometimes augmented with manure or other natural fertilizers. Chemical fertilizer is the rice grower's greatest single expense.

At least two weeks before the start of plowing, rice seeds are planted in a specially prepared seedbed. Transplanting the rice seedlings into the plowed field requires a great

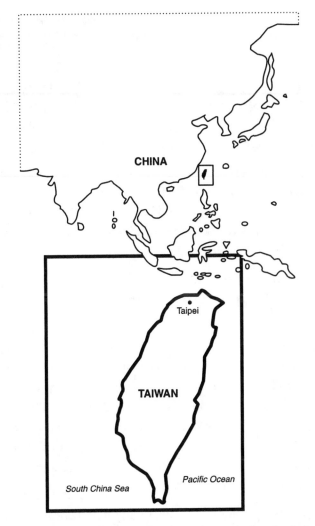

Figure 8.2: Wet-rice farmers in Taiwan practice intensive agricultural subsistence, but their system differs from that of the Afghanistan wheat farmer. Instead of a locally based, locally controlled system, the Taiwanese system traditionally has been based on a large governmental bureaucracy and on local sociocultural institutions.

deal of labor. First, the rice seedlings are cut from the seedbed, then carried in baskets on bamboo poles to the fields, where they are planted 10 to 12 inches apart in the flooded fields.

After planting, the field is flooded with at least 4 inches of water. While the plants are growing, the fields must be weeded three times, as well as sprayed with carefully selected insecticides and fungicides. Rice plants are prey to a number of insects and diseases, so selecting the right spray requires expertise.

Rice is harvested by using a sickle. After the fields have been drained and dried for several weeks, portable threshers are brought to a convenient location. These are powered by foot pedal or a small gasoline engine and have wire teeth that separate the grain from the stalk. Then the heavy sacks of rice are carried to the nearest road, where they are loaded on a farm wagon and hauled to the farmhouses.

Rice from the fields is dried on cement courtyards. It must be repeatedly turned to ensure even drying and, if rain threatens, the rice must be piled and covered. This job is usually done by the farm wife.

Rice farming requires intensive labor and sophisticated knowledge to choose the best varieties to plant during each season, the ones that resist disease and provide the greatest yields, and to select the proper fertilizers and chemicals. Nearly all Taiwanese rice farmers belong to farmers' associations that provide experts on the latest techniques in rice farming. Farmers can also borrow money from the associations to buy farming equipment and machinery. Since 1950, agricultural experiment stations have been established in Taiwan. These are often funded by the Chinese and American Joint Commission on Rural Reconstruction.

The Taiwanese rice-farming complex is not a locally based, locally controlled system like that of the Afghanistan wheat farmer. The Taiwanese system has traditionally been based on a large governmental bureaucracy and on local sociocultural institutions. Before the Nationalist Chinese took over, most of the population consisted of peasants who cultivated the land as small landowners, or tenants and laborers who had no rights to land. Most of the land, and thus nearly all of the power, was held by a small group of highly educated government officials and influential people, often referred to as gentry. The government handled problems by dealing with the resident gentry rather than with the peasants.

Through a series of laws, the Nationalist government reduced tenant rents to 37.5 percent of the annual main crop and protected the tenant against arbitrary eviction. Then the government took part of the landlords' land away and sold it to former tenants on an installment arrangement, spreading payments over ten years. The landlords were paid in land bonds, redeemable in two semiannual installments, and by stock shares in the paper, mining, and cement industries.

The object of redistribution was to increase rice production. The Nationalist government also expanded the irrigation network. Increased rice production was necessary to feed Taiwan's expanding population. But the government also wanted to produce a surplus to export to foreign markets for cash to finance its multilevel bureaucracy and military establishment. Also, it used cash from agriculture to finance a move toward industrialization.

The Taiwan and Afghanistan examples represent different approaches to intensive agricultural systems. However, these examples do not begin to exhaust the number of potential approaches to providing food through agriculture.

Study Activities

Vocabulary Check

Check your understanding of terms by writing the letter of the appropriate definition in the space next to the corresponding term. Check your choices with the Answer Key at the end of the lesson.

_____ 1. horticulture   _____ 5. nonindustrial cities
_____ 2. intensive agriculture   _____ 6. specialization of labor
_____ 3. New World dry lands   _____ 7. slash-and-burn horticulture
_____ 4. New World tropical wetlands _____ 8. land ownership

a. first became necessary in horticultural communities
b. areas where such crops as rice and yams are produced
c. areas where such crops as manioc are produced
d. subsistence food production using simple hand tools
e. variety of full-time occupations first appearing in nonindustrial cities
f. areas where such crops as maize, beans, and squash are produced
g. also known as swidden farming
h. communities made possible from intensive agriculture
i. often employ irrigation, fertilizers, and plows to produce a surplus

Completion

Fill each blank with the most appropriate term from the list immediately following that paragraph.

1. Evidence suggests that the first changes from food foraging to food producing may have occurred between _____ years ago. It is possible that many societies made this change out of necessity, such as a shortage of game and plants for food. The change was dramatic in its consequences, involving the development of new _____ and the loss of old ones. It is pointed out that a contemporary farmer probably could not survive if placed in a wilderness area and forced to hunt for food. For example, the farmer would lack such basic knowledge as which wild plants were _____.

             5,000 and 7,000   13,000 and 15,000   skills

             9,000 and 11,000   edible

2. Farming, however simple, made it possible for groups to develop _____ settlements to replace the camps of nomadic peoples. Material goods could be accumulated to a greater extent when people stayed in one area. Heavy utensils and tools became practical. Once surplus food was available, some individuals began _____ in the new crafts, thus beginning a new type of division of labor.

        specializing   permanent

3. Horticulture is a distinctive type of farming marked by the use of _____ tools on comparatively small plots of land. Individual plots of land, or gardens, are frequently located around a _____. Even though complex social systems are usually not developed by horticulturists, some kind of arrangement of _____ is necessary.

           complex   land ownership

           hand   village

4. In an intensive agricultural society, there can also be a division of labor. The Aq Kupruk, however, are chiefly farmers, although there are some _____ and shop owners; they maintain an existence comparatively isolated from urban centers. The Aq Kupruk are _____ agriculturalists, rather than horticulturists, because they use more complex technology, such as animal-drawn plows and _____, in addition to hand tools.

           intensive   tradespeople

           irrigation

5. Horticultural farming has been introduced both in dry _____ regions and in _____ wetlands. In dry regions of southwest Asia, the crops planted include wheat and _____, while in the wet regions, tubers and _____ are cultivated. In the Americas, different plants have been cultivated: maize, beans, squash, and _____ in the dry regions and manioc in the wet areas. Thus, distinct crop complexes have developed with these and other plants.

           barley   rice   upland

           potatoes   tropical

6. Nonindustrial urban areas are associated with many changes in the social order. Specialization of labor, social _____ based on occupation or family, and specialized _____ institutions develop to meet new needs. In the Aztec city of Tenochtitlán, the production of food surpluses made increasing population size and density possible. Many were employed in nonagricultural pursuits: artisans, warriors, merchants, _____, and nobles.

classes   priests

political

Self-Test

Objective Questions

Select the one best answer.

1. The most significant result of the change from food foraging to food production was that

   a. people could spend less time and effort to obtain food.
   b. kinship ties were weakened, allowing greater individuality.
   c. the nature of human society began to undergo significant change.
   d. food shortages became more severe.

2. It is believed that the transition from food foraging to food production began

   a. 6,000 to 8,000 years ago.
   b. 9,000 to 11,000 years ago.
   c. 12,000 to 15,000 years ago.
   d. 16,000 to 20,000 years ago.

3. The horticultural pattern of subsistence is characterized by all of the following features EXCEPT

   a. little or no surplus food production.
   b. use of hand tools.
   c. individual garden plots.
   d. irrigation from canals.

4. The "prestige garden" kept by Gururumba families is maintained principally for

    a. a decorative "front yard" for the family dwelling.
    b. a supply of good quality vegetables to exchange.
    c. growing ornamental plants and flowers used at festivals.
    d. growing a surplus that can be sold for profit at the end of the season.

5. Slash-and-burn horticulture is practiced by the

    a. Nuer of the Sudan.
    b. Bakhtiari of western Iran.
    c. Chinese farmers of Taiwan.
    d. Maya of the Yucatán.

6. Maize, beans, squash, and potatoes are typically grown in the

    a. dry areas in the Americas.
    b. tropical wetlands in the Americas.
    c. dry areas in southeast Asia.
    d. tropical wetlands in southeast Asia.

7. The development through intensive agriculture that made possible the rise of nonindustrial cities was

    a. new strains of food plants.
    b. kinship group organization.
    c. complex political structures.
    d. surplus food production.

8. A stratified society, in which people were ranked according to their work or their family, first appeared in

    a. food-foraging societies.
    b. horticultural societies.
    c. nonindustrial cities.
    d. pastoral societies.

9. The governmental structure of the Aztec city of Tenochtitlán is best described as

   a. a huge bureaucracy managing social order, taxation, and storehouses.
   b. an informal government of the leading farmers of the community.
   c. a king and a few advisors who settled disputes between landowners.
   d. a council of elders based on kinship groups.

10. The immediate purpose of the Nationalist Chinese redistribution of land to peasants in Taiwan was to

   a. decrease the rigid stratification of the society into social classes.
   b. increase the variety of crops grown.
   c. increase rice production.
   d. return to traditional farming methods.

Short-Answer Essay Questions

1. Explain why kinship units probably became important as people began farming in groups.

2. Why were nonindustrial cities able to develop in conjunction with intensive agriculture, but not with horticulture or pastoralism?

Suggested Activities

1. Use the *Statistical Abstract of the United States* (which you can find in your local library) and other references to learn the percentage of U.S. population directly engaged in agriculture at the present, 50 years ago, and 100 years ago. What developments in agricultural techniques have changed this proportion?

2. For an in-depth picture of the culture, organization, and urban life of the Aztecs, read *The Aztecs of Central Mexico: An Imperial Society,* by Frances F. Berdan (Harcourt Brace College Publishers, 1982).

3. Read Gideon Sjoberg's *The Preindustrial City: Past and Present* (Free Press, 1965); then compare the preindustrial "agricultural revolution" with industrial city patterns.

Answer Key

Vocabulary Check

1. d   4. c   7. g
2. i   5. h   8. a
3. f   6. e

Completion

1. 9,000 and 11,000, skills, edible
2. permanent, specializing
3. hand, village, land ownership
4. tradespeople, intensive, irrigation
5. upland, tropical, barley, rice, potatoes
6. classes, political, priests

SELF-TEST

Objective Questions

(Page numbers refer to the textbook.)

1. c (Objective 1; pages 167–169; Background Notes 8A)
2. b (Objective 1; page 167)
3. d (Objective 2; pages 167–169; video program)
4. b (Objective 2; page 173)
5. d (Objective 2; video program)
6. a (Objective 3; page 173)
7. d (Objective 4; page 176; Background Notes 8A)
8. c (Objective 5; pages 176–177; video program)
9. a (Objective 5; page 180)
10. c (Objective 5; video program; Background Notes 8C)

Short-Answer Essay Questions

1. Explain why kinship units probably became important as people began farming in groups.

   Your answer should include:

   - Ownership of land became important when people began to invest their time and efforts in planting and harvesting. The horticulturist or agriculturalist needed to know that the land and the crop would be "his" at harvest time.

   - The growth of settlements meant that more people shared the same resources, such as land and water.

   - Strong kinship groups probably served as the organizing units to determine ownership of parcels of land; the same organizations probably helped settle the question of obtaining adequate work parties for gardens or farms. Kinship organizations also provided a structure for access to land, sharing crops, and inheritance of property.

2. Why were nonindustrial cities able to develop in conjunction with intensive agriculture, but not with horticulture or pastoralism?

   Your answer should include:

   - Population growth is one key factor in the rise of cities. Such growth is related to improved agricultural techniques and higher crop yields, but the cause-and-effect relationship is not certain.

   - Production of substantial food surpluses makes it possible to free some people from food-producing activities. Thus, individuals can specialize in arts and crafts, or become politicians, priests, or warriors on a full-time basis. The surpluses also require a system for distributing the food and other products, usually a marketplace for the exchange of goods. The market becomes the focal point of the region and the basis of a village or a city. Some people accumulate greater wealth and prestige and become leaders with authority to command the labor of others.

- Development of formal political organizations, new inventions, and wider trade created opportunities for construction and other large-scale projects. A modern example of the impact of strong political organization is the island of Taiwan, which has directed large agricultural efforts to make industrialization possible.

- In contrast, food-foraging and pastoral societies practiced population mobility. Storage of food surpluses was not practical, nor was accumulation of excess material goods.

Economic 9 Anthropology

Assignments

Before viewing the video program	• Read the Overview and the Learning Objectives for this lesson. Use the Learning Objectives to guide your reading, viewing, and thinking. • Read textbook Chapter 7, "Economic Systems," pages 184–213. • Review the section on "Adaptation" in textbook Chapter 6, pages, 152–159, on the relationship between natural resources and culture.

View video program 9, "Economic Anthropology"

After viewing the video program	• Review the terms used in this lesson. In addition to those terms in the Learning Objectives, you should be familiar with these:

balanced reciprocity	informal economy
conspicuous consumption	Kula ring
craft specialization	market exchange
generalized reciprocity	money

• Review the reading assignments for this lesson.
• Complete each of the Study Activities and the Self-Test in this study-guide lesson; check your answers with the Answer Key at the end of this lesson.
• According to your instructor's assignment or your own interests, complete one or more of the Suggested Activities. You also may be interested in the readings listed at the end of Chapter 7 in the textbook.

Overview

For many people in industrialized Western societies, "economics" appears to be a field of vast, impersonal, vaguely understood forces. The size of a federal government budget for a single year, or the amounts involved in a country's gross national product, for example, stagger the imagination. The international markets and global economy discussed in daily newspapers seem impersonal, far beyond the control of individuals or even governments. Also, to people in an industrial society, the use of currency, money, seems "natural," and money is very useful. It is easier to place a money-value, like $25, on a shirt than to define the value of the garment in terms of a number of chickens or liters of oil. Even so, currency introduces new factors into economics that further complicate its understanding. Economic theories in Western industrial societies deal with huge business enterprises, huge governments, vast amounts of money, and the exchange of goods and services for profit.

For anthropologists, the "Westernized" interpretation of economics has limited value in studying the economics of nonindustrial societies because many traditional cultures studied by anthropologists do not use either money or profit as bases for their economics. These cultures do not encourage the accumulation of material goods for personal wealth, and they often do not permit private ownership of property or land. Such economies, therefore, cannot be interpreted in light of industrialized Western money-based systems or the technologies and values governing work and property in those societies.

To begin your study of economic anthropology in this lesson and the following one, it might help to view economics from the standpoint of the individual and the group. Perhaps it has occurred to you that very few persons are "self-sufficient." Virtually everyone on Earth consumes some food or uses something that someone else has produced. Some societies feature sharing as the means for distribution, but in many there is a formalized exchange of goods and services. In either case, the pattern of the culture determines the form and circumstances of sharing or exchange. As you learned in previous lessons, human beings have survived and subsisted in nearly every type of climate and terrain through cultural adaptation. The economics of a society is simply one part (and a very important part) of the society's adaptation to existing conditions. Like all adaptation, economics is partly dictated by environmental conditions, but in a larger sense, it is a highly creative response to those conditions. Some kind of division of labor, for instance, exists in all societies, but exactly how work is assigned to men, women, and children varies widely. Cultural attitudes toward wealth vary just as widely. Accumulation of wealth is virtually impossible in some societies, while in others accumulation is encouraged only for the purpose of giving the wealth away again.

Anthropologists feel that economic systems must be studied in the context of the cultures in which they exist. Therefore, this lesson will give you glimpses of striking contrasts between the values and practices of Western and non-Western cultures. You will see seemingly opposite economic practices used effectively to satisfy similar needs of both Western and non-Western cultures, while practices that otherwise are similar in both cultures are being used to satisfy different motives and purposes.

Early in this course it was suggested that every human culture is unique, having its own worth and value. For this reason alone, the economies of other societies should be studied and understood. The textbook identifies an even more urgent reason for cultural understanding: the expansion of Western economic practices into third-world countries. Governments of some nonindustrial countries attempt to superimpose industrial patterns on their present economies, frequently in sincere efforts to improve the quality of life for their peoples. Businesses from the United States and other Western countries establish new operations that until now have followed older, traditional cultural patterns. History tells us that the Industrial Revolution in Europe and the United States, while eventually improving the quality of life for most of their peoples, initially led to misery and deprivation for large numbers for much more than a generation. Today, suddenly imposed economic changes can deprive much of a society of its security, livelihood, and health.

Western economic values are not the only legitimate economic values, and cultural change should be approached with caution and concern for the society's members. The insights that can be gained through the discipline of anthropology are needed in a time when Western markets and industries seek expansion into third-world countries.

Video Program: From the generalized reciprocity among the !Kung to the balanced reciprocity of the Yanomamo and the Trobriand Islanders, this program explains that the economies of many non-Western societies are based on principles other than currency. In the highlands of New Guinea, the Mendi are shown engaging in balanced reciprocity when they barter a bride price in pearl shells and in redistribution when they engage in a cassowary contest in which they give away their holdings to gain prestige. A third system of distribution—the marketplace—is illustrated with scenes of Ashanti women in Ghana and of nomads in Afghanistan. The Ashanti women, who trade fruits and vegetables, are shown negotiating within a network of economic interdependency that reflects traditional social relationships. In Afghanistan, the nomads are seen negotiating within an economy based on both barter and cash. The program concludes with an examination of how a market system and a cash economy change the nature of distribution and social relationships in modern Western society.

As you view the video program, look for:

- examples of generalized reciprocity among food-foraging societies.

- scenes of the Kula trade of the Trobriand Islanders.

- the importance of gender roles among the Mendi horticuturists and in the Ashanti market place.

- an Afghan marketplace and the functions it serves.

- economic behavior and problems of industrialized cultures.

Learning Objectives

When you have completed all assignments in this lesson, you should be able to:

1. Define *economic system*. TEXTBOOK PAGE 186; VIDEO PROGRAM

2. Recognize that raw materials, labor, and technology are essential resources for the production of goods and services. TEXTBOOK PAGES 188–195

3. Describe three patterns for the sexual division of labor and a typical pattern of division of labor by age in a traditional society. TEXTBOOK PAGES 188–191

4. Describe various ways land resources may be allocated for economic production. TEXTBOOK PAGE 193

5. Define *technology* and describe two examples of technological knowledge in nonindustrial societies. TEXTBOOK PAGES 194–195

6. Define and describe three systems of distributing goods in nonindustrial societies: *reciprocity, redistribution,* and *market exchange.* TEXTBOOK PAGES 195–197, 200–202, 206–208, AND 210; VIDEO PROGRAM

7. Describe barter (including silent trade) as a form of negative reciprocity. TEXTBOOK PAGES 197–200; VIDEO PROGRAM

8. Describe the conditions necessary for redistribution to emerge as a system of economic distribution. TEXTBOOK PAGES 200–201

9. Explain the Big Man feast of many societies in Papua New Guinea as a display of wealth and a "leveling mechanism." TEXTBOOK PAGES 201–205

10. Describe the functions of the marketplace in nonindustrial societies. TEXTBOOK PAGES 206–208, 210; VIDEO PROGRAM

11. Explain why expansion of business ventures into third-world countries makes the study of economic anthropology important. TEXTBOOK PAGES 210–211

Study Activities

Vocabulary Check

Check your understanding of terms by writing the letter of the appropriate definition in the space next to the corresponding term. Check your choices with the Answer Key at the end of the lesson.

_____ 1. economic system   _____ 7. leveling mechanism
_____ 2. craft specialization   _____ 8. barter
_____ 3. negative reciprocity   _____ 9. balanced reciprocity
_____ 4. tools   _____ 10. redistribution
_____ 5. reciprocity   _____ 11. conspicuous consumption
_____ 6. generalized reciprocity

a. requires production of a surplus and the existence of a centralized government
b. a form of barter without verbal communication
c. artifacts used in the production of goods
d. display of wealth to gain prestige
e. the overall process by which goods are produced, distributed, and consumed in a society
f. exchange of goods and services of about equal value
g. an exchange in which the giving and the receiving are specific as to the value of the goods and the time of their delivery.
h. one type of division of labor common in more complex societies
i. an exchange in which neither the value of what was given is calculated nor the time of repayment specified
j. exchange of goods between two groups, each of which calculates relative value
k. social obligations that function so that no individual accumulates more wealth than another in a society
l. an exchange in which the giver tries to get the better of the exchange

Completion

Fill each blank with the most appropriate term from the list immediately following that paragraph.

1. An economic system involves the _____, _____, and _____ of goods. Economic systems are studied by anthropologists because culture defines the wants or demands of people in a society, dictates how and when available goods will be distributed, and establishes the division of labor—all needed for an economic system. The culture also determines the society's _____ to the environment and supplies the technologies that will be used to exploit natural _____.

    adaptation   distribution   resources

    consumption   production

2. All societies assign certain tasks to members of each _____, although in modern industrial societies, the importance of this kind of division of labor is diminishing. People of various ages also have different roles. The exact pattern for all division of labor is established by the culture. Landownership patterns also vary among nonindustrial societies—in one common pattern, the land is owned by a _____ group. In other societies, however, there is a feudal pattern in which land ultimately belongs to the _____. Individuals who work the land have some "ownership rights," but cannot sell or give their land away without approval. Individual ownership of land is rare in nonindustrial societies.

    chief or king   sex

    kinship

3. Taxes and government expenditures in the United States are a form of _____. In nonindustrial societies, a similar pattern can be part of the economic system. Some of the goods go to the government, which in turn distributes them according to its needs, thus replacing one-to-one exchange. For this process to exist, there must be a fairly substantial _____ of goods, combined with a complex _____ organization.

    political   surplus

    redistribution

4. "Market exchange" in modern industrial societies refers to the methods by which price is established through the balancing of _____ and _____. In nonindustrial societies, market exchange is carried out in an actual marketplace. In these marketplaces, people exchange goods grown, raised, or made by _____. The marketplaces in these societies also have _____ functions, which are as important as economic functions.

demand	political	supply
outsiders	social	themselves

Self-Test

Objective Questions

Select the one best answer.

1. In addition to production, the essential parts of an economic system are

   a. reciprocity and distribution.
   b. distribution and consumption.
   c. consumption and taxation.
   d. taxation and redistribution.

2. To produce goods, a nonindustrial society needs

   a. only labor.
   b. labor and technology.
   c. technology and raw materials.
   d. labor, technology, and raw materials.

3. In the division of labor by age found in nonindustrial societies,

   a. both children and the elderly are likely to have important roles.
   b. younger children are usually not permitted to work, but the elderly have important ceremonial and advisory roles.
   c. elderly persons are usually honored but contribute little work, while children are expected to be productive at an early age.
   d. neither elderly persons nor children usually make any significant contribution to the economy of the family or group.

4. The basis for sexual division of labor in traditional societies is related to

   a. environmental factors.
   b. technological factors.
   c. cultural patterns.
   d. biological factors.

5. In sexually segregated societies,

   a. men and women perform identical tasks.
   b. tasks usually performed by one sex may be performed by the other.
   c. a person of one sex would seldom perform a task normally done by the other.
   d. each sex has recognized tasks, but neither sex is thought inferior to the other.

6. In !Ju/'hoansi societies, ownership of land is traditionally recognized as held by

   a. band members who have lived longest in the area.
   b. each individual adult male who uses the land.
   c. the entire band.
   d. the chief or "king."

7. In some west-African societies, the typical pattern of landownership is

   a. individual ownership.
   b. feudal ownership.
   c. band ownership.
   d. descent-group ownership.

8. The technology of a nonindustrial society is reflected in part in its

   a. land holdings.
   b. hunting or agricultural skills.
   c. traditions and rituals.
   d. tools and artifacts.

9. An example of technology typical of a horticultural society is the

   a. hoe.
   b. arrow.
   c. threshing machine.
   d. tent.

10. A system of reciprocity where neither the value of what is given is calculated nor the time of repayment specified is called

    a. balanced.
    b. open ended.
    c. generalized.
    d. negative.

11. The Kula ring involves barter and an element of

    a. negative reciprocity.
    b. generalized reciprocity.
    c. redistribution.
    d. silent trade.

12. Of the following societies, the one that developed a sophisticated redistribution system is the

    a. Trobriand Islanders.
    b. Kwakiutl.
    c. Kota.
    d. Inca.

13. The conditions essential for the establishment of a system of redistribution are

    a. conspicuous consumption and a surplus.
    b. a leveling mechanism and a surplus.
    c. a central administration and a surplus.
    d. a central administration and a leveling mechanism.

14. The Big Man feast is considered a leveling mechanism because it

    a. is also an occasion to renew friendships and exchange gossip.
    b. tends to distribute goods so that no one retains more than anyone else.
    c. is a procedure that involves balanced reciprocity.
    d. involves conspicuous consumption of wealth.

15. Which of the following is NOT a function of a nonindustrial marketplace?

    a. the display of wealth for social prestige
    b. the display and sale of goods produced or grown by the people
    c. the opportunity for social exchanges
    d. a location for the exchange of goods produced in a region

16. Which of the following institutions is similar to a nonindustrial marketplace?

    a. New Orleans cotton exchange
    b. New York stock exchange
    c. a flea market
    d. a Big Man feast

17. The history of business ventures such as Western-style farming operations in third-world countries suggests that

    a. such projects usually improve the income and health of rural populations.
    b. such projects often deprive much of the population of their means of livelihood.
    c. such projects would improve living conditions if the local populations were willing to work.
    d. large corporations do not need to understand the culture and society affected by their operations.

Short-Answer Essay Questions

1. Define each of these terms in relation to nonindustrial societies: technology, balanced reciprocity, generalized reciprocity, negative reciprocity.

2. What are the social and economic aspects of barter and silent trade?

3. In what ways does generalized reciprocity resemble the Big Man feast, and how do these two practices differ?

4. List several problems that might arise when Western industrial practices are imposed on societies with non-Western cultures.

Suggested Activities

1. Haviland has listed several advances and trends in industrial societies that tend to reduce division of labor by sex. From your own observations or additional reading, what evidence is there that roles assigned based on sex are disappearing in North America? Do you see indications that some such roles are remaining firmly entrenched? You may wish to read the article "Society and Sex Roles," by Ernestine Friedl, in *Human Nature*, 1 (April 1978): 68–75.

2. Carefully observe exchanges in some of the following situations: birthday parties, weddings, holiday gifts, and in flea markets or garage sales. Then make a report on the exchange patterns. Can you describe these patterns in terms of balanced, generalized, and negative reciprocity?

3. The "profit motive" has generally been cited as the driving force behind successful industrial enterprise and much individual achievement. Many have considered it "universal." Based on the information in this lesson, would you agree or disagree with the concept of a "prestige motive"? In North American society, are "profit" and "prestige" identical? How do they differ?

Answer Key

STUDY ACTIVITIES

Vocabulary Check

1. e	5. f	9. g
2. h	6. i	10. a
3. l	7. k	11. d
4. c	8. j	

Completion

1. production, distribution, consumption, adaptation, resources
2. sex, kinship, chief or king
3. redistribution, surplus, political
4. supply, demand, themselves, social

SELF-TEST

Objective Questions

(Page numbers refer to the textbook.)

1. b (Objective 1; page 186; video program)
2. d (Objective 2; page 188)
3. a (Objective 3; pages 190–191)
4. c (Objective 3; pages 188–190)
5. c (Objective 3; pages 188–190)
6. a (Objective 4; page 193)
7. b (Objective 4; page 193)
8. d (Objective 5; page 194)
9. a (Objective 5; page 194)
10. c (Objective 6; page 197; video program)
11. a (Objective 7; pages 198–200; video program)
12. d (Objective 8; page 200)
13. c (Objective 8; pages 200–201)
14. b (Objective 9; pages 201–205)
15. a (Objective 10; pages 206–208; video program)
16. c (Objective 10; page 210)
17. b (Objective 11; page 210)

Short-Answer Essay Questions

1. Define each of these terms in relation to nonindustrial societies: technology, balanced reciprocity, generalized reciprocity, negative reciprocity.

    Your answer should include:

    *   Technology is the capability to apply knowledge for practical purposes. Examples could include ability to make tools and weapons or identify plants that can be used as food.

    *   Balanced reciprocity: an exchange of goods or services of about equal value with agreement about relative values and the times for exchange to take place.

    *   Generalized reciprocity: a system of exchange in which neither the value of goods given is calculated nor a time of repayment specified. For example, general distribution of food to group members from a hunt is considered generalized reciprocity.

    *   Negative reciprocity: an exchange in which one party tries to obtain the better value in the trade. This type of exchange may involve deceit or even use of force.

2. What are the social and economic aspects of barter and silent trade?

    Your answer should include:

    *   Barter is a type of exchange that usually takes place between people from different groups.

    *   To minimize negative reciprocity and help ensure a balance, much bargaining may take place in the calculation of relative value.

    *   Barter allows exchange to take place despite potential hostility and competition between the respective groups.

    *   Silent trade is a form of barter without any verbal communication. For example, goods offered for trade are displayed, and the opposite group in turn displays what it offers in exchange. Acceptance may be shown when the first group takes possession of the traded goods.

    *   Silent trade makes exchange possible when the groups are prohibited from openly communicating with each other, when verbal communication might lead to hostility, or when there is no common language.

3. In what ways does generalized reciprocity resemble the Big Man feast, and in what ways do these two practices differ?

Your answer should include:

- Generalized reciprocity and the Big Man feast both serve as leveling mechanisms: They tend to prevent great accumulation of wealth and encourage distribution of wealth throughout the group.

- They also resemble each other in that both are viewed as social obligations within the group.

- They are different in several respects. The Big Man feast is an elaborate celebration with ceremonial features; reciprocity need not be an elaborate occasion. The potential for prestige is probably much greater in the Big Man feast than in most instances of generalized reciprocity. As described in the textbook, generalized reciprocity usually does not involve the extensive accumulation of surpluses necessary for a Big Man feast.

4. List several problems that might arise when Western industrial practices are imposed on societies with non-Western cultures.

Your answer should include:

- Traditional economic patterns are usually disrupted by new economic activities imposed on a society. Familiar types of work might disappear, and allocation of land use or other resources could change drastically.

- Economic activities are integrated into the larger cultural pattern so that changes in that area might have a profound effect on other aspects of life in the society affected by change. For example, traditional ways of earning a living may be closely related to the concept of "manhood" or "womanhood." In extreme cases, a disruption of the familiar ways of doing things might lead to complete culture loss.

- Changes might occur so rapidly that many individuals cannot adjust to unfamiliar new situations or find ways to earn a living. So-called "economic improvement" under such conditions often leads to extreme poverty, hunger, health problems, and large-scale discontent.

- Problems are compounded by Westerners who implement economic changes without understanding the cultural basis of the affected society.

The Highland Maya: A Case Study in Economic Anthropology 10

Assignments

Before viewing the video program	• Read the Overview and the Learning Objectives for this lesson. Use the Learning Objectives to guide your reading, viewing, and thinking.
	• Read Background Notes 10A, "The Highland Maya," in this study-guide lesson.
	• Review textbook Chapter 7, "Economic Systems," paying special attention to the section "Leveling Mechanisms" (page 195).

View video program 10, "The Highland Maya: A Case Study in Economic Anthropology"

After viewing the video program	• Review the terms used in this lesson. In particular, check your understanding of these:

        cargo   *mayordomo*   *milpa*
        leveling mechanism   *mestizo*   stratified system

• In Figure 10.1, locate the region of the Highland Maya.
• Review the reading assignments for this lesson.
• Complete each of the Study Activities and the Self-Test in this study-guide lesson; check your answers with the Answer Key at the end of this lesson.
• According to your instructor's assignment or your own interests, complete one or more of the Suggested Activities. You may also be interested in reading *The Zinacantecos of Mexico: The Modern Way of Life*, by Evon Z. Vogt (Holt, Rinehart and Winston, 1970) for a more detailed picture of the life and culture of the Highland Maya.

Overview

Are you somewhat uncomfortable with the idea that people in some societies give away economic surpluses to gain honor and prestige, even at the risk of making themselves destitute? When you learned about the Enga subclan in Papua New Guinea and the intricate Big Man feast in Lesson 9, you may have felt that such a philosophy is quite alien to your own lifestyle. And, in truth, the practice of giving away valued possessions, rather than accumulating them, *is* quite foreign to most people living in industrial societies. It is not so unusual, though, in present-day nonindustrial societies, and the Enga subclan in Papua New Guinea is not the only society that bases its economic system on the practice of divesting its members of their wealth.

After studying the "cargo system" of the Highland Maya in this lesson, you may not find the idea of giving wealth away so strange. The Highland Maya have institutionalized the practice of exchanging their surplus goods solely for the rewards of social approval. In their system, a Maya male may become destitute and fall deeply in debt, but he has won prestige and the respect of his society. To the Maya, the reward is greater than simple "approval." He who gives is taking the major available pathway for advancing his status and prestige in the society. Attaining status and prestige in turn binds him to specific civic and religious responsibilities important to the Highland Maya society.

The economic practices of the Highland Maya are called a "cargo system." Cargo, in this case, does not refer to "goods" but to a "burden." The cargo holder carries out civil and religious "burdens," or responsibilities, for an entire year, receiving no payment from the community, although that person bears the costs, sometimes sizable, of performing these duties.

A culture is, of course, integrated; each part of the pattern reinforces other parts of the culture. At times, as you watch the video program, it may seem that the cargo system is, more than anything else, religious in nature. While it is true that the cargo system gives essential support to religious observances and other Highland Maya community interests, the system also is important politically and economically. The cargo system may function as a leveling mechanism, preventing, or at least restricting, accumulation of wealth by individuals. The system keeps surplus money and goods in circulation within the region. The system also ensures that certain civic functions and social events will be carried out. The fiestas, or social and religious activities, serve, too, as major symbols of the community's sense of identity. Just as important, perhaps, is the fact that the system guarantees that men will devote their time and efforts to the community.

Video Program: This program examines complex interweaving of economics and religion known as the "cargo" system among the Highland Maya of Mexico and Guatemala. Featured in the program is Augustin Gomez, a corn farmer, who, by passing through all four levels of the cargo system, is influential and highly respected in the community. The program also illustrates the strength of the obligation to the cargo system in a segment with Enrique Olvera, another Highland Maya. Olvera continues to fulfill his cargo obligation, at great financial sacrifice, years after he left his village and moved to the United States. Anthropologist Frank Cancian defines the different levels of cargoes as the program shows the two men carrying out their duties. He questions in what ways the cargo system is a "leveling device" and observes that a secondary effect of the system is to ensure fulfillment of community service and community loyalty.

As you view the video program, look for:

- the meaning and significance of the cargo system.

- Augustin Gomez and his lifestyle and position in the community.

- the close relationship between civil and religious functions, unlike the United States, where church and state are separate.

- the hierarchy of the cargo system; the roles of the *capitan*, the *mayordomo*, and the *alferez*; and the duties undertaken by various cargo holders.

- the economic burden placed on some families by the cargo system.

Learning Objectives

When you have completed all assignments in this lesson, you should be able to:

1. Describe the subsistence pattern of the Highland Maya. VIDEO PROGRAM; BACKGROUND NOTES 10A

2. Describe the functions and importance of cargo positions in the Maya society. TEXTBOOK PAGE 195; VIDEO PROGRAM; BACKGROUND NOTES 10A

3. Explain in what ways the cargo system serves as a leveling mechanism among the Maya. TEXTBOOK PAGE 195; VIDEO PROGRAM; BACKGROUND NOTES 10A

4. Discuss how the cargo system contributes to a feeling of community and regional solidarity and the importance of such solidarity. TEXTBOOK PAGE 195; VIDEO PROGRAM; BACKGROUND NOTES 10A

5. Explain how the cargo system of the Maya helps to maintain inequalities between the Maya Indians and the *mestizos*. VIDEO PROGRAM; BACKGROUND NOTES 10A

THE HIGHLAND MAYA

The Maya Indians shown in the video program live in the highlands of southern Mexico and northern Guatemala. They are farmers, and corn is their primary crop. Their lands are at high altitudes, often above 6,000 feet. At these altitudes, the weather is too cold to grow much of a surplus crop for selling, because corn is particularly vulnerable to frosts. The Maya diet consists mainly of corn tortillas, beans, and a variety of green vegetables; meat and poultry are eaten only on ceremonial occasions.

Nuclear families live in one-room adobe houses on lands owned by the extended family. The Highland Maya use an intensive form of shifting agriculture called slash-and-burn, or *milpa*, farming. They cut forest and undergrowth from a plot of land, burn it, and plant corn with a digging stick. After four or five years, the yield declines and the plot is allowed to reforest.

Social organization of the Highland Maya is shaped by the cargo system. (The name "cargo" comes from the Spanish word for "burden.") Males gain prestige in a community by undertaking periods of service to the community. The period of service, or cargo, lasts for one year. Types of services performed are ranked, so that a man works his way up through a series of graded steps, like rungs on a ladder, alternating between civil and religious offices.

Young men enter the system by doing menial tasks, such as running errands for older men. As they grow older, they hold political offices, equivalent to mayor, council member, or sheriff. Cargo holders on the first level of religious office may sweep the floors or change the flowers in the church. As they progress, they sponsor religious festivals. This includes providing food and liquor, as well as paying for church services, musicians, dancers, and bullfighters.

Taking part in the cargo (or burden) is time-consuming and expensive. Young men may be reluctant to enter a cargo, but they can be coerced into it by social pressure. When they enter the cargo, they are expected to perform their duties joyfully and give most of their financial resources, so that they are in debt at the end of their cargo term. Anthropologist Frank Cancian says, "The cargo must be a financial burden to the cargo holder, and he must accept this burden in good spirits, happy that he is sacrificing for the gods and the saints" (*Economics and Prestige in a Maya Community: The Religious Cargo System in Zinacantan* [Stanford: Stanford University Press, 1965], p. 97).

However, the cargo holder gains in prestige what he loses in time and money. A senior cargo holder always has authority over a junior cargo holder. On ceremonial occasions, cargo holders address each other by the names of their cargos, rather than by their personal names. If two men meet on a path, the junior stops to let the senior pass, and if they are walking together, the senior walks ahead. Cancian writes, "Who is senior and who is junior is almost always a question of great importance in Zinacantan [the town he studied], whatever the situation" (p. 32). He describes the following drinking behavior:

"When drinking formally, the older person is served first and is bowed to as he toasts the younger. He extends his hand, touching the younger's forehead, and thus indicates that the latter may raise his head. When the younger person is served, he bows to the older as he speaks the words of toast" (p. 32).

In the hierarchy, the ranking applies to the cargos and not to the ages of the men.

Some anthropologists have suggested that the cargo system is a leveling device that redistributes resources in the society. According to this theory, the cargo prevents individuals from accumulating wealth. Because each man participating in the cargo system must "give until it hurts," the rich give more than the poor.

However, Cancian feels that the cargo system may, in fact, maintain stratification, since the cargo hierarchy has many positions at the bottom and very few at the top. Thus, few males are able to occupy the top positions. He adds that cargos in Zinacantan involve

Figure 10.1: The economy of the Highland Maya, who live at a high altitude in southern Mexico and northern Guatemala, is based on the growing of corn by the slash-and-burn system, or *milpa* farming.

expenditures of 50 to 14,000 pesos in a community where the average man is fortunate to clear 1,000 pesos a year. Thus, poor men can afford only the less-expensive cargos, while the rich take the more-expensive cargos. He writes, "This is leveling in some sense, but in fact the rich seem to be so rich that they do not lose their relative standing" (p. 292). Thus, the rich are able to maintain their standard of living and gain prestige through the cargo system. Also, prestige afforded by the more-expensive cargos gives them an advantage, such as arranging favorable marriages, in community exchange.

Population growth has significant influence on the availability and cost of cargo positions. As the population grows, the number of men eligible for the positions grows as well, but the number of offices is relatively inflexible. Opportunity to serve, therefore, is increasingly restricted. Increased population means larger fiestas and greater expense for those who finance the events.

The Maya are descendants of Maya Indians who lived in the area prior to the Spanish conquest of Central America. Today, the Indians coexist with *mestizos* living in the region. As you'll learn in Lesson 17, the word *mestizo* is derived from the Spanish word for "mixed," but the difference between Indians and *mestizos* is more cultural than biological. Indians speak a Maya dialect, wear Indian clothes, and take part in the cargo system. *Mestizos* speak Spanish, wear modern dress, and consider themselves aligned with the nation's elite.

Mestizos don't take part in the cargo system, but they benefit from it. The cargo system reinforces economic differences between Indians and *mestizos* that keep the Indians subordinate to *mestizos*. The merchants and shopkeepers who sell supplies for religious festivals are *mestizos*. Also, the fiestas require large expenditures of cash. Since the Maya are able to grow only enough for their subsistence needs, with very little left over to sell, they have little cash. When they complete their cargo service, they have accumulated prestige, but are destitute and in debt. One way of acquiring cash to pay their debts is to sign on as cheap labor for *mestizos*.

As the Maya example illustrates, the economic system of a society is far more complex than a balance sheet or a bank statement. Cash may not even be the most important commodity exchanged. In the cargo system, goods, services, and prestige are all important considerations. Success in the economic arena may not be determined simply by accumulations of wealth and goods, but it is related to the role of each individual in the community.

Cancian says the cargo system helps to integrate the community by coercing members into reinvesting their resources in the community. Individuals are forced to commit themselves to the Maya way of life by participation in the cargo system for which they receive more intangible rewards. Also, the rich are required to invest time and money in community service. Thus, the cargo system represents more than just economic activity; it integrates the economic arena with social and religious traditions.

Study Activities

Vocabulary Check

Check your understanding of terms by writing the letter of the appropriate definition in the space next to the corresponding term. Check your choices with the Answer Key at the end of the lesson.

_____ 1. cargo
_____ 2. *milpa*
_____ 3. *mayordomo*

_____ 4. leveling mechanism
_____ 5. stratified system
_____ 6. *mestizos*

a. encourages accumulation of wealth
b. discourages accumulation of wealth
c. Spanish-speaking people living in the highlands with the Maya
d. derived from the Spanish word for burden
e. slash-and-burn corn farming
f. religious leader of the community
g. cargo position with the largest number of "openings" each year
h. second rank in civil-religious hierarchy
i. encouraged by relative scarcity of upper-level positions and population growth

Completion

Fill each blank with the most appropriate term from the list immediately following that paragraph.

1. The Maya Indians of the highlands of southern Mexico and northern Guatemala are agriculturalists, producing _____ as their primary crop to meet their needs, but little in the way of a surplus. They practice a _____ system of agriculture, in which the fields of an individual family are allowed to return to forest after about five years. The towns used by the Highland Maya for ceremonial occasions are nearly _____ most of the time.

   corn   slash-and-burn

   potatoes   vacant

2. Taking part in the cargo system is called a _____ , yet most men do so, for this is an important, socially accepted pathway to _____ and _____ in the community. A young man begins in one of the lower positions in the hierarchy, serving in this position for a full year, and performing mostly menial tasks. Later, the man may advance through the hierarchy, taking more important positions. All of this work might be described as volunteer labor, for the men receive no compensation. Instead, they are required to spend money out of their own assets and frequently go into debt. Through the cargo system, important _____ and _____ offices are filled without a redistribution system such as taxation.

    burden   prestige   religious

    civil   status

3. An important function of the town is to provide a center for _____ organized and carried out by members of the cargo hierarchy, who also bear all costs. The festivals are essentially _____ in nature, and the ceremonies have roots in both the Roman Catholic and the traditional _____ religions. Taking care of the religious materials, such as statues of the _____ , is one of the responsibilities of those who have taken on cargo burdens.

    festivals   religious

    Maya   saints

4. Other residents of the area, *mestizos*, benefit from the cargo system, although they do not take part in it and are not part of the Highland Maya subculture. *Mestizo* merchants sell the wine and other goods necessary for the festival celebrations. They also provide work, at _____ wages, for the Maya. Such work is virtually the only way the Maya can obtain sufficient money to pay the _____ he has contracted as a result of his _____ of cargo service.

    debts   year

    menial

Self-Test

Objective Questions

Select the one best answer.

1. The chief product of Highland Maya subsistence activities is

   a. poultry.
   b. beans.
   c. cattle.
   d. corn.

2. The level of surplus the Highland Maya Indians typically produce is

   a. sufficient to cover the cost of social obligations, such as festivals.
   b. almost none, chiefly because of the climate.
   c. often less than enough for family survival, which makes work in the cities necessary.
   d. frequently sizable because of good climate and fertile ground.

3. Augustin Gomez has achieved the prestige he enjoys in his society because he has

   a. reached the level of *mayordomo*.
   b. passed through all four levels of the cargo system.
   c. accumulated sufficient wealth to discontinue farming.
   d. ancestors who were *mestizos*.

4. The cargo holder might best be described as

   a. a volunteer.
   b. a paid civil servant.
   c. part of the priesthood.
   d. an elected official.

5. Cargo holders receive their positions through

   a. kinship status, which determines their rank.
   b. purchase of the rank they hold.
   c. working their way up through a hierarchy of positions.
   d. assignment based on consensus of the elders of the community.

6. The expenses of the highest-ranking cargo holder during his term of service could be as much as

   a. 50 pesos.
   b. 400 pesos.
   c. 2,000 pesos.
   d. 14,000 pesos.

7. The cargo system influences distribution of wealth because

   a. money tends to be held by the wealthiest farmers.
   b. those who are wealthiest tend to contribute more to the community activities.
   c. those who are cargo holders tend to hold the concentration of wealth.
   d. cargo holders cannot retain any money or economic resources.

8. Which of the following is NOT an effect of the cargo system?

   a. Cargo holders have an opportunity to gain prestige in the community.
   b. Cargo holders are required to commit themselves to their society.
   c. Cargo holders carry out the duties of both civic and religious offices.
   d. Cargo holders generally gain greater income opportunities from participation.

9. In the Highland Maya culture, the chief contribution of the festivals is that they

   a. provide a time when families from several villages join together as a community.
   b. provide a socially accepted means for contact with the *mestizo* subculture.
   c. are a time for rewarding the cargo holders for their service.
   d. provide a time when the oldest members of the community are honored.

10. "Vacant towns" are

   a. villages that are abandoned due to loss of fertility in the land.
   b. mock villages that have been constructed to be dwellings for ancient Maya gods.
   c. towns that mostly are visited on special ceremonial occasions.
   d. towns that are avoided because of traditional taboos.

11. The Highland Maya are dependent upon the *mestizos* because

   a. *mestizo* cities provide most of the Highland Maya food, as well as other goods.
   b. employment by *mestizos* is virtually the only way to gain cash.
   c. the *mestizo* leadership controls the cargo system.
   d. the *mestizos* perform menial labor for the Maya.

12. The effect of cargo responsibilities upon most participating Maya is a tendency to

   a. lose prestige.
   b. go into debt.
   c. leave Indian society.
   d. acquire better farm holdings.

Short-Answer Essay Questions

1. Explain how the cargo system serves as a leveling mechanism for the Highland Maya, but at the same time does not create an egalitarian society.

2. In what ways do the offices and the festivals that are part of the cargo system serve to knit the Maya society together?

Suggested Activities

1. In a brief essay, compare and contrast the cargo system with the Big Man feast as leveling mechanisms.

2. In what ways is the cargo system and its obligations similar to those of U.S. civic-service organizations such as Kiwanis and Lions? In what ways is it similar to government-sponsored programs such as VISTA the Peace Corps? Or the military service?

3. Read and write a brief report on *Economics and Prestige in a Maya Community: The Religious Cargo System in Zinacantan*, by Frank Cancian, Stanford University Press, 1965. This book is a thorough analysis of the cargo system in and around the town of Zinacantan, a Highland Maya community.

4. What would be the impact on the cargo system if the Highland Maya were faced with any of the following problems: increase in wealth, increase in population, or increase in access to Western goods?

Answer Key

STUDY ACTIVITIES

Vocabulary Check

1. d	3. g	5. i
2. e	4. b	6. c

Completion

1. corn, slash-and-burn, vacant
2. burden; status, prestige (either order); civil, religious (either order)
3. festivals, religious, Maya, saints
4. menial, debts, year

SELF-TEST

Objective Questions

(Page numbers refer to the textbook.)

1. d (Objective 1; video program; Background Notes 10A)
2. b (Objective 1; video program; Background Notes 10A)
3. b (Objective 2; video program; Background Notes 10A)
4. a (Objective 2; video program; Background Notes 10A)
5. c (Objective 2; page 195; video program; Background Notes 10A)
6. d (Objective 3; Background Notes 10A)
7. b (Objective 3; page 195; video program; Background Notes 10A)
8. d (Objective 4; page 195; video program; Background Notes 10A)
9. a (Objective 4; page 195; video program; Background Notes 10A)
10. c (Objective 4; video program; Background Notes 10A)
11. b (Objective 5; Background Notes 10A)
12. b (Objective 5; video program; Background Notes 10A)

Short-Answer Essay Questions

1. Explain how the cargo system serves as a leveling mechanism for the Highland Maya, but at the same time does not create an egalitarian society.

   Your answer should include:

   - The cargo system tends to prevent people from accumulating large surpluses; those with more money are expected to donate more during cargo service.

   - Since prestige and status result from cargo activities, and not from wealth, simply holding wealth is discouraged.

   - The system does not create an egalitarian society in practice. Instead, the society is stratified, and the richer members seem to have enough wealth that cargo obligations do not adversely affect them.

   - The rich are better able to afford the more expensive offices in the cargo hierarchy. Thus, they tend to have more prestige, which gives them social advantages. Social advantages, in turn, may give them economic advantages.

   - Population growth also makes the cargo positions, especially the higher-ranking ones, more difficult to obtain. Hence, the opportunity for increasing one's status is less available.

2. In what ways do the offices and the festivals that are part of the cargo system serve to knit the Maya society together?

   Your answer should include:

   - Highland Maya society may especially need a mechanism to knit it together because Maya normally live and work in isolated areas, away from each other.

   - The festivals, which are managed by the cargo holders, give the larger community a time to be together in celebration.

   - The religious celebrations, and especially the statues of saints, may add to the sense of continuity, since the Maya identify the saints with the ancient gods.

   - The cargo holders commit themselves to the continuation of the community by their service and their economic contributions.

Sex and Marriage 11

Assignments

Before viewing the video program	• Read the Overview and the Learning Objectives for this lesson. Use the Learning Objectives to guide your reading, viewing, and thinking. • Read the textbook Introduction to Part III, pages 216–217, and Chapter 8, "Sex and Marriage," pages 218–245.

View video program 11, "Sex and Marriage"

After viewing the video program	• Review the terms used in this lesson. In addition to those terms in the Learning Objectives, you should be familiar with these:
	
	    affinal kin consanguineal
	    conjugal polygamy
	
	• Review the reading assignments for this lesson.
	• Complete each of the Study Activities and the Self-Test in this study-guide lesson; check your answers with the Answer Key at the end of this lesson.
	• According to your instructor's assignment or your own interests, complete the Suggested Activity. You also may be interested in the readings listed at the end of Chapter 8 in the textbook.

Overview

Love stories are popular themes in our culture: in the movies, on television, and in scores of paperback romances. The story often ends with wedding bells. In the popular culture of North America, marriage is part of that "happily ever after" that no one cares to delve into too deeply. This attitude reflects very accurately the culture's perception of marriage as the culmination of a romantic ideal. Marriage is the end of the story.

But society's interest in marriage doesn't stop there. In fact, that is just the beginning. By getting married, a couple takes on a new set of social rights and obligations. By bearing children, the couple ensures that society will survive. Because the family is a focal point for society, it is of great interest to anthropologists.

For many years, anthropologists have debated whether marriage is universal. Do all societies have some form of marriage? It appears that they do, although marriage can take many forms. Monogamy, the taking of a single spouse, is the form of marriage most common in industrialized societies. Some anthropologists suggest that serial marriage is also typical of North American society. In this form, a man or woman marries or lives with a succession of partners.

Polygamy is a form of marriage involving multiple partners. There are two general types of polygamy. In polygyny, a man takes more than one wife; in polyandry, a woman takes more than one husband.

Polygyny is useful in societies where a woman's labor is valuable, as in small-scale horticultural societies such as those found in the New Guinea highlands, where women work in the fields and tend the pigs. However, it is difficult for a young man there to acquire more than one wife. The man must rely on his kin to provide the wealth to acquire a wife, and only older men have the influence to acquire multiple wives. Thus, this system allows older men to maintain power over younger ones by controlling access to women.

Polygyny is also practiced where wives are viewed as a form of wealth, as in some Middle Eastern countries. In both cases, multiple wives are associated with wealth. But, in New Guinea, wives contribute to a man's wealth; while in the Middle East, wives are a form of display, since only wealthy men can afford multiple wives.

Polyandry usually occurs where there is a shortage of land, such as in some mountainous areas of Tibet and Nepal. In these cases, a woman may marry all the brothers of a particular family. Since all resulting children are born of one mother—and all potential fathers are brothers—land owned by the family can be passed on to the next generation without dividing it.

In some societies, a woman is expected to marry her husband's brother if her husband dies. This practice is known as the levirate. Cases in which a man is expected to marry his wife's sister are known as the sororate. The levirate provides security for a woman and her children and ensures that her husband's family maintains control over her reproductivity, so that her children are not lost to the lineage. The levirate and sororate maintain ties between the man's and woman's kin group even after one of them dies.

In spite of their diversity, all marriage forms have several key elements in common. They should be viewed as contracts between social groups, rather than simply relationships between individuals. They involve exchanges of rights and obligations, usually between kin groups. Though sexual rights are always part of a marriage alliance, they may not be exclusive rights. Nor are they the primary object of marriage. It is more accurate to say that marriage assigns control over reproductive rights. Children are usually valued new members of a kin group, and marriage rules determine who has rights to them.

Marriage rules also assign rights to labor and property. In New Guinea, a woman raises pigs and works in gardens, and these products become part of her husband's wealth and prestige. In the United States, a man is expected to earn a salary to provide for the material needs of his wife and children, and property is usually owned jointly, as "community property." However, some property, such as personal clothing, may be viewed as belonging to the individual.

Principles of alliance can clearly be seen in the marriage customs of North American society. Before the ceremony even begins, each family has a set of obligations. Traditionally, the bride's family pays for the ceremony, and the groom's family for the rehearsal dinner. The rehearsal dinner functions to bring both families together formally and privately before the public display of the new couple at the wedding. And both families are expected to contribute gifts that help the new couple establish their home. As the wedding begins, the families of the bride and groom are ushered to opposite sides of the church, stressing descent-group solidarity. The father of the bride gives his daughter away, symbolically transferring her labor, loyalties, and offspring from his descent group to her husband's, since North American society exhibits a patrilineal bias. The exchange takes place in the center aisle, symbolizing the linking of the two descent groups.

The bride wears white, traditionally a sign of virginity. Before modern forms of birth control, the bride's virginity was especially important, because it assured the new husband that children of the union (or at least the first one) would be his. Thus, he could be sure of passing his property on to his own child, not to someone else's. Marriage also provides that children of a sexual union will be assigned a social identity, a name, and a place in a kinship network. Therefore, the child is assured of being cared for and socialized within the society's norms.

Marriage, in its many manifestations, is a basic form of alliance in any society. It is also the basic unit of socialization—of inducting new members into society and teaching them what they need to know as members of society.

Video Program: This program focuses on the unique customs and practices related to marriage in societies throughout the world. It explains that marriage is a social contract and that its customs reflect the economic needs of the group. Among the societies featured are the Turkana of northwest Kenya and the Zaire pygmies. The Turkana practice polygyny to ensure that a man will have an adequate number of wives to care for his cattle, and the Zaire pygmies marry outside of their own communities to make alliances with other tribes and gain access to other hunting areas. The program also shows Ashanti women and men talking about their attitudes toward polygamy, an arranged marriage and the accompanying elaborate wedding preparations among Laotian Mien in their new community in North America, and the bride market held by the Berber of Morocco.

As you view the program, look for:

- the importance of the family in the nurturance of children.
- a dispute over bride price among the Turkana.
- the importance of marriage in establishing the social identity of children.
- how marriage establishes a social and economic contract.
- the diversity of marriage customs throughout the world.

Learning Objectives

When you have completed all assignments in this lesson, you should be able to:

1. Define *marriage* from a cross-cultural perspective. TEXTBOOK PAGES 221–223, 225–227, AND 230–232; VIDEO PROGRAM

2. Define *incest taboo* and suggest several explanations for its cultural universality. TEXTBOOK PAGES 223–225

3. Distinguish between *endogamy* and *exogamy* and describe their purposes. TEXTBOOK PAGES 225–227; VIDEO PROGRAM

4. Define the following forms of marriage: *monogamy, polygyny, polyandry, group marriage, serial monogamy, levirate,* and *sororate* and indicate their relative frequency. Suggest reasons for polygyny. TEXTBOOK PAGES 230–232; VIDEO PROGRAM

5. Contrast the mate selection patterns of more traditional societies with those of present-day North American societies. TEXTBOOK PAGES 232–234; VIDEO PROGRAM

6. Describe the customs of bride price, bride service, and dowry. TEXTBOOK PAGES 239–240

7. Recognize the wide variety of customs and traditions regarding divorce. TEXTBOOK PAGES 241–242

Study Activities

Vocabulary Check

Check your understanding of terms by writing the letter of the appropriate definition in the space next to the corresponding term. Check your choices with the Answer Key at the end of the lesson.

_____ 1. marriage
_____ 2. incest taboo
_____ 3. polygyny
_____ 4. affinal kin
_____ 5. endogamy

_____ 6. exogamy
_____ 7. polyandry
_____ 8. bride service
_____ 9. levirate

a. forbids sexual relationships between specified relatives
b. marriage within a certain group or category
c. custom that a widow marries a brother of her dead husband
d. marriage outside the group
e. includes rights of sexual access and eligibility to bear children
f. requires that a man marry his deceased wife's sister
g. prohibits marriage within a certain group
h. marriage form in which the woman takes more than one husband at the same time
i. marriage form in which the man takes more than one wife at the same time
j. people who are related by marriage
k. an obligation undertaken by a husband to the bride's family
l. related by blood

Completion

Fill each blank with the most appropriate term from the list immediately following that paragraph.

1. Marriage is a contract that establishes rights of _____ access and the _____ of the woman to _____ children. One of the most unusual marriage patterns is that of the Nayar, in which the man never _____ with the woman. In present-day North America, some spouses do not remain married, but they divorce and remarry in what the textbook calls _____ monogamy.

   bear   lives   sexual

   eligibility   serial

2. Other marriage patterns include the most common form, or _____, a less common but preferred form involving more than one wife, or _____, and two rare forms: more than one husband, or _____, and _____ marriage.

| group | monogamy | polygyny |
| levirate | polyandry | sororate |

3. Choices of marriage partners are restricted to some degree by all cultures. For example, all cultures have a taboo against _____, which has led some observers to believe that this prohibition is ingrained in "human nature." However, the specific category of persons excluded by this taboo varies _____ from culture to culture. It always includes the _____, and, usually, siblings, but in some cases the excluded group may be much larger.

| incest | parents |
| little | widely |

4. Still other marriage choices are determined by the culture. In many instances, marriages must be outside of a specifically defined group, or _____. The opposite cultural requirement is marriage within a specific group, or _____. One hypothesis for the first form is that such marriages help form _____. It is thought that the second form, which is much less common, is practiced to preserve cultural heritage and to consolidate resources.

| alliances | exogamous |
| endogamy |

Self-Test

Objective Questions

Select the one best answer.

1. From a cross-cultural standpoint, all of the following statements about marriage are true **EXCEPT** for the statement that marriage

    a. makes the wife eligible to bear children.
    b. includes rights of sexual access.
    c. is socially sanctioned.
    d. is a contract between one man and one woman.

2. Although incest taboo is

    a. not found in all societies, anthropologists can satisfactorily explain its occurrence.
    b. found in some form in all societies, anthropologists do not have completely satisfactory explanations for its occurrence.
    c. found in some form in all societies, it sometimes does not include restrictions on sexual relations between parents and children of the opposite sex.
    d. not found in all societies, it always includes restrictions on sexual relations between parents and children of the opposite sex.

3. One probable explanation for the practice of exogamy is that it

    a. helps to cement alliances between groups.
    b. overcomes the incest taboo.
    c. prohibits mixing with "outsiders."
    d. is inherited as a part of "human nature."

4. The two most common forms of marriage in the world today are

    a. polygyny and group marriage.
    b. polygyny and monogamy.
    c. polyandry and monogamy.
    d. polyandry and polygyny.

5. Polyandry is a marriage custom in which a

    a. husband has more than one wife.
    b. group of men has sexual access to a group of women.
    c. man or woman may have a series of mates.
    d. wife has more than one husband.

6. The marriage custom of levirate is best described as a

    a. woman marrying her dead sister's husband.
    b. widower marrying his dead wife's sister.
    c. widow marrying her dead husband's brother.
    d. man marrying all of the sisters in a family.

7. The manner by which North Americans select their mates differs significantly from mate selection practices in traditional societies in that North Americans

    a. make selections at a comparatively early age.
    b. select their own mates, rather than allowing their families to make such decisions.
    c. generally base their mate selections on the needs of their family group.
    d. tend to base their evaluation of prospective mates on less emotional and transitory values.

8. The purpose of bride price is to

    a. give the bride an opportunity to prove her worth to the husband's family.
    b. enable the bride to remain with her family after she marries.
    c. allow the man to determine whether or not his prospective wife will be an economic asset.
    d. repay the bride's family for the economic loss of their daughter.

9. Payment of a woman's inheritance to the husband at the time of marriage is called the

    a. bride service.
    b. bride price.
    c. sororate.
    d. dowry.

10. Divorce rates in Western societies are
    a. considerably lower than those of many matrilineal societies.
    b. higher than those of virtually any traditional society.
    c. lower than those of most traditional societies.
    d. about the same as those in most matrilineal societies.

Short-Answer Essay Question

1. In what ways have North American patterns of mate selection departed from traditional methods of matchmaking?

Suggested Activity

1. Assume you are going to debate the proposition that arranged marriages are more stable and long-lasting. Present your arguments in favor of the proposition, using a cross-cultural perspective to prove your points.

Answer Key

Vocabulary Check

1. e	4. j	7. h
2. a	5. b	8. k
3. i	6. d	9. c

Completion

1. sexual, eligibility, bear, lives, serial
2. monogamy, polygyny, polyandry, group
3. incest, widely, parents
4. exogamous, endogamy, alliances

SELF-TEST

Objective Questions

(Page numbers refer to the textbook.)

1. d (Objective 1; pages 221–222, 230–232; video program)
2. b (Objective 2; pages 232–235)
3. a (Objective 3; page 226; video program)
4. b (Objective 4; page 230)
5. d (Objective 4; page 232)
6. c (Objective 4; page 232)
7. b (Objective 5; pages 233–234; video program)
8. d (Objective 6; page 239)
9. d (Objective 6; page 239)
10. a (Objective 7; page 241)

Short-Answer Essay Question

1. In what ways have North American patterns of mate selection departed from traditional methods of matchmaking?

    Your answer should include:

    • In North American society, marriage choice and selection of mate have become matters of individual and independent decision, to be made by the individuals themselves. To a great extent, these decisions are influenced by the impermanent factors of youth, beauty, and romantic love.

    • In traditional societies, where the family is a powerful social institution, marriages are most often arranged for the economic and political good of the families and the community.

    • Arranged marriages may involve extensive investigation and negotiation by family members, but neither of the prospective mates may be involved in any way. Other family members make or approve the selection and settle economic arrangements, which usually involve gifts of money or property that will go either to one of the families or to one of the persons to be married.

Family and 12
Household

Assignments

Before viewing the video program	• Read the Overview and the Learning Objectives for this lesson. Use the Learning Objectives to guide your reading, viewing, and thinking. • Read textbook Chapter 9, "Family and Household," pages 246–271. • Review, in textbook Chapter 8, the section "Marriage and the Family," pages 229–230.

View video program 12, "Family and Household"

After viewing the video program	• Review the terms used in this lesson. In addition to those terms in the Learning Objectives, you should be familiar with these:
	
	    conjugal family nurturance
	    consanguine polygamous family
	
	• Review the reading assignments for this lesson.
	• Complete each of the Study Activities and the Self-Test in this study-guide lesson; check your answers with the Answer Key at the end of this lesson.
	• According to your instructor's assignment or your own interests, complete the Suggested Activity. You also may be interested in the readings listed at the end of Chapter 9 in the textbook.

Overview

By this point in *Faces of Culture,* you realize that humans have fashioned a wide and diversified variety of customs and practices in their societies. Descriptions in the textbook and, especially, some of the segments in the video programs probably help you realize that the values and traditions of any society seem "natural " and "right" to anyone who has grown up within that society. These feelings exist within members of a society because the practices and beliefs are familiar, and because the overall cultural pattern works well, no matter how strange it may seem to North American or Western minds.

But if it is still difficult to look at unfamiliar practices without feeling an "ours-are-better" attitude, it may be a relief to know that the "institution" of the family, along with the "institution" of marriage that you learned about in the previous lesson, is virtually universal in some form. On the other hand, you will have to relinquish the culture-bound picture that "family" unavoidably brings to mind for most people living in Canada and the United States. Your concepts of family are probably related to what anthropologists call the "nuclear family," which is only one possible arrangement. The nuclear family, in fact, is not the preferred arrangement in the vast majority of societies. By studying many cultures, anthropologists have developed cross-cultural definitions for each of them, definitions that include the customs and behaviors you are familiar with as well as many others that different societies have developed.

Anthropology teaches us that every culture is intrinsically valuable. It is worth the effort that must be made to understand the many unfamiliar family forms and practices described in this lesson. Everything from the residence patterns to the everyday lifestyles may be strange, although most of these practices have been followed far longer than those now in vogue in your community.

This point in the course seems an especially good time to remind you to employ the objectivity suggested in the first lesson—that you ask yourself, what is the value of each custom? How effectively does it contribute to the survival of that particular society and to the well-being of its members? In this lesson, you will find that every arrangement reflects values important to their societies, but that each has significant problems in the present-day world. It is not a matter of selecting "the best," but rather of discovering new ways to provide for the survival and fulfillment of members of the respective societies.

Video Program: "Family and Household" explores how families throughout the world carry out basic functions: economic production and consumption, inheritance, child rearing, and provision of shelter. Among the societies featured are the Mbuti, whose mothers and fathers are shown teaching their daughters and sons vital food-foraging skills; a typical North American nuclear family instilling a sense of independence and concern for cleanliness in their toddler; and an extended family in northern India in which all family members contribute to the economic viability of the unit. The program also includes information on the Ashanti of Ghana and their matrilineal inheritance and patrilocal residence patterns, the neolocal residence pattern in North America and the related problems of single motherhood, and the impact of culture change on the family groups of the Yanomamo and !Kung.

As you view the video program, look for:

- socialization of children in the families of the Mbuti and food-foraging people.
- an extended family and its functions in India.
- the kinds of pressures exerted by present-day industrial society that make it difficult to retain the structure and traditions of extended families.
- the assignment of responsibility for child care to women among the Ashanti of Africa and in North America.

Learning Objectives

When you have completed all assignments in this lesson, you should be able to:

1. Define *family* and *household* from a cross-cultural perspective and describe the basic functions of these units. TEXTBOOK PAGES 229–230, 253–256; VIDEO PROGRAM

2. Define *nuclear family* and describe conditions in industrial societies that favor the existence of nuclear families. TEXTBOOK PAGES 229–230, 257–258; VIDEO PROGRAM

3. Define *extended family*, contrast it with a nuclear family, recognize its frequency in traditional societies, and describe the economic functions served by it. TEXTBOOK PAGES 256–261; VIDEO PROGRAM

4. Explain the importance of marital residence patterns and recognize and define the five patterns: *patrilocal, matrilocal, ambilocal, neolocal,* and *avunculocal.* TEXTBOOK PAGES 261–263

5. Briefly describe several problems of the nuclear family and of female-headed households in modern society. TEXTBOOK PAGES 256–267, 269; VIDEO PROGRAM

Study Activities

Vocabulary Check

Check your understanding of terms by writing the letter of the appropriate definition in the space next to the corresponding term. Check your choices with the Answer Key at the end of the lesson.

_____ 1.	nurturance	_____ 4.	neolocal residence
_____ 2.	nuclear family	_____ 5.	conjugal family
_____ 3.	patrilocal residence	_____ 6.	extended family

a. marriage outside the group
b. the common residence pattern in North America
c. family formed on the basis of marital ties
d. taking care of the young; an important function of the family
e. a married couple living in a locality associated with the husband's father's relatives
f. a family unit composed of husband, wife, and dependent children
g. a collection of nuclear families related by ties of blood

Completion

Fill each blank with the most appropriate term from the list immediately following that paragraph.

1. The residence pattern in which a married couple lives in the locality associated with the husband's father's relatives is known as _____. The residence pattern in which the husband lives with his wife in her parent's household is called_____. A society in which married couples can choose to live with the relatives of either spouse is_____ . In one of the least common residence patterns, a married couple can live with the brother of the husband's mother. This pattern is known as _____ residence.

ambilocal	matrilocal	patrilocal
avunculocal	neolocal	

2. Industrial societies do not lend themselves to maintaining large and stable _____ families. As new kinds of jobs become available in new areas, workers move to those jobs, taking their _____ families with them. This type of family structure poses problems for members, including being _____ from both sets of kin and thus lacking the psychological and economic support of extended family members.

extended	nuclear
isolated	

Self-Test

Objective Questions

Select the one best answer.

1. One of the basic functions of the family is to

    a. protect property.
    b. equalize labor patterns between the sexes.
    c. nurture children.
    d. provide for mobility of the nuclear family.

2. The basic residential unit that provides for functions such as production, consumption, inheritance, and shelter is termed the

    a. family.
    b. neolocal residence.
    c. household.
    d. nuclear family.

3. The nuclear family is typically found in

    a. the Nayar society.
    b. the Mbuti society of Zaire.
    c. the United States and Canada.
    d. India.

4. An economic environment in which the elderly become a burden rather than an asset favors development of

    a. extended families.
    b. matrilineal families.
    c. nuclear families.
    d. endogamous families.

5. One explanation for the existence of extended families in many cultures is that
   a. raising children is more difficult in traditional societies.
   b. religious beliefs make it difficult for children to leave home.
   c. a lack of money or wealth makes it impossible for family members to leave.
   d. the need for a large labor pool and cooperation in economic activities keeps family members together.

6. The residence pattern in which a woman leaves her family after marriage to live with the family in which her husband grew up is the
   a. patrilocal residence pattern.
   b. neolocal residence pattern.
   c. matrilocal residence pattern.
   d. ambilocal residence pattern.

7. A distinct problem of nuclear families in Western industrialized societies such as the United States is
   a. control of important decisions by relatives.
   b. isolation of spouses or single parents from the support of other relatives in dealing with family responsibilities.
   c. conflict with near relatives such as aunts and cousins who are outside the nuclear family.
   d. the dependence of children on their parents after they are reared.

Short-Answer Essay Questions

1. Summarize the basic functions of the family found in virtually all societies. Compare the terms *family* and *household*.

2. Contrast nuclear and extended families. Briefly summarize the suitability of each in nonindustrial and industrial societies. What special problems does each type encounter in modern industrial societies?

Suggested Activity

1. Investigate at least two living patterns for the elderly in or near your community. For example, there may be a "retirement home" under any of several names, such as "nursing home" or "retirement community"; or there may be an apartment complex that restricts residents to ages over 55. If possible, visit these residences firsthand or obtain information from reading articles or promotional brochures. Try to answer these questions: What social advantages do these lifestyles have for the residents? What social and economic advantages and disadvantages are realized by the community or by younger members of families of the residents? How do these patterns differ from the position of the elderly in traditional extended families?

Answer Key

STUDY ACTIVITIES

Vocabulary Check

1. d   4. b
2. f   5. c
3. e   6. g

Completion

1. patrilocal, matrilocal, ambilocal, avunculocal
2. extended, nuclear, isolated

SELF-TEST

Objective Questions

(Page numbers refer to the textbook.)

1. c (Objective 1; page 254; video program)
2. c (Objective 1; page 256)
3. c (Objective 2; page 257; video program)
4. c (Objective 2; page 257)
5. d (Objective 3; pages 257–261; video program)
6. a (Objective 4; page 261)
7. b (Objective 5; page 265; video program)

Short-Answer Essay Questions

1. Summarize the basic functions of the family found in virtually all societies. Compare the terms *family* and *household*.

   Your answer should include:

   - Two primary functions of the family are providing for survival through group living and nurturing children. Living in groups is a basic human characteristic. Children require years of protection, nurturance, and interaction with members of both sexes.

   - A "family" includes the woman, her children, and at least one adult male joined by marriage or blood ties. Although a "household" is usually a family, it is more correctly defined as a residential unit for economic production, consumption, inheritance, and child rearing.

2. Contrast nuclear and extended families. Briefly summarize the suitability of each in nonindustrial and industrial soceities. What specific problems does each type encounter in modern industrial soceities?

Your answer should include:

- The nuclear family consists of mother, father, and dependent children, while the extended family is a much larger group, composed of more than one nuclear family, all related by a combination of conjugal and consanguineal ties.

- The extended family lives and works together in settings, such as farming, that require much cooperative labor. It is especially suited to environments where "many hands" are needed for a number of tasks. The nuclear family is better suited to the requirement for mobility found in industrialized societies.

- Extended families find it difficult to survive as a unit in complex, industrialized societies. Either because of dissatisfaction or economic need, younger members may wish to move away from the family to seek new job opportunities not available in the immediate area.

- Nuclear families also face many problems in complex industrialized societies. In a neolocal residence away from kin, the family has no certain support in such matters as childbirth, child rearing, or resolving conflicts between the two adults. Except for raising children, the role of the woman is uncertain. Since the children will also leave home to start their own nuclear families, there is no expectation that anyone will care for the parents when they are old.

The Yucatec Maya: A Case Study in Marriage and the Family 13

Assignments

Before viewing the video program	• Read the Overview and the Learning Objectives for this lesson. Use the Learning Objectives to guide your reading, viewing, and thinking. • Read Background Notes 13A, "The Yucatec Maya," and 13B, "Chan Kom and Xaibe," in this study-guide lesson; note the map showing the Yucatec region of Mexico and the state capital, Merida. • Review textbook pages 129–131 ("Dependence Training"); 253–255 ("Functions of the Family"); 257–258 ("The Nuclear Family"); 258–261 ("The Extended Family"); and pages 264–265 ("Extended Families" [problems of]).

View video program 13, "The Yucatec Maya: A Case Study in Marriage and the Family"

After viewing the video program	• Review the terms used in this lesson. In particular, check your understanding of these terms:

extended family	multiple family	patrilocal
milpa	nuclear family	slash-and-burn

- Review the reading assignments for this lesson.
- Complete each of the Study Activities and the Self-Test in this study-guide lesson; check your answers with the Answer Key at the end of this lesson.
- According to your instructor's assignment or your own interests, complete one or more of the Suggested Activities. You also may be interested in the readings listed at the end of Chapter 9 in the textbook.

Overview

In North America and Western Europe, marriage is usually viewed as a culmination of romantic love. In many societies, however, romantic love is not considered a significant aspect of marriage. Although views of marriage differ, marriage is important throughout the world, because it is a key link in that most basic of social institutions, the family. And the family is the principal unit for socialization and economic cooperation.

The various forms of families, such as nuclear, patrilocal, and matrilocal extended families, are described in the textbook. From their studies of families throughout the world, anthropologists have found considerable evidence that the structure of families is related to subsistence.

As described in Lesson 12, different styles of family organization develop as a means of meeting and solving problems intrinsic to the environment and to the kind of society. In other words, structuring the family so that it functions as a group is an *ecological adaptation*. This lesson looks at details of family adaptation to conditions in a particular region. In some situations, adaptations are not simple. Sometimes a family must exercise limited and difficult choices to find adaptations that will allow the family to prevail under new or changing conditions.

This lesson closely examines moments in the lives of extended families. The video program includes the field research of Hubert L. Smith and profiles of a traditional extended family group and an extended family that attempts to cope with changes from traditional practices. The conditions under which they live, called "the system" by Smith, largely govern the organization of these families. You will recognize values that North American culture shares with these peoples: the importance of children; the love for and from parents and grandparents; the delights of humor; loyalty; and the value of work and achievement.

In Background Notes 13B, you will read a summary of changes that occurred in two other Maya villages during the middle third of the twentieth century. These studies document the existence of nuclear as well as extended-family arrangements among the Maya during very early periods in their history. The video program and the readings illustrate that, no matter what difficulties or environmental changes occur, the family remains a most durable and adaptable unit in human society.

Video Program: The lives of two extended Yucatec Maya are the subjects of this program. Film footage and commentary by Hubert L. Smith, whose field research spanned many years in the Maya community of Chican, follow the traditional extended-family group of Prudencio Colli Canche as its members companionably share the daily chores, do *milpa* farming, and teach the youngsters in a never-ending cycle. The second family, that of Reymundo Colli Colli, experiences change and stress because two sons want to break out of the farming lifestyle, seek more schooling, and move to the city. The "dependency" training of extended families is revealed by this challenge, and the sons, unable to cope with a new environment, return home.

As you view the video program, look for:

- the depiction of slash-and-burn horticulture on the *monte*, and how the extended-family structure adapts to this subsistence pattern.

- the forces of change felt by Reymundo Colli Colli and his family, and the resulting stress on this extended-family organization. In particular, note the reactions of his sons Audomaro and Romaldo to school experiences. Reymundo's wife is Agrifina, and his other sons are Bernardino and Santos.

- the family of Prudencio Colli Canche, the relationship of this man to others in his family, including his sons, his wife Maria, and his grandchildren.

Learning Objectives

When you have completed all assignments in this lesson, you should be able to:

1. Describe the slash-and-burn (*milpa*) agriculture of the Yucatec Maya and explain how the labor pattern of the extended family is appropriate to that process. VIDEO PROGRAM; BACKGROUND NOTES 13A AND 13B

2. Describe the characteristics of the extended family of Prudencio Colli Canche as shown in the video program. VIDEO PROGRAM

3. Describe the changes occurring in the extended family of Reymundo Colli Colli and suggest reasons for those changes. VIDEO PROGRAM

4. Describe the personality traits prized and fostered by the traditional extended-family organization. TEXTBOOK PAGES 129–131, 258–261; VIDEO PROGRAM

5. Discuss characteristics of the extended family that make it difficult to adapt to changing economic patterns and other consequences of modernization occurring in the region. TEXTBOOK PAGES 258–261, 264–265; VIDEO PROGRAM

6. Describe the changes in family organization that occurred in the village of Xaibe and the reasons for those changes. BACKGROUND NOTES 13B

THE YUCATEC MAYA

The Yucatec Maya are a good example of how family structure varies as a result of economic reality. The Yucatec Maya take their designation from the peninsula of Yucatán, a low, level limestone shelf that juts out into the southern part of the Gulf of Mexico. The peninsula has no significant watercourses because the limestone is too porous to hold standing water. The area is diversified only by small hills and depressions. But differences in rainfall produce great changes in vegetation in different parts of the area and, therefore, in the suitability of the land for human occupation. Toward the east and south, scrubby bush gives way to taller bushes that give way to a tropical rain forest.

The Yucatán contained a flourishing complex society long before the Spanish arrived in Central America. The Maya built cities featuring massive architecture and carved stone monuments. They developed a writing system, based on a system of glyphs, with which they recorded historical and calendrical events. However, most of the large cities were abandoned by the time the Spaniards arrived, perhaps because the Maya's elaborate social institutions organized around powerful priests overtaxed the environment.

The Spanish entered the area in 1527, establishing Spanish and Catholic rule by 1545. Following the Spanish Conquest, epidemics of disease greatly reduced the Maya populations and obliterated entire villages. Bloody uprisings of Maya Indians against the Spanish further drastically reduced the Indian population.

As were their ancestors, present-day Mayans are agriculturalists, who practice a form of cultivation known as *milpa*. The soil is made ready for cultivation by cutting and burning the bush. The shallow topsoil makes it impossible to raise corn, their primary crop, on the same plot for more than two or three consecutive years and requires that the land lie uncultivated for many years before it is planted again. The farmer must travel farther and farther from his village in search of good land. Eventually, his cornfields become so remote from his village that he remains at his fields during periods of agricultural labor. As the farmer's family and others from the village join him at the new site, it becomes a *milperia*, or kind of *milpa* colony, and may become a new village.

The Maya society illustrates the remarkable resilience of the human family through time. The Yucatec Maya are especially interesting to anthropologists because their family structures seem to refute the generally accepted notion that the nuclear family is a product of modernization. Anthropologist Evon Z. Vogt suggests that nuclear families among the Maya represent a breakdown of patrilocal extended families (*The Zinacantecos of Mexico: A Modern Maya Way of Life* [New York: Holt, Rinehart and Winston, 1970]). However, Joseph J. Gross cites historical sources that indicate the nuclear-family group is a tradition for the Maya. He notes that records of households paying tribute in 1574 indicate the average household had about five members. He adds, "Large extended families could not have been the statistical norm among the Maya of sixteenth-century Guatemala" ("Marriage and Family among the Maya" in Arnaud F. Marks and Rene A. Rooner, eds., *Family and Kinship in Middle America and the Caribbean* [Leiden, The Netherlands: University of the Netherlands Antilles Curacao and the Department of Caribbean Studies of the Royal Institute of Linguistics and Anthropology, 1975], p. 74).

 The complete story of Mayan family development and change may be even more complex. The situation of Maya families in 1574, for example, may have resulted from deliberate policies of Spanish rule that encouraged the breakup of extended families.

However, it is important to recognize that changes in social patterns can proceed in virtually any direction. Gross says that anthropologists are mistaken if they assume that family structure always evolves from extended families to nuclear families. He writes, ". . . those who use the presence of the nuclear-family as an indicator of social change or 'modernization,' particularly among the Maya, are holding a false yardstick" (p. 80). Gross's argument points out the dangers of assuming that social institutions always evolve in a particular direction. Unless we have historical records, we really don't know what was normative before the anthropologist begins observations. And certainly it is

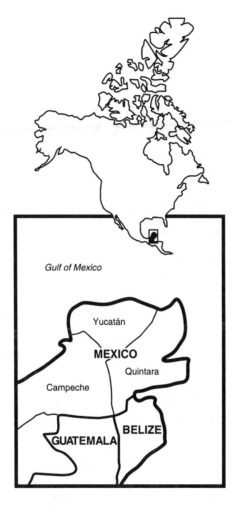

Figure 13.1: Extended- and nuclear-family patterns are exhibited in the rural communities of Maya Indians, horticulturists living in the Yucatán Peninsula of Mexico.

risky to assume that all societies follow the same evolutionary steps. However, the data of several anthropologists suggest that the family, as an economic unit, is responsive to changes in subsistence requirements.

CHAN KOM AND XAIBE

The relationship between family structure and subsistence patterns among the Yucatec Maya is illustrated in two case studies by anthropologists Robert Redfield and Ira Abrams in the villages of Chan Kom and Xaibe.

Redfield worked primarily in the village of Chan Kom in the northeastern part of the Yucatán Peninsula. Most of his fieldwork took place in the early 1930s, but he revisited the village in 1948. When Redfield studied the village in 1931, he noted that "Maize (corn) is the people's food, their work and their prayer—it fills the days and the talk" (p. 51). The people grew twice as much corn as needed for subsistence and the surplus was traded for market goods. Some of the men in Chan Kom also planted beans, sweet potatoes, *jicama* (a root crop similar to a sweet turnip), squashes, and chili peppers. People who did not plant these minor crops bought them from their neighbors. A few of the men owned cattle, but all families raised poultry. Poultry was eaten primarily at festivities. Fruit was also grown.

Redfield writes, "In 36 out of 42 cases, *milpas* were made by individual laborers and the harvests consumed as the individual property of these single agriculturalists in individual small-family households" (p. 56). He adds, "The small family in Chan Kom is much as
it is with us, consisting of the mating couple and their children" (nuclear family) (pp. 87–89). According to Redfield, the mating couple recognized kinship ties to both the wife's and the husband's relatives. However, "the ties that are emphasized are those between husband and wife" (p. 89). Redfield further notes that in two cases *milpas* were

made by patrilocal extended families. In the remaining four cases, groups of relatives joined to clear, sow, and harvest a common plot of land. However, within each plot the separate *milpas* of each laborer were marked off and the harvests were "consumed in the individual small-family households of the separate men" (p. 56).

When Redfield studied the village of Chan Kom in 1931, the villagers went to markets in surrounding towns for the services of merchants, musicians, or artisans. But when he returned to the village in 1948, Chan Kom had developed its own artisans and merchants as specialists and did not depend much on other towns for such services. Redfield writes, "The leather workers and the principal baker spend so much time at these manufactures that their work in the *milpa* is much reduced. . . ." (*A Village That Chose Progress: Chan Kom Revisited* [Chicago: The University of Chicago Press, 1964], p. 60).

The nuclear family was predominant in 1948, as it was in 1931. Redfield writes, "The single-family households preponderate as they did before. As before, the family consisting of parents and children is by far the commonest arrangement" (p. 80). However, he notes that the two extended patrilocal families that he studied in 1931 had broken up. Each of the sons had his own *milpa* and arrangements for meals, and many of the sons had their own houses.

Ira R. Abrams studied a Mayan village in northern Belize, which is in the southern part of the Yucatán Peninsula. According to Abrams, the village, Xaibe, is characterized by two developmental periods in this century ("Cash Crop Farming and Social and Economic Change in a Yucatec Maya Community in Northern British Honduras," Ph.D. dissertation, [Harvard University, 1973]). Until the 1960s, Xaibe was composed largely of subsistence agriculturalists and part-time wage laborers. In response to efforts by the government and local political forces, a few individuals began to farm sugar cane commercially after 1950. In 1956, the government purchased the village and most of the land in the district from its single owner and redistributed it to prospective cane farmers, along with cane-production licenses and loans to cover the costs of beginning a cane field. By 1963, there was a large-scale shift to cane farming in Xaibe.

The change from subsistence agriculture and wage labor to commercial agriculture was correlated with a change in family structure. Prior to the introduction of sugar-cane agriculture, Abrams says there was not one incidence of the patrilocal extended family serving as an economic unit; 44 percent of the people lived in what Abrams calls multiple-family groups, which he views as significantly different from the traditional patrilocal pattern. In these multiple-family groups, the married sons lived with their fathers, but maintained their families in separate homes as separate economic units. The majority of the families (54 percent) were single nuclear families. After the introduction of sugar-cane agriculture, 41 percent of the households were extended families, 47 percent were multiple families, and only 12 percent were single families. These figures indicate a shift from independent nuclear families to larger cooperating family groups. Abrams suggests that, "In pre-cane days, there was little incentive for a son to form an extended family household with his parents. Part-time wage labor, in which men spent most of their time, was an activity that each man entered into independently" (p. 32).

Abrams says that *milpa* was not practiced throughout the year so it did not justify common households or pooled economic resources. "The long duration and large percentage of yearly income derived from commercial agricultural activities could provide more of a basis for making cooperative labor between a father and son a focus for household organization than did small-scale subsistence level *milpa* agriculture" (p. 36).

Extended families engaged in commercial agriculture could pool credit and earnings to buy a truck, which cut transportation costs and could be hired out to others. Abrams says three extended families in commercial cane agriculture had a "level of material wealth" that was 165 percent over the community average. "There had been only one extended family household in the community that had developed without the aid of cane farming. The members of this household were, however, also commercial agriculturalists; they grew commercial crops of plantains and oranges" (p. 39). Abrams concludes that his data show "with some certainty that the post-cane extended family household represents the addition of a new domestic pattern altogether for Xaibe" (p. 43).

Study Activities

Vocabulary Check

Check your understanding of terms by writing the letter of the appropriate definition in the space next to the corresponding term. Check your choices with the Answer Key at the end of the lesson.

_____ 1. *milpa*
_____ 2. Yucatán
_____ 3. Prudencio
_____ 4. Reymundo

_____ 5. Romaldo
_____ 6. Chan Kom
_____ 7. Xaibe
_____ 8. patrilocal

a. father of an extended family that is under stress as it attempts to adapt to changing conditions
b. a large region in southeastern Mexico
c. a Maya village in which families joined together in larger groups to solve the problems of new agricultural practices
d. member of a Maya family who elected to leave the traditional family pattern
e. the elder male of a patrilocal family who follows traditional practices
f. agricultural method in which the use of farmed land is rotated
g. a Maya village in which the nuclear-family pattern predominates
h. family dwelling pattern based on the father's family

Completion

Fill each blank with the most appropriate term from the list immediately following that paragraph.

1. Slash-and-burn agricultural practices are employed where there is sufficient land, usually forest, to allow periodic _____ of one particular area. For one or two years, the land is farmed, then allowed to return to its _____ to restore fertility. The slash-and-burn agricultural patterns of the Yucatec Maya often encourage formation of extended family groups. For example, a larger family group supplies more _____ for the work that needs to be done under this labor-intensive agricultural system. Property such as horses can be owned by the entire group or by several members of the extended family.

    cultivation   natural state

    laborers

2. In other instances, slash-and-burn agriculture may yield such limited returns that it is more economical for a _____ family to farm a small plot of land, as Abrams concluded from his studies in Xaibe. In this village, the arrival of commercial agriculture, in which the cash crop was sugar cane, resulted in the rapid growth of larger family units based on the extended family. In these larger family units, known as _____, married sons continue to live with the father and work cooperatively with him, but they maintain their individual families separately.

    multiple families   nuclear

3. Reymundo and Prudencio head extended families that practice a _____ residence pattern. The children of Prudencio and his wife work their land, and some share in the ownership of property. All of them share in the work that needs to be done, and all of them share the benefits of even a small prize. Such sharing serves as a symbol and reminder of the family's _____.

    interdependence   neolocal

    matrilocal   patrilocal

4. The major source of income for the family of Reymundo is raising beans, squash, and _____ on the family plots of land. Financial pressures on the family's resources occurred when two sons went to _____ in the nearby city of Merida.

    corn   school   work

    rice   wheat

5. In the Maya village of Chan Kom, Redfield found that the nuclear family predominated in 1931. Returning in 1948, he found that the only two former _____ had disappeared as working units, with each son working his own *milpa* and, usually, maintaining an independent residence. A major change that Redfield noted was that some villagers had developed _____ in various crafts, so that villagers did not have to travel to other communities for such services.

    extended families   specialties

Self-Test

Objective Questions

Select the one best answer.

1. The kind of agriculture called *milpa* involves

    a. continuous use of land by different family groups.
    b. clearing of land for permanent use by a particular settlement.
    c. clearing of land and allowing it to return to its natural state after a few years.
    d. intensive farming with modern technology.

2. The greatest advantage the extended family offers in a *milpa* agricultural pattern is that

    a. a larger work force is held together by strong loyalties.
    b. there are more opportunities for supplemental income through part-time work.
    c. there is more freedom for individual members to determine their own activities.
    d. there are opportunities for younger members to exercise leadership.

3. The position that Prudencio holds in his family group is

    a. youngest son in a patrilocal group.
    b. family head in a patrilocal group.
    c. one of several elders who lead the community.
    d. an older individual who primarily looks after children.

4. As portrayed in the video program, the family of Prudencio Colli Canche

    a. began to form a larger group from small nuclear families.
    b. experienced the loss of two sons to full-time jobs in the city.
    c. appeared happy and content with the farming and large family group.
    d. was forced off the land by government order.

5. As shown in the video program, a major change that occurred in the family of Reymundo is that

   a. a crop was lost to drought.
   b. educational opportunities threatened to break up the family.
   c. opportunity for city employment threatened to break up the family.
   d. the family had to sell the corn supply, animals, and home-woven hammocks.

6. The first opportunity that attracted Reymundo Colli Colli's youngest sons away from the family and to the city was

   a. employment.
   b. festivals.
   c. revolution.
   d. school.

7. The Maya standard of behavior for adults is

   a. fierce and aggressive.
   b. even-tempered and harmonious.
   c. independent and competitive.
   d. complete lack of emotion.

8. In the two families shown in the video program on the Yucatec Maya extended family, responsibility for final decisions was usually held by

   a. the eldest son.
   b. the mother.
   c. the father.
   d. adult males, through mutual agreement.

9. Audomaro's and Romaldo's experience with schooling in a strange city suggests that

   a. Maya youth are strongly motivated to leave the family farm for the city.
   b. Maya youth usually find it easier to break family ties than do older people.
   c. rebellion against traditional ways of life is encouraged by the Maya culture.
   d. even young people find it difficult to leave the traditional family.

10. In traditional extended families, the younger adults
    a. compete with one another for leadership.
    b. defer to the decision of the family leader.
    c. compete with older males for dominance.
    d. usually specialize in a single skill or craft.

11. The characteristic of the "multiple families" identified by Abrams in Xaibe was that
    a. several families were joined in a patrilocal group.
    b. separate nuclear families worked a *milpa* together.
    c. sons lived with their fathers but separately maintained their own families.
    d. unrelated families were joined in a corporate venture.

12. The major change Abrams observed in Xaibe was
    a. the introduction of commercial farming, which led to an increase in extended families.
    b. the introduction of commercial farming, which led to an increase in nuclear families.
    c. a return to traditional farming, which led to an increase in extended families.
    d. the introduction of new farming techniques, which led many families to leave the village for the city.

Short-Answer Essay Questions

1. Briefly describe the cooperative efforts, interdependence, and personality traits that are illustrated by the family of Prudencio and Maria.

2. What kind of difficulty in adjustment to new conditions can be illustrated by Reymundo's attempt to send two younger boys to school?

3. Why did the family organization patterns change so greatly in Xaibe? What does this and other studies suggest about the evolution of extended and nuclear families?

Suggested Activities

1. What do the video program and the Background Notes suggest about the adaptability of the family to new circumstances? Does the evidence of any society mentioned in the last two lessons indicate that the family may be disappearing? Use examples to support your opinion.

2. Using local library resources, read about developments in the Yucatán Peninsula. What agricultural and economic changes is the Mexican government attempting to introduce into the area? Characterize the relationship between the indigenous Maya and other groups living in the region. What do you think will be the future of the various family patterns of the area?

Answer Key

STUDY ACTIVITIES

Vocabulary Check

1. f	4. a	7. c
2. b	5. d	8. h
3. e	6. g	

Completion

1. cultivation, natural state, laborers
2. nuclear, multiple families
3. patrilocal, interdependence
4. corn, school
5. extended families, specialties

SELF-TEST

Objective Questions

(Page numbers refer to the textbook.)

1. c (Objective 1; video program; Background Notes 13A)
2. a (Objective 1; video program; Background Notes 13A)
3. b (Objective 2; video program)
4. c (Objective 2; video program)
5. b (Objective 3; video program)
6. d (Objective 3; video program)
7. b (Objective 4; video program)
8. c (Objective 4; video program)
9. d (Objective 5; video program)
10. b (Objective 5; page 264; video program)
11. c (Objective 6; Background Notes 13B)
12. a (Objective 6; Background Notes 13B)

Short-Answer Essay Questions

1. Briefly describe the cooperative efforts, interdependence, and personality traits that are illustrated by the family of Prudencio and Maria.

   Your answer should include:

   - All members of the family look to Prudencio, the father, for his leadership. His authority is not challenged because his wisdom and experience are invaluable in this traditional agricultural environment.

   - All members of the family contribute to the common effort. Sharing is important, not only because it assures that everyone will get his or her necessities, but because sharing symbolizes the interdependence of the family.

   - The oldest members watch the children, freeing younger members for heavier duties, and providing a role model for the children.

   - Maya adults strive to maintain a calm, considered, gentle manner in all activities.

2.   What kind of difficulty in adjustment to new conditions may be illustrated by Reymundo's attempt to send two younger boys to school?

Your answer should include:

- Although Reymundo wanted to give his younger sons, Audomaro and Romaldo, the opportunity for schooling, he voiced concern that they were not like his eldest son, who wanted to work in the fields.

- The conflict between traditional and new ways became evident when the boys entered, and then withdrew from, school because they missed their family.

- After the single attempt at sending the boys to school, Reymundo let them remain at home. Audomaro eventually took up farming, although Romaldo later took a job in the city. Breaking free of traditional ways is difficult, because new ways are strange and the family ties are strong.

3.   Why did the family organization patterns change so greatly in Xaibe? What does this and other studies suggest about the evolution of extended and nuclear families?

Your answer should include:

- The family organizations changed after the government introduced commercial agriculture with sugar-cane crops. Before sugar cane was farmed, the traditional *milpa* farming was practiced by individual nuclear families or multiple families in which the sons lived with the father but maintained separate homes for their families. After sugar cane was introduced, the multiple family pattern was maintained, and many families joined in extended-family living patterns. The proportion of nuclear families declined from more than 50 percent to 12 percent.

- Abrams believed that *milpa*, as practiced in Xaibe, did not offer enough incentive for people to join in larger family groups. Individual men could earn more by farming their own plots and working away from the farms part-time. The commercial farming made it possible for larger work forces to gain more income, by combining their labor and purchasing power to obtain modern equipment.

- The Xaibe experience suggests that families do not simply evolve from extended families to nuclear families as new technology and economic systems are introduced. Families are adaptable to changing conditions, and may attempt different organizational patterns according to the problems posed by a specific set of conditions.

Kinship and Descent, Part I 14

Assignments

Before viewing the video program	• Read the Overview and the Learning Objectives for this lesson. Use the Learning Objectives to guide your reading, viewing, and thinking. • Read textbook Chapter 10, "Kinship and Descent," pages 272–290. (The balance of the chapter will be assigned in the next lesson.)

View video program 14, "Kinship and Descent, Part I"

After viewing the video program	• Review the terms used in this lesson. In addition to those in the Learning Objectives, review the definitions for *consanguineal* and *affinal* (Lesson 11) and consult a dictionary to clarify the usage of the term *kinship*. • Review the reading assignments for this lesson. You may also find that the introduction to Part III of the textbook (pages 216–217) provides a useful perspective on kinship, descent, and other devices for organizing societies. • Complete each of the Study Activities and the Self-Test in this study-guide lesson; check your answers with the Answer Key at the end of this lesson. • According to your instructor's assignment or your own interests, complete one or more of the Suggested Activities. You also may be interested in the readings listed at the end of Chapter 10 in the textbook.

Overview

Many North Americans are interested in genealogy. Some people are encouraged by their religion to locate all ancestors. For others, genealogy is a serious hobby, and they spend hours poring over census records, correspondence, church baptismal and burial lists, and passenger ship manifests, searching for those who were parents-of-parents long ago. For many, the pursuit of such information probably stems from the excitement of solving the mystery or the puzzle. For others, it perhaps helps answer the unspoken question, "Who am I?"

In the 1970s, the novel *Roots* enjoyed popularity in its printed form and as a television miniseries. Beginning mostly with oral traditions maintained for generations in his family, author Alex Haley painstakingly traced the story of his forebears from the time of one man's kidnapping from Africa through years of slavery in the Colonies and the United States, and, finally, to his own parents. In the novel, Haley recounts how his family stories were confirmed by an oral historian in an African village who recounted the memorized history of the village and its families, including the disappearance of Haley's ancestor. In discovering this story, Haley conveyed to many a new sense of the dignity and worth of those who had been torn away from their homes and suffered through years of slavery and intolerance.

Most present-day U.S. residents lack knowledge about their ancestry, and little cultural importance is attached to many aspects of kinship. But in the vast majority of societies through human history, kinship and the tracing of lines of descent have played an important role. Knowledge of one's ancestors often defines more than family membership. It confirms membership within a social group, has strong influence on the status of the individual within the society, determines residence patterns, defines what natural resources are available to the individual, and makes available a dependable force of persons under mutual obligation for defense and aid. Kinship ties are often basic to the definition of "self." Many nonindustrial societies still depend on the kinship ties traced through descent. In those societies, kinship and descent patterns provide the organizational arrangements necessary to handle functions that in more complex societies may be the functions of governments and religious, military, and special-interest groups.

In this lesson, the first of two describing the structure and function of kinship in human societies, you will learn about the importance of kinship and descent in shaping the culture. This lesson concentrates on descent as a social bond. In the following lesson, you will explore more fully the structure and functions of kinship relationships.

Video Program: This program focuses on how kinship and descent provide the underpinning for political, economic, and religious functions in many societies. Featured societies include the Yanomamo and their strong patrilineal organization; the Mendi, whose clans have strong economic and religious importance; and the Trobriand Islanders, with a matrilineal descent pattern. The program also notes the relative unimportance of kinship and descent in modern North American society.

As you view the video program, look for:

- a fight among members of two descent groups in a Yanomamo village; the fight reveals complexities of kinship obligations in that culture.

- the cassowary contest of the Mendi of New Guinea and how it reveals clan alliances as the basis of social organization in that culture.

- the economic and political activities of the Trobriand Islanders based on their matrilineal descent patterns.

- examples of descent-group traditions still found in the British Isles.

Learning Objectives

When you have completed all assignments in this lesson, you should be able to:

1. Define *kinship* and *descent groups*. TEXTBOOK PAGES 273, 274; VIDEO PROGRAM

2. Identify the basic functions of descent groups in nonindustrial societies. TEXTBOOK PAGES 273, 274, 285–287; VIDEO PROGRAM

3. Describe *patrilineal descent* and organization as a type of unilineal descent, and describe the organization and functions of patrilineal descent groups in traditional China and among the Yanomamo. TEXTBOOK PAGES 274–278; VIDEO PROGRAM

4. Describe *matrilineal descent* and organization as a type of unilineal descent, and describe the organization and functions of matrilineal descent groups found among the Hopi and the Trobriand Islanders. TEXTBOOK PAGES 280–283; VIDEO PROGRAM

5. Define *double descent* and briefly describe how this applies to the Yakö of eastern Nigeria. TEXTBOOK PAGE 284

6. Define *ambilineal descent* and briefly describe how this applies to organizations of Jews in New York City. TEXTBOOK PAGES 284–285

7. Define and describe the basic features of *lineage, clan, phratry,* and *moiety.* TEXTBOOK PAGES 285–287; VIDEO PROGRAM

Study Activities

Vocabulary Check

Check your understanding of terms by writing the letter of the appropriate definition in the space next to the corresponding term. Check your choices with the Answer Key at the end of the lesson.

_____ 1. consanguineal
_____ 2. affinal relationship
_____ 3. patrilineal
_____ 4. matrilineal
_____ 5. phratry
_____ 6. double descent

_____ 7. ambilineal descent
_____ 8. lineage
_____ 9. clan
_____ 10. totemism
_____ 11. moiety

a. residing near either the groom's or the bride's family
b. a unilineal descent group composed of at least two clans that supposedly share a common ancestry
c. each group that results from division of a society into two parts on the basis of descent
d. descent that can be traced through either parent for purposes of group membership
e. a group claiming relationship to a common ancestor for purposes of group membership, although relationship cannot actually be traced
f. relationships by birth
g. descent traced through each parent, each for separate purposes
h. one of several groups that includes two or three clans in a society, each group claiming relationship to a particular common ancestor
i. a corporate descent group whose members can trace their links to a common ancestor
j. belief that people are related to animals, plants, or natural objects because of their descent from common ancestral spirits
k. descent traced through females
l. cousin or uncle
m. relationship defined by marriage
n. descent traced through males

Completion

Fill each blank with the most appropriate term from the list immediately following that paragraph.

1. In some societies, the family organization of husband, wife, and children may confront problems that require more than the efforts of a few to resolve. In industrial societies, a formal _____ may be formed to manage these larger social functions. In nonindustrial societies, the _____ group is a way of handling matters larger than possible for individual families. Such groups have a variety of functions including mutual aid, a means of sharing resources such as land, and cooperative work forces for tasks larger than a single family could undertake.

    kinship   political system

2. Groups that trace ancestry exclusively through either the male or female line are termed _____. Until World War II, rural Chinese traditional society was _____. Each family belonged to a larger group, the _____, which was the most important social unit. Membership of the male in this larger group assured him _____ support and supportive aid to assist in special gatherings for important occasions. Residence in this traditional society was usually _____.

    ambilineal   patrilineal   *tsu*

    economic   patrilocal   unilineal

    matrilocal   political

3. While patrilineal societies are usually associated with _____ and intensive agricultural subsistence patterns, groups that trace descent through matrilineal lines are usually found in _____ societies where the women perform much of the productive work. In most such matrilineal societies, descent is reckoned through _____, although power is exercised by _____. Family bonds are formed through the wife's lineage; for example, strong bonds are expected to be maintained throughout life by lineage "brothers" and "sisters"—this group includes the children born to the wife's _____.

    brothers   horticultural   pastoral

    females   males   sisters

4. Among the Hopi, descent groups are _____. The head of each subclan or lineage is a senior _____, although the "medicine bundle" and considerable power are in the hands of a _____. Women exert strongest authority within the _____, but they also have strong influence over decisions made by the chief and village council.

brother or maternal uncle	man	patrilineal
household	matrilineal	woman

5. In many non-Western societies, descent is established exclusively through the male or female line. This system is known as _____ descent. A rare descent system, in which descent is reckoned matrilineally for some purposes and patrilineally for others, is known as _____ descent. Still a third form of descent, in which an individual may affiliate with either parent's descent group, is known as _____ descent.

ambilineal	unilineal
double	

Self-Test

Objective Questions

Select the one best answer.

1. *Kinship* is a term most precisely used to refer to

   a. ancestors.
   b. descendants.
   c. relatives.
   d. family.

2. To be described as a descent group, the group must have

   a. siblings.
   b. clans.
   c. an ancestor.
   d. a totem.

3. One important function of descent groups in many nonindustrial societies is

   a. providing for religious and ceremonial observances.
   b. providing security and services for its members.
   c. encouraging political and defensive alliances.
   d. exercising control of natural resources.

4. A descent group that is a corporate group

   a. ceases to exist when key members leave the group.
   b. is formed at the pleasure of potential members.
   c. is a long-lasting organization that survives changes in membership.
   d. is interested in control only of property.

5. A descent group that traces its ancestors exclusively through the male or female line is called

   a. an ambilineal group.
   b. a unilineal group.
   c. a patrilineal group.
   d. a matrilineal group.

6. In patrilineal descent groups,

   a. the line is traced through male descent for some purposes and through female descent for others.
   b. group membership is determined through the male line.
   c. group membership is determined through the female line.
   d. all children and grandchildren trace descent through the ancestors of both parents.

7. In the former traditional Chinese society, the *tsu* functioned as a

   a. patrilineal descent group that owned the land.
   b. matrilineal descent group that owned the land.
   c. patrilineal descent group that gave economic and social support.
   d. matrilineal descent group that gave economic and social support.

8. In matrilineal societies,

   a. women usually hold exclusive authority.
   b. women share authority with their husbands.
   c. the tie between husbands and wives is usually strong.
   d. unsatisfactory marriages are more easily ended than in patrilineal societies.

9. Among the Hopi, the lineage owns the

   a. land, and descent is traced through the woman's line.
   b. horses, and descent is traced through the woman's line.
   c. agricultural tools, and descent is traced through the man's line.
   d. religious symbols, and descent is traced through the man's line.

10. Among the Trobriand Islanders, primary responsibility for raising children belongs to the

    a. mother.
    b. father.
    c. father's brother.
    d. mother's brother.

11. A descent system in which the matrilineal line confers some rights and the patrilineal line confers others is termed

    a. lineage descent.
    b. unilineal descent.
    c. double descent.
    d. ambilineal descent.

12. Among the Yakö people of eastern Nigeria, an individual might inherit ritual privileges from

    a. the matrilineal line.
    b. the patrilineal line.
    c. both lines.
    d. neither line.

13. The "family circles" of Jewish descendants from Eastern European societies are open to membership for anyone who can trace descent from specific ancestors through

    a. either male or female lines.
    b. the father's line.
    c. the mother's line.
    d. a friend's ancestors.

14. The term for a group that allows membership to anyone who can trace descent through either the father's or mother's line to an ancestor is

    a. lineage descent.
    b. unilineal descent.
    c. double descent.
    d. ambilineal descent.

15. A common feature of lineages is that marriage

    a. within the lineage is usually required.
    b. with someone from a specific related lineage is usually required.
    c. with someone from another lineage is usually required.
    d. choices are usually not restricted by lineages.

16. In clans, all members belong to a

    a. noncorporate descent group and claim descent from a common ancestor.
    b. corporate descent group and claim descent from a common ancestor.
    c. noncorporate descent group and live close to each other.
    d. corporate descent group and are dispersed through a large area.

17. In a society with moieties, the number of moieties is

    a. two.
    b. four.
    c. eight.
    d. ten.

Short-Answer Essay Questions

1. List the important functions of unilineal descent groups.

2. Explain the general purposes of the Jewish "family circle" societies of New York City; briefly describe how the accepted descent pattern compares with unilineal and double descent patterns.

3. Define and list several features of *lineage, clan, phratry,* and *moiety*.

Suggested Activities

1. If you have never charted your genealogy, prepare a simple chart tracing descent through your father's male and mother's female lines. While you may include the brothers and sisters of each generation, the key aspect of this descent exercise is to determine how far back (that is, how many generations) you can trace your ancestry. Use the symbols illustrated on textbook page 276 in preparing your chart. If you have previously traced your family's descent, interview a friend and attempt to develop a genealogical chart for that person.

2. Does descent serve any function in your immediate or larger society? Try to list several specific aspects of life that are influenced by descent. Do you see a relationship between descent groups and nationality groups in the United States such as German-American or Irish-American societies?

Answer Key

STUDY ACTIVITIES

Vocabulary Check

1. f	4. k	7. d	10. j
2. m	5. b	8. i	11. c
3. n	6. g	9. e	

Completion

1. political system, kinship
2. unilineal, patrilineal, *tsu*, economic, patrilocal
3. pastoral, horticultural, females, males, sisters
4. matrilineal, woman, brother or maternal uncle, household
5. unilineal double, ambilineal

SELF-TEST

Objective Questions

(Page numbers refer to the textbook.)

1. c (Objective 1; page 274; video program)
2. c (Objective 1; page 274; video program)
3. b (Objective 2; page 274; video program)
4. c (Objective 2; page 286)
5. b (Objective 3; pages 274–275; video program)
6. b (Objective 3; page 275; video program)
7. c (Objective 3; page 277)
8. d (Objective 4; page 281; video program)
9. a (Objective 4; pages 281–282)
10. d (Objective 4; video program)
11. c (Objective 5; page 284)
12. a (Objective 5; page 284)

13. a (Objective 6; page 284)
14. d (Objective 6; page 284)
15. c (Objective 7; page 286)
16. a (Objective 7; page 286)
17. a (Objective 7; page 287)

Short-Answer Essay Questions

1. List the important functions of unilineal descent groups.

   Your answer should include:

   - As a corporate group, the unilineal descent group has a perpetual existence despite the birth and death of individual members, providing security and stability for its membership.

   - They are a source of mutual support and aid within the group, and through alliances with other groups, they support and assist in resolving conflicts with other groups.

   - They frequently own and regulate the use of land and other resources.

   - They determine who is eligible for marriage to members.

   - They provide continuation of religious and ceremonial traditions.

2. Explain the general purposes of the Jewish "family circle" societies of New York City; briefly describe how the accepted descent pattern compares with unilineal and double descent patterns.

   Your answer should include:

   - The "family circles" and "cousins clubs" have been organized in New York City and other cities in the twentieth century. They represent an attempt to preserve and restructure the strong family ties traditional in Jewish cultures from Eastern Europe and have functioned to preserve family ties and to provide mutual aid.

- Membership depends upon descent from an ancestral pair; however, the descent may be traced through either the male or female links, without any set order or pattern. In ambilineal descent, descent through either line is sufficient for the same purpose, that of membership.

- This kind of descent reckoning differs from unilineal, which allows tracing of descent only through the father's (male) or mother's (female) line; and from double descent patterns, which trace patrilineal and matrilineal descents, but each for specific purposes.

3. Define and list several features of *lineage, clan, phratry,* and *moiety.*

    Your answer should include:

    - Lineage: a corporate descent group permitting membership only to those who can trace their genealogical links to a specific known ancestor. In many societies, lineage membership confers status for political and religious purposes. A lineage is a self-perpetuating, usually exogamous group, which, in many cases, controls land and other resources.

    - Clan: a noncorporate descent group claiming descent from a common ancestor without being able to trace the specific genealogical links to the ancestor. A clan results from the fission of a lineage and lacks residential unity. Clans are exogamous and tend to gather together for ceremonial or similar purposes, identify themselves with totems, and offer special hospitality and aid to members of the clan.

    - Phratry: a unilineal descent group composed of two or more clans claiming common ancestry. The feeling of kinship among members of a phratry is generally weaker than that among members of a clan or lineage. Phratries are useful in controlling marriage (exogamous) and for ceremonial purposes.

    - Moiety: each of two groups resulting from the division of a society into two parts based on descent.

Kinship and Descent, Part II 15

Assignments

Before viewing the video program	• Read the Overview and the Learning Objectives for this lesson. Use the Learning Objectives to guide your reading, viewing, and thinking. • Read textbook Chapter 10, "Kinship and Descent," pages 290–297. • Review pages 274–278, 280–283, and 285–290.

View video program 15, "Kinship and Descent, Part II"

After viewing the video program	• Review the terms used in this lesson. In addition to those terms in the Learning Objectives, you should be familiar with these:
	
	    Crow system Hawaiian system Omaha system
	    Eskimo system Iroquois system Sudanese system
	
	• Review the reading assignment for this lesson.
	• Complete each of the Study Activities and the Self-Test in this study-guide lesson; check your answers with the Answer Key at the end of this lesson.
	• According to your instructor's assignment or your own interests, complete one or more of the Suggested Activities. You may also be interested in the readings listed at the end of Chapter 10 in the textbook.

Overview

Do you know the names of your great-great grandparents? Or, for that matter, can you recall the names of your great grandparents? If so, you probably rank among an exceedingly small percentage of those studying *Faces of Culture*. Nor is this surprising. Except in the case of a relatively few families distinguished by great wealth or achievement (or both), one's descent does not usually have much significance in North America today. Does this mean that Western industrial society has, in general, lost interest in relatives? Not really, because the nuclear family is still very important, although its structure and functions may be undergoing stresses, such as those described in earlier lessons. Like most North Americans, you are probably more aware of close relatives, those who are part of your nuclear family and those who have been members of the nuclear families in which your parents were children.

A grouping of relatives from both sides of the family that an individual recognizes as relatives is called a *kindred*. As social organizations, kindreds are weaker than unilineal descent groups, since they don't have fixed boundaries and are not corporate—they cannot make decisions in common. However, kindreds are more flexible than unilineal descent groups, so they are typically found in societies where mobility is an advantage.

Another interesting aspect of kinship explored in this lesson is the pattern by which the kindred names its members, thereby signifying their importance in the group. English names for close relatives (uncle and cousin, for example) do not have universal parallels. In fact, anthropologists have identified six distinct systems for naming the members of one's kindred, and each of these systems says something about the comparative importance of specific individuals. For example, some societies extend the use of the term "mother" to include all the sisters of both father and mother, as well as to the female parent. What conclusions might you draw about such a society?

After studying these two lessons on kinship and descent, you may have a greater appreciation for your family and relatives and the functions they serve.

Video Program: This program continues the examination of kinship and descent, paying particular attention to how kinship systems provide a blueprint for ideal social behavior and reflect a culture's values. Illustrative examples in the program include the kinship terms of the Baruya, the Navajo clans and matrilineal kinship organization, the Yanomamo and their patrilineal descent organized around lineages, and the patterns in the Greek village of Kypseli that reflect both patrilineal and matrilineal descent practices. Several of the six major systems of classifying kin and kinship terminology are diagrammed and illustrated in this program.

As you view the video program, look for:

- French anthropologist Maurice Godelier investigating the kinship terms used by the Baruya of New Guinea. He's speaking a kind of pig Latin and works through an interpreter.
- textbook author William A. Haviland explaining the importance of kinship and descent systems.
- the Navajo matrilineal kinship organization and terminology system.
- the social patterns of men, women, and children of the Greek village of Kypseli reflecting patrilineal and matrilineal descent practices.

Learning Objectives

When you have completed all assignments for this lesson, you should be able to:

1. Give examples to illustrate how matrilineal and patrilineal descent systems influence residence patterns. TEXTBOOK PAGES 276–278, 280–283; VIDEO PROGRAM

2. Define *bilateral kinship*. TEXTBOOK PAGES 287–289; VIDEO PROGRAM

3. Distinguish between unilineal descent and bilateral kinship and identify the types of societies in which each system is commonly found. TEXTBOOK PAGES 274–276, 287–290; VIDEO PROGRAM

4. Define *kindred* and *ego* as used in studying bilateral kinship and explain the ways in which a kindred differs from a descent group. TEXTBOOK PAGES 287–289; VIDEO PROGRAM

5. Identify symbols used by anthropologists in kinship and descent diagrams. TEXTBOOK PAGE 276; VIDEO PROGRAM

6. Recognize that different societies categorize relatives differently and have developed specialized kinship terminology systems to reflect those differences. TEXTBOOK PAGES 290–295; VIDEO PROGRAM

7. Briefly describe six major kinship terminology systems and identify the kinship terminology system commonly used by Anglo-Americans. TEXTBOOK PAGES 290–295; VIDEO PROGRAM

Study Activities

Vocabulary Check

Check your understanding of terms by writing the letter of the appropriate definition in the space next to the corresponding term. Check your choices with the Answer Key at the end of the lesson.

_____ 1. bilateral kinship	_____ 5. kinship terminology
_____ 2. kindred	_____ 6. siblings
_____ 3. ego	_____ 7. Eskimo kinship terminology system
_____ 4. Sudanese kinship terminology system	_____ 8. Omaha kinship terminology system
	_____ 9. triangle

a. often identifies the comparative importance of various relatives to an individual
b. the individual at the center of a kindred
c. a system in which an individual feels related equally to all near relatives of both parents
d. a system in which cross cousins on the mother's side are merged with the mother's generation
e. the most precise of kinship terminology systems
f. identifies a male in a kinship diagram
g. a relatively limited group of people related to one living individual through both parents
h. brothers and sisters
i. a system used in Anglo-American and Inuit societies
j. identifies a female in a kinship diagram

Completion

Fill each blank with the most appropriate term from the list immediately following that paragraph.

1. The focus of a lineal-descent system is an _____, while the "center" of a kindred is a living individual called the _____. In a unilineal descent system, the line that traces relationships to the _____ determines which relatives are more important to the individual. A system in which both lines include relatives who are equally important is known as a _____ system.

ambilineal	bilateral	father or mother
ancestor	ego	

2. In each of the following diagrams, identify each symbol marked with an "x" according to the following kinship terminology system. Note: In these diagrams, ego is represented by a shaded triangle or circle, depending on the sex of the person. Terms can be used more than once.

aunt	father's sister	nephew
brother	mother	niece
cousin	mother's brother	sister
father		

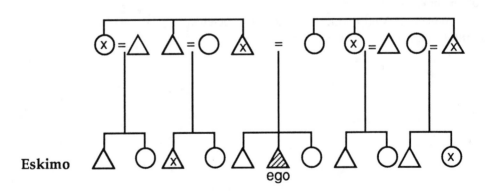

Eskimo

ego

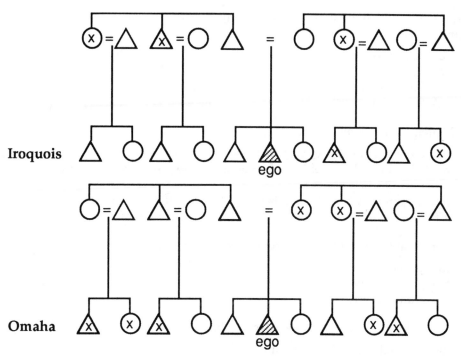

Iroquois

Omaha

Self-Test

Objective Questions

Select the one best answer.

1. A society in which a married woman and her husband are expected to reside with the wife's mother is the

    a. Trobriand society.
    b. Navajo society.
    c. rural Chinese society.
    d. Bakhtiari society.

2. A society in which the wife leaves the home of her family to live with the husband's family is the

   a. rural Chinese society.
   b. Navajo society.
   c. Hopi society.
   d. Eskimo society.

3. In bilateral kinship, an individual is

   a. related to the mothers of both parents, but not to the fathers.
   b. related to his father's relatives for some purposes and his mother's relatives for other purposes.
   c. free to gain membership in either his father's or his mother's descent group.
   d. affiliated with a large number of relatives of both parents.

4. In a bilateral kinship system, descent is traced through

   a. four grandparents.
   b. two grandparents.
   c. one grandparent.

5. Bilateral kinship is typical of societies in which

   a. large extended families are common.
   b. large tracts of farmland are held by the same family over many generations.
   c. nuclear families predominate.
   d. members trace their descent for many generations.

6. Unilineal descent is commonly found in

   a. all nonindustrial societies.
   b. agricultural and horticultural societies.
   c. all nonagricultural societies.
   d. food-foraging and pastoral societies.

7. One characteristic of many societies that organize relationships according to bilateral kinship is

    a. advanced technology.
    b. pastoralism.
    c. intensive agriculture.
    d. mobility.

8. A kindred includes

    a. all descendants of great grandparents.
    b. descendants of a single significant ancestor.
    c. all near relatives of a living person.
    d. brothers and sisters of the parents.

9. One function performed by kindreds is to

    a. assign unchanging status to individuals.
    b. hold title to property or pass it on.
    c. render assistance when requested.
    d. continue existence through several generations.

10. In a bilateral kinship system, the individual from whom relationships to a large number of relatives are traced is called

    a. ancestor.
    b. ego.
    c. kindred.
    d. sibling.

11. A kindred ends when

    a. ego dies.
    b. it fissions into two groups.
    c. a child is born to ego.
    d. the grandparents die.

12. In kinship diagrams, the symbol Δ (triangle) indicates

    a. a male.
    b. an ancestor of either sex.
    c. a female.
    d. a descendant of either sex.

13. The principal purpose of kinship terminology systems is to

    a. indicate positions occupied by persons in a society.
    b. trace descent from a specific ancestor.
    c. categorize each individual according to his or her generation.
    d. distinguish the nuclear family from all other relatives.

14. The kinship terminology system that links certain cousins with the parents'
    generation is the

    a. Omaha system.
    b. Iroquois system.
    c. descriptive system.
    d. Eskimo system.

15. The kinship terminology system used by Anglo-Americans is the

    a. Omaha system.
    b. Iroquois system.
    c. Eskimo system.
    d. unilinear system.

16. In the Eskimo system of kinship terminology,

    a. only members of the mother's family are specifically recognized.
    b. all relatives of the same sex and generation are referred to by the same term.
    c. no distinction is made between generations among certain kinsmen.
    d. no distinction is made between maternal and paternal sisters and brothers or
       their children.

Short-Answer Essay Questions

1. Give examples from the textbook and the video programs for Lessons 11, 12, and 15 to illustrate the relationships of patrilineal and matrilineal descent patterns with residence patterns.

2. In what types of societies are kindred organizations found? Why are they found in these particular societies?

3. Contrast the names given some near relatives in the Eskimo and Crow systems of kinship terminology; explain how each naming system indicates the relative importance of specific relatives.

Suggested Activities

1. Examine your local newspaper for one or two weeks for announcements of weddings, funerals, reunions, and other events in which there is a mention of kindred groups or of individuals who are kindred but not immediate family. During this period, did you find mention of any kind of activities involving descent—even the meeting of a genealogical society or a dispute among heirs over the disposition of an estate? Write a brief summary of the events you identify, and compare their frequency with events held for other types of groups. What conclusion can you draw about the importance of kinship relationships in your region?

2. William A. Haviland, the author of the textbook, suggests that mobility and individuality weaken kinship ties in Western industrial society. What institutions and organizations have taken over the various functions served by kinship organizations in other societies? In your opinion, are there values Western society has lost as a result of weakened kinship ties?

Answer Key

STUDY ACTIVITIES

Vocabulary Check

1. c	4. e	7. i
2. g	5. a	8. d
3. b	6. h	9. f

Completion

1. ancestor, ego, father or mother, bilateral
2. If you completed the diagrams of the kinship system accurately, the terminology should match that on the following charts.

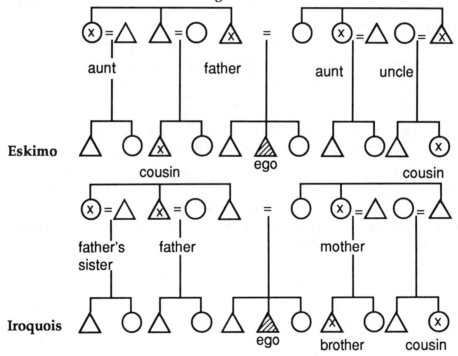

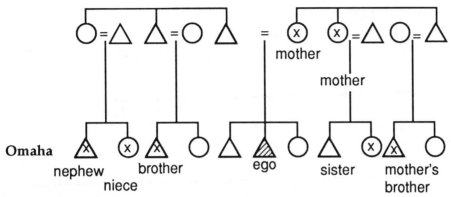

Omaha

nephew   brother   ego   sister   mother's
    niece   brother

SELF-TEST

Objective Questions

(Page numbers refer to the textbook.)

1. b (Objective 1; video program)
2. a (Objective 1; pages 277–278; video program)
3. d (Objective 2; pages 287–289; video program)
4. a (Objective 2; page 288; video program)
5. c (Objective 3; pages 287–289; video program)
6. b (Objective 3; pages 275, 288–289; video program)
7. d (Objective 3; page 289)
8. c (Objective 4; page 288; video program)
9. c (Objective 4; page 289)
10. b (Objective 4; page 288; video program)
11. a (Objective 4; pages 288–289)
12. a (Objective 5; page 276; video program)
13. a (Objective 6; page 290; video program)
14. a (Objective 7; page 294)
15. c (Objective 7; page 291)
16. d (Objective 7; page 291)

Short-Answer Essay Questions

1. Give examples from the textbook and the video programs for Lessons 11, 12, and 15 to illustrate the relationships of patrilineal and matrilineal descent patterns with residence patterns.

    Your answer should include:

    *   Societies with patrilineal descent patterns may have the custom of patrilocal residence or residence near the father's relatives. In the Yanomamo and Bakhtiari societies, for example, a married pair is expected to live in the vicinity of the husband's family.

    *   In societies with matrilineal descent, residence preference may be determined by the residence of maternal relatives. In Navajo society, for example, women are shown living with their maternal relatives, and a husband, at marriage, joins his wife in her home. In some societies with matrilineal descent, however, the residence pattern after marriage may still be patrilocal, as in the case of the Ashanti, whose women live in their husbands' village.

    *   Traditions vary widely. In the Kypseli village of Greece, a married couple lives in a house provided by the wife's relatives, although patrilineal descent determines status and inheritance.

    *   Many other factors influence residence patterns. One of the most important factors is economic, based on whether the male or female members of the society are the main providers of subsistence. These same factors help determine whether the society reckons descent through the male or female lines.

2. In what types of societies are kindred organizations found? Why are they found in these particular societies?

    Your answer should include:

    *   Kindred organization is typical of many food-foraging and industrial societies.

    *   In both types of societies, the nuclear family is often of primary importance. After the nuclear family, a kindred organization of close relatives is more likely to rank next in importance.

- Kindred organization is common in mobile societies where contact with a large group of relatives is impractical.

- Mobility weakens ties with a large group of relatives; industrial societies tend to encourage a high degree of mobility, making it unlikely that one would remain living in an area with one's lineage. To a lesser extent, the mobility characteristic of food-foraging societies is also a deterrent to the formation of descent groups.

3. Contrast the names given some near relatives in the Eskimo and Crow systems of kinship terminology; explain how each naming system indicates the relative importance of specific relatives.

Your answer should include:

- In the Eskimo kinship terminology system, brothers and sisters of the father and mother are termed aunts and uncles. In the Crow kinship terminology system, the father and his brother are called by the same term, as are the mother and her sister. In contrasting these kinship terminology systems, the Eskimo system indicates that ego's biological parents are of greater importance than the parents' brothers and sisters. In the Crow system, on the other hand, the parents' siblings of the same sex are considered about equal in importance.

- In the Eskimo system, all children of the parents' brothers and sisters are labeled with a single term regardless of sex. In the Crow system, such offspring may be termed brother and sister if they are children of the father's brother or mother's sister. Thus, the relationship of the father and his same-sex sibling or the mother and her same-sex sibling is emphasized over other children of the same generation. Children of the father's sister are identified with the parent's generation, while children of the mother's brother are identified with the generation of ego's own children (that is, called son and daughter or niece and nephew). This terminology serves to identify the importance of the lineage, because the "son and daughter" are, in effect, the product of ego's lineage.

Age, Common Interest, and Stratification 16

Assignments

Before viewing the video program	• Read the Overview and the Learning Objectives for this lesson. Use the Learning Objectives to guide your reading, viewing, and thinking. • Read textbook Chapter 11, "Grouping by Sex, Age, Common Interest, and Class," pages 298–321. • Review textbook Chapter 10 (especially pages 285–290) on the forms and functions of descent groups.

View video program 16, "Age, Common Interest, and Stratification"

After viewing the video program	• Review the terms used in this lesson. In addition to those terms in the Learning Objectives, you should be familiar with these: egalitarian society symbolic indicators gender stratification verbal evaluation open class society • Review the reading assignments for this lesson. • Complete each of the Study Activities and the Self-Test in this study-guide lesson; check your answers with the Answer Key at the end of this lesson. • According to your instructor's assignment or your interests, complete one or more of the Suggested Activities. You may also be interested in the readings listed at the end of Chapter 11 in the textbook.

Overview

Anthropologists have long known that people of all origins, ages, preferences, purposes, and both sexes tend to come together in groups of one kind or another. At this point, midway through your study of *Faces of Culture*, you, too, must have noticed that the inclination to "group" together is basic to humankind and is thus universal. Traditional societies have grouped together in family or kinship units for purposes of self-defense, resource-sharing, and pooling of labor. Within these groups and cutting across the boundaries of kinship relations are other significant groupings. The groups serve societies by resolving problems not effectively dealt with by family organization alone.

In this lesson, you will study four types of groups found in a wide range of societies: sex, age, common interest, and social class. Grouping by sex sometimes indicates a significant inequality of the sexes, but sometimes it does not. Grouping by age is a way of organizing groups to perform specific functions. Although common-interest groups have been in existence for thousands of years, today, they are particularly prominent in industrial societies. Grouping by social class, which is inherently discriminatory in determining one's share of status and resources, is characteristic of intensive agricultural and industrial societies.

As you are introduced by the textbook and the video program to examples of these types of social organizations, you will find it easy to identify counterparts in U.S. and other Western societies, perhaps many in your community. For example, would you say that the practice of processing all criminal offenders below a certain age through a system of special laws, courts, and detention facilities is a manifestation of age grading? How would you describe unions and professional associations and the tradition in which some young women make their "debut" at a so-called "coming-out" ball? Do you view yourself as a member of a social class? If so, which one?

At the same time you are identifying counterparts, however, you will realize, as you progress through this lesson, that age grouping among the Nuer, common-interest groups among the Crow Indians, and the caste system in India do not follow the same patterns or share the same functions as their counterparts in Western societies.

Video Program: In this program, the pastoralist society of Africa's Masai, where young boys live cooperatively in a training compound apart from their families, illustrates the concept of age grading, one of several ways in which people are grouped in nearly all societies. The program describes practices that promote group unity, such as the braiding of each other's hair among the Masai warriors. Common-interest associations, a second grouping of people in societies, are illustrated with footage of New England contra dancers and through the story of the Brotherhood of Sleeping Car Porters, a black labor union in the United States. Stratification, a third means of organizing people within a society, is illustrated with footage that contrasts the daily activities of an affluent U.S. family with the white domination of the blacks of South Africa under the apartheid system that once existed in that country and with the caste system of India.

As you view the program, look for:

- the importance of male age sets for the Masai of Africa.
- the variety of common-interest associations found in pluralistic industrial societies and the various purposes they serve.
- the origins and history of the Brotherhood of Sleeping Car Porters, a black labor union in the United States.
- examples of stratification in the United States, India, and South Africa.

Learning Objectives

When you have completed all assignments in this lesson, you should be able to:

1. Define and describe at least three examples of social groupings based on age or sex. TEXTBOOK PAGES 300–305; VIDEO PROGRAM

2. Describe some functions of age groupings. TEXTBOOK PAGES 301–305; VIDEO PROGRAM

3. Distinguish between age grade and age set. TEXTBOOK PAGES 303–304

4. Define and describe common-interest associations and state the functions of common-interest associations in both traditional and present-day industrial societies. TEXTBOOK PAGES 305–308; VIDEO PROGRAM

5. Compare kinship groups, age groups, and common-interest associations as methods of organizing society. TEXTBOOK PAGES 285–290 [CHAPTER 10] AND PAGES 301–308; VIDEO PROGRAM

6. Define and describe *social stratification* and its manifestation in social classes and castes. TEXTBOOK PAGES 308–312; VIDEO PROGRAM

7. Describe conditions that lead to the development of a stratified society and explain the role of mobility in such a society. TEXTBOOK PAGES 313–317, 319–321; VIDEO PROGRAM

Study Activities

Vocabulary Check

Check your understanding of terms by writing the letter of the appropriate definition in the space next to the corresponding term. Check your choices with the Answer Key at the end of the lesson.

_____ 1. age grade

_____ 2. age set

_____ 3. mobility

_____ 4. common-interest association

_____ 5. egalitarian society

_____ 6. verbal evaluation

_____ 7. stratified society

_____ 8. social class

_____ 9. symbolic indicator

_____ 10. caste

_____ 11. open-class society

a. a society in which the number of valued positions is equal to the number of people capable of filling them
b. a set of families and individuals who enjoy nearly equal prestige
c. a kind of social class in which membership is determined at birth and remains fixed for life
d. a category of people based on age
e. a group not based on age, kinship, marriage, territory, or rank
f. a group of people initiated into an age grade at the same time
g. permits a great deal of social mobility
h. the ability to change one's class position
i. valued positions that exist for every person capable of filling them
j. division of society into groups with unequal sharing of resources, prestige, and influence
k. what people say about others in their own society
l. activity or possession indicative of a given social class

Completion

Fill each blank with the most appropriate term from the list immediately following that paragraph.

1. Some kind of age grouping is nearly _____ among human societies. Different life stages are recognized, and the purposes and resulting organizations vary widely. In some instances, the separation is of the youth, adults, and _____. In others, there are practices that may teach skills or otherwise aid the _____ from one stage of life to another. Age groups may aid in maintaining social continuity, ensuring that important social roles will be filled, and in transmitting the society's cultural heritage.

elders	universal
transition	

2. The Tribal Unions of West Africa are common-interest associations whose chief purpose is preservation of _____ traditions. A typical characteristic of common-interest groups found in traditional cultures is concern for the well-being of the entire _____, not just for their own members.

    Labor unions in the United States arose from movements in the nineteenth and twentieth centuries to improve working conditions and wages. Their efforts are typical of common-interest associations in rapidly changing societies that give _____ to members through _____ of existing institutions or the development of new ones to meet the challenges posed by industrialization and _____.

adaptation	community	urbanization
assistance	cultural	

3. Social stratification systems are more complex than age or common-interest groupings. Some anthropologists subscribe to the theory that social inequality first arose in food-producing societies when members could accumulate a surplus of goods. This occurrence gave some (those who controlled the surplus) more power than others. Exercise of power led to still greater stratification of societies in terms of _____, influence, _____, and prohibitions. Other influences, such as political organization beyond the local community, may also have served to intensify the development of a class structure. Social stratification systems range from the most rigidly stratified, such as the _____ system of India, to more _____ class societies where opportunities for mobility between classes exist.

caste	open	status
closed	privileges	

Self-Test

Objective Questions

Select the one best answer.

1. Among the Five Nations Iroquois
    a. men lived in the villages and raised crops.
    b. women lived in the villages and raised crops.
    c. men lived in the villages and built houses and palisades.
    d. women lived in the villages and built houses and palisades.

2. Of the following groups, the one that is based on an age grade is the
    a. Brotherhood of Sleeping Car Porters.
    b. castes in India.
    c. warriors of the Tiriki.
    d. kindred.

3. Masai males are first grouped into age grades at about age
    a. 6.
    b. 12.
    c. 18.
    d. 21.

4. The general purpose of age groupings is best described as a means of
    a. identifying and separating those who are not productive due to age.
    b. identifying a number of life stages.
    c. preserving certain privileges for selected groups.
    d. organizing those with a specific set of concerns and needs into one organization.

5. An *age set* is best defined as

   a. all the people of the same age in a given population.
   b. an organized group of people based on age.
   c. a group of people, based on age, who move through a series of stages together for much of their lives.
   d. the individuals who actually hold membership in an organization based primarily on age.

6. Common-interest associations are found in

   a. advanced industrial societies.
   b. rapidly changing urban societies.
   c. traditional nonindustrial societies.
   d. all of the above.

7. Of the following groups, the one that requires a deliberate act of joining, though not necessarily voluntary, is

   a. age class.
   b. caste.
   c. common-interest association.
   d. social class.

8. The purpose of the Tribal Unions of West Africa is

   a. preserving cultural heritage.
   b. providing sufficient members for various social roles.
   c. adaptating to urbanization.
   d. preserving stratification systems.

9. The major purpose of associations formed in rapidly changing and newly urbanized societies is usually

   a. preserving traditions.
   b. providing members for various social roles.
   c. political action.
   d. adapting to new conditions.

10. The Brotherhood of Sleeping Car Porters was organized to

    a. preserve the traditions of a historic era.
    b. combat segregation and discrimination.
    c. improve working conditions for its members.
    d. assist in making rail travel more popular.

11. In general, as societies become industrialized and more complex,

    a. both kinship groups and common-interest groups increase in importance.
    b. both kinship groups and common-interest groups decrease in importance.
    c. kinship groups increase in importance.
    d. common-interest groups increase in importance.

12. The term *stratified society* refers to

    a. formation of groups based on age.
    b. a nobility or priesthood class.
    c. ranking of classes based on wealth, power, and prestige.
    d. the existence of a slave class.

13. In a stratified society,

    a. it is virtually impossible to move from one social level to another, except possibly by marriage.
    b. various groups are unequal in resources, power, and prestige.
    c. an individual's position in society depends largely on his or her skills.
    d. social mobility between classes is quite easy.

14. In an egalitarian society,

    a. there are great differences in rank and privilege.
    b. various groups are unequal in power and prestige.
    c. an individual's position in society depends largely on sex, age, and skills.
    d. an individual's ranking depends upon his or her birth.

15. The classic example of a system of social caste is found in

    a. India.
    b. South Africa.
    c. Polynesia.
    d. Western Europe.

16. Social mobility refers to the

    a. breakup of the extended family or kinship group influence.
    b. amount of modern transportation available.
    c. ease with which one moves from one common-interest association to another.
    d. possibility of changing one's social class membership.

17. Of the following factors, the one that may adversely affect mobility is

    a. an extended-family organization.
    b. extensive age grouping.
    c. availability of educational opportunity.
    d. industrialization.

Short-Answer Essay Questions

1. Explain how age sets in Tiriki society might function more effectively than kinship groups in ensuring that key social roles are filled.

2. Describe how the functions of common-interest associations in rapidly changing societies might differ from those found in traditional societies. Cite an example of traditional and Western common-interest groups having similar functions.

Suggested Activities

1. Analyze factors related to four or five of your closest friendships: In each friendship, what parts do kinship, age, common interests, and social class play? Are you and any of your friends members of the same common-interest groups, political parties, or groups that indicate social class?

2. Make an anthropological study of a nearby, but fairly large, newsstand or magazine display. How many common-interest groups (even if not formally organized groups) are reflected by the magazine titles? Based on the number of magazines appealing to particular interests, which groups seem to be the largest? Which of these groups seem to be seeking political or social power, as indicated by a quick check of the titles of articles in the magazines? Categorize the primary function of each group according to the following list: preservation, help members to change and adapt, desire to change some aspect of society.

Answer Key

STUDY ACTIVITIES

Vocabulary Check

1. d	5. a	9. l
2. f	6. k	10. c
3. h	7. j	11. g
4. e	8. b	

Completion

1. universal, elders, transition
2. cultural, community, assistance, adaptation, urbanization
3. status, privileges (either order), caste, open

SELF-TEST

Objective Questions

(Page numbers refer to the textbook.)

1. b (Objective 1; page 300)
2. c (Objective 1; page 304; video program)
3. a (Objective 1; video program)
4. b (Objective 2; pages 303–304)
5. c (Objective 3; page 304)
6. d (Objective 4; page 305; video program)
7. c (Objective 4; page 305; video program)
8. a (Objective 4; page 305)
9. d (Objective 4; page 308)
10. c (Objective 4; video program)
11. d (Objective 5; page 308)
12. c (Objective 6; page 309; video program)
13. b (Objective 6; page 309; video program)
14. c (Objective 6; page 309)
15. a (Objective 6; page 311; video program)
16. d (Objective 7; pages 313–314)
17. a (Objective 7; page 314)

Short-Answer Essay Questions

1. Explain how age sets in Tiriki society might function more effectively than kinship groups in ensuring that key social roles are filled.

   Your answer should include:

   • Young men in a given age grade are joined in formal association in an age set, regardless of family. Therefore, there is a social unity, which is communitywide, going beyond the family.

- Through the Tiriki system of age grouping, each of four "vital" social positions always has adequate membership. It is possible that individual kinship groups might not supply sufficient numbers at any one time for all four positions. It is also possible that kinship group preparation and training might concentrate on the needs of that group rather than the needs of the entire community.

2. Describe how the functions of common-interest associations in rapidly changing societies might differ from those found in traditional societies. Cite an example of traditional and Western common-interest groups having similar functions.

   Your answer should include:

   - Common-interest associations of individuals living in rapidly changing societies help individuals adapt to new conditions in new environments.

   - Common-interest associations such as political clubs, unions, and women's groups in industrial societies may also be a vehicle for introducing change to society. In contrast, common-interest groups in traditional societies tend to preserve the traditional patterns of behavior. However, some contemporary common-interest groups may exist to help preserve traditional values and lifestyles. These groups may include organizations such as ethnic membership clubs, Daughters of the American Revolution, and historical societies.

The Aymara: A Case Study 17
in Social Stratification

Assignments

Before viewing the video program	• Read the Overview and the Learning Objectives for this lesson. Use the Learning Objectives to guide your reading, viewing, and thinking. • Review textbook Chapter 11, "Grouping by Sex, Age, Common Interest, and Class," especially the "Social Stratification" section, pages 308–317 and 319–321, and the chapter summary. • Read Background Notes 17A, "The Aymara," in this study-guide lesson.

View video program 17, "The Aymara: A Case Study in Social Stratification"

After viewing the video program	• Look at the Bolivia map in Lesson 6 in this study-guide lesson. • Check your understanding of these names and terms:

Andes	feudal	social stratification
Ayata	*mestizo*	symbolic indicators
Aymara	mobility	verbal evaluation
chuno	MNR	Viracocha
class	sharecroppers	Vitocota

• Review the reading assignments for this lesson. A thorough second reading of the Background Notes is suggested.
• Complete each of the Study Activities and the Self-Test in this study-guide lesson; check your answers with the Answer Key at the end of this lesson.
• According to your instructor's assignment or your own interests, complete one or more of the Suggested Activities.

Overview

Stratification, or division by social class, is most apparent in societies that have large and heterogeneous populations and centralized control, including North American society. You probably became aware at an early age that North Americans discriminate by social class in the sharing of resources and the bestowing of status and prestige, although some may want to deny this reality. You should know, however, that division or definition by social class is by no means a phenomenon peculiar to present-day or industrial societies; social class distinctions also characterized all ancient civilizations. Although the division is not always clear, social classes in stratified societies can be based on birth, wealth, legal status, and other distinctions. Whatever the basis, stratification means that members of different social classes will not share equally in status or resources.

When you first studied stratification in Lesson 16, did you realize that class structures are very difficult to change? In the case study for this lesson, you will learn how the social-class system of northern Bolivia, which has roots dating back more than 400 years, deeply affects the lives of the Aymara Indians living there. Listen to the words spoken by members of the different social classes in the video program for this lesson; note what people say to and about one another, and observe how they interact. You will learn that the pattern of stratification is woven into many social institutions of this society, and religious practices perpetuate the social structure.

During the second half of this century, the Bolivian government has attempted to improve the conditions of the Aymara. After viewing the program, you may feel that progress is terribly slow. "But compared to the past ," one Aymara says, "we are like free and radiant doves." Perhaps you will find yourself reflecting on what it means to be "free" and what it means to be denied access to social and economic resources.

Video Program: Through footage made in northern Bolivia, where the heterogeneous population is socially and economically stratified, this program provides a close look at the inequities of a sharp class division between the Spanish-speaking *mestizos* and the subordinate Aymara Indians. The class system depicted, typical of much of Latin America, is apparent not only in the fields, but in religious practices, the celebratory fiestas, the classroom, and even in medical care. Although a revolution in 1952 brought some changes in Bolivia, this program shows that the Aymara are still bound by many of the economic and social patterns that existed before the revolution.

As you view the program, look for:

- the attitudes shown by the *mestizos* (the Spanish-speaking landholders) toward the Aymara throughout the program.

- the educational, economic, social, and other differences between the *mestizo* town of Ayata and the Aymara village of Vitocota.

- evidence of the limited resources available to the Aymara such as educational opportunity, medical care, and political and economic opportunities.

- evidence of class distinctions shown in the Flag Day celebration near the end of the program.

Learning Objectives

When you have completed all assignments in this lesson, you should be able to:

1. Briefly describe the origins of the stratification system of the Aymara and the *mestizos* in Bolivia. VIDEO PROGRAM; BACKGROUND NOTES 17A

2. Describe the indicators of the power and influence of the *mestizos* and the indicators of the lower-class status of the Aymara. TEXTBOOK PAGES 308–317, 319–321; VIDEO PROGRAM; BACKGROUND NOTES 17A

3. Describe indicators of mobility in the stratification system of the Aymara. VIDEO PROGRAM; BACKGROUND NOTES 17A

4. Identify the ways in which the Aymara and the *mestizos* are mutually interdependent. VIDEO PROGRAM; BACKGROUND NOTES 17A

5. Describe how the Bolivian revolution of 1952 changed the relationship between the Aymara and the *mestizos*. VIDEO PROGRAM; BACKGROUND NOTES 17A

6. Discuss indications of class attitudes and economic conditions present in scenes of Aymara and *mestizo* children. VIDEO PROGRAM

THE AYMARA

The Aymara are agriculturalists who live in the Andes in Bolivia. The video program focuses on a village, Vitocota, and a town, Ayata, that are located near Lake Titicaca 12,000 feet above sea level. Because of the altitude, it is often cloudy, and frost at night is common. The Aymara depend on the weather for survival. They are sometimes plagued by hail, winds, and drought, and the ground they farm is not very fertile. Due to the short growing season and infertile soil, the Aymara can produce only one crop a year.

The Aymara farm much as they did before the Spanish conquered the area in the sixteenth century. Men break up the sun-hardened ground with a wooden footplow, and both women and men use stones to break up the soil even more.

Land is now individually owned, and the Aymara try to have plots of land at various altitudes. This dispersed pattern of landownership allows the Aymara a greater chance for growing enough food. If frost damages the crop in a plot of land higher up the mountain, the yield from a lower-lying plot might prevent them from going hungry. If too much rain destroys the lower crop, the crop on higher terrain might still be available for harvest. Multiple plots give them access to crops from a variety of weather zones. The Aymara enhance the fertility of the soil by adding manure and by using a sophisticated eight-year cycle of crop rotation.

Potatoes are the primary crop for the Aymara. Up to 300 varieties are grown, and a family may grow as many as forty varieties, some for their taste and some because they are frost-resistant. Potatoes provide about two-thirds of the Aymara diet. They are consumed principally in the form of *chuno*, which are potatoes preserved by alternately freezing and sun-drying. Prepared in this way, the potatoes last almost indefinitely.

The Aymara also grow other tuber crops and grain. They raise guinea pigs and sheep, but they usually trade or sell the meat and eat only the edible intestines. Consequently, the Aymara diet is low in protein.

The Aymara live in close-knit extended family groups headed by an elder male. All children, male and female, inherit land equally. There is sexual division of labor in most agricultural tasks. Women select the seed and prepare manure to use as fertilizer. They decide how much seed will be sown, how much *chuno* will be prepared, and which potatoes will be sold. Women dominate most matters involving livestock, and they control the family finances. Men do the heavier plowing tasks, help with the planting and harvesting, and conduct rituals associated with planting and harvesting. Harvests are often carried out as community efforts and become times of social interaction and merriment. The Aymara also exchange labor and hire themselves out as labor. Successful Aymara are expected to sponsor religious festivals and other ritual events. Sponsoring a fiesta involves them in a series of gift exchanges—in the form of food, alcohol, and coca leaves—and enhances their prestige. For the Aymara, coca serves much the same social and stimulant functions that coffee does in Western society; it is also important in rituals.

Although the Aymara use many of the same planting and harvesting techniques they did before they were conquered by the Spanish, their social, political, and economic roles have changed considerably. The Spanish established a system of feudal landownership and forced labor in the tin and silver mines. When Bolivia achieved independence from Spain in 1825, forced labor in the mines was abolished, but the system of landownership remained essentially unchanged. In 1950, fewer than 5 percent of the people owned 90 percent of the land. Under this ownership pattern, most of the farmers were tenants who were bound to the land and could legally be bought and sold with the land they worked.

Many of the landowners were *mestizos*. *Mestizo* is a Spanish word meaning "mixed" and usually refers to racially mixed people. But, in Bolivia, the *mestizos* are distinguished from the Aymara not so much by race as by language, occupation, residence, culture, and style of living. *Mestizos* speak Spanish, the official language of the country, and wear Western dress. The Aymara speak their own language, one of two major native language groups in the area, and wear handwoven clothing. *Mestizos* are largely urban; the Aymara are rural peasants. *Mestizos* have access to Western medicine; the Aymara, as a rule, do not. *Mestizos* control certain ritual duties needed by the Aymara. For example, most priests are *mestizos*, and the Aymara must hire *mestizos* to conduct parts of religious festivals in Latin.

Mestizos and Aymara are educated differently. *Mestizo* children are taught in combined primary-secondary schools, which can prepare them for professional training. Aymara children may attend the first few grades in a peasant school. If they seek further schooling, they go to a "central" school, perhaps in another community, where they can complete the primary grades. Few continue with secondary or professional education. Salaries and working conditions for teachers in rural schools are inferior to those in urban schools. The curriculum for peasant children is aimed at teaching Spanish, reading, writing, arithmetic, and a few vocational skills. This education is inadequate for staying in a rural community or preparing for further study. The inadequacy of peasant education is reflected in Bolivia's illiteracy rate, which is 17 percent for urban dwellers over the age of fifteen and 85 percent for the rural population over fifteen.

The *mestizos* and the Aymara distrust each other. In the video program, Aymara boys talking on the soccer field are convinced that food is available to the school, but it is not being distributed equally to the *mestizo* and the Aymara children. On the other hand, *mestizos* living in town fear the growing power of the rural areas, a power that was sparked by the "great revolution" of 1952. The peasants did not start the 1952 revolution. It was brought about by the Nationalist Revolutionary Movement (Movimiento Nacional Revolucionario, or MNR), a loose coalition representing a variety of interests, including miners, factory workers, and intellectuals. About the only thing the 1952 revolutionists had in common was their opposition to the tiny urban elite who had previously taken turns occupying seats of power through a series of "revolutions" that had little effect on the vast majority of the populace.

The Nationalist Revolutionary Movement came to power in 1952 after brief but bloody fighting. The movement immediately initiated sweeping changes, some of which were aimed at securing the support of the peasants. Education for rural children was assigned to the Ministry of Peasant Affairs and extended into some of the most remote areas of the country. The present form of rural education exists primarily because of the revolution.

The MNR also instituted major agrarian reforms. Large landholdings were broken up and the land redistributed to the peasants who had been farming it. The MNR was faced with the problem of dividing a limited amount of tillable land in the highlands, where the Aymara live, among a vast number of people. Thus, the MNR began resettlement of people into less-populated and more tropical areas in the eastern lowlands. However, in the mountainous region, the fact that the Aymara became landholders was an important change in the stratification patterns relating Aymara and *mestizo*. The MNR tried to set up an internal transportation system and improve roads, which was difficult because of the mountainous terrain of the Andes. The MNR also nationalized Bolivia's tin mines and extended the vote to greater numbers of people.

After 1952, inflation and mismanagement led to new concentrations of power in Bolivia's central government. Some political scientists have described Bolivia's political system as "internal colonialism." Wealth and power are concentrated in the capital, which drains off the economic resources of the rest of the country. But the changes brought about by the revolution of 1952 were too far-reaching to be erased. The Aymara have demanded a greater voice in determining their social and economic roles. And they are seeking better educational opportunities for their children. Limited land combined with a rapidly expanding population means that future generations cannot hope to keep dividing the family plot among siblings, so they must find jobs away from the land. For the Aymara, education may be the key to a better economic future and a way to break down barriers between them and the *mestizos*. Anthropologist William E. Carter writes, "Their sons, they claim, also want to be doctors" (*The Children Know*, film essay from the series *Faces of Change*, produced by The American University's Field Staff, 1976, page 5).

Study Activities

Vocabulary Check

Check your understanding of terms by writing the letter of the appropriate definition in the space next to the corresponding term. Check your choices with the Answer Key at the end of the lesson.

_____	1. Andes	_____	5. Vitocota
_____	2. feudal	_____	6. *chuno*
_____	3. Viracocha	_____	7. Ayata
_____	4. *mestizo*	_____	8. MNR

a. system in which owning the land involves virtual ownership of the people who work the land
b. vegetable grown by the Aymara
c. mountain region in which the Aymara live
d. literally means "mixture"
e. Aymara village
f. "revolutionary" government that instituted land and education reforms
g. church official
h. preserved potatoes
i. a god of the indigenous religion in Bolivia, and a term used by Aymara in referring to *mestizos*
j. *mestizo* town

Completion

Fill each blank with the most appropriate term from the list immediately following that paragraph.

1. The Spanish conquest of Bolivia imposed many changes on the Aymara-speaking Indians in the region, although some aspects of their life remain largely unchanged. For example, the Aymara still use the same _____, and _____ practices remain largely as before the conquest. Some aspects of the older _____ beliefs still survive, although these are now blended with Roman Catholic ritual. However, the Spanish imposed a _____ pattern of landownership and _____ labor in the mines.

agricultural	forced	religious
feudal	language	

2. The *mestizos* are the _____ landowners, a class that resulted from Spanish rule. Generally, they live in _____ areas, speak Spanish, and have an _____ system that can lead to _____ training. The Aymara, in contrast, are rural people, habitually speak their own language, and were provided limited formal education only in the last half of the twentieth century.

educational   professional

middle-class   urban

3. Reforms instituted in the 1952 revolution that have affected the Aymara include _____ and _____. The Aymara and *mestizos* _____ each other, and the contrast in opportunities for services such as medical care is still great. According to the video program, *mestizos* view the Aymara as _____ and given to drinking too much, while one Aymara views his fellow villagers as spending too much effort and money on _____.

distrust   fiestas   lazy

education   landownership   respect

Self-Test

Objective Questions

Select the one best answer.

1. The term *mestizo* identifies a group in Bolivia that is primarily
   a. the aristocracy of La Paz.
   b. a Spanish nobility class.
   c. small-town landowners.
   d. tenant farmers and laborers.

2. The present stratification system of the Aymara and the *mestizos* in Bolivia had its origins in
   a. the feudal landholding patterns established by the Spanish.
   b. establishment of a priest class.
   c. linguistic, educational, and ethnic differences between the *mestizos* and the Aymara.
   d. reforms instituted by the MNR.

3. The status of the *mestizos* is reflected in their
   a. rural residence patterns.
   b. religious preference.
   c. education and wealth.
   d. political party.

4. Which of the following statements was still true at the time the ethnographic film shown in the video program for this lesson was made?
   a. Landowners use Aymara labor to work the farms.
   b. The Aymara are required to work in mines.
   c. No educational opportunities are provided for the lower class.
   d. All farming land is owned by individual farmers.

5. A criticism frequently leveled against the Aymara by the *mestizos* is that the Aymara
   a. do menial work.
   b. are ignorant.
   c. do not take part in politics.
   d. drink too much.

6. The language of the Aymara affects their status because it is
   a. the official language of the nation.
   b. difficult to understand.
   c. not the official language of the nation.
   d. now spoken by very few residents.

7. The obstacle that makes it difficult for the Aymara to receive professional education is that

 a. the Aymara are prohibited by law from entering most professions.
 b. the elementary education available to the Aymara does not adequately prepare them for further schooling.
 c. values derived from their old religion prevent young Aymara from seeking education.
 d. no professional education is available in Bolivia.

8. Which of the following statements is NOT true of elementary education in Aymara communities?

 a. All instruction is in Aymara.
 b. Teachers in rural schools are paid less than those in urban schools.
 c. All instruction is in Spanish.
 d. Students usually have to leave their community for upper-grade education.

9. Many Aymara depend on *mestizo* society for their religious practices because

 a. all churches are located in *mestizo* cities.
 b. the Aymara still follow the older worship of Viracocha.
 c. religious clergy are supported by the government.
 d. the clergy are from the *mestizo* society.

10. For the mestizos, the Aymara of Vitocota primarily provide

 a. household servants.
 b. field labor.
 c. teachers, police, and similar work.
 d. office and shop workers.

11. In the land reforms instituted by the Bolivian revolutionary government after 1952,

 a. all farmland was nationalized.
 b. peasant farmers began owning land.
 c. landownership was taken over by *mestizos*.
 d. modern agricultural methods were introduced widely.

12. After the Nationalist Revolutionary Movement came to power,

    a. educational opportunities decreased greatly because many schools were closed.
    b. native languages, as well as Spanish, were used in primary-school instruction.
    c. peasant schools were established in Aymara villages.
    d. comprehensive high schools were established to teach vocational skills important to rural communities.

13. The *mestizo* population distrusts the rural Aymara population because

    a. some of the revolutionary government's reforms were designed to gain peasant support, and the Aymara are beginning to demand a larger voice in government.
    b. the peasants led the 1952 revolution, causing the *mestizos* to fear further political changes.
    c. the rural populations have become a strong political force, but they are not as literate as those of the cities.
    d. the Aymara are moving rapidly into the cities and threatening to disrupt city life.

14. The Flag Day celebration shown in the video program suggests that Aymara and *mestizo* children

    a. are able to ignore the social barriers and play together.
    b. have habitually played together in the past.
    c. do not mix or play together.
    d. play together now, as they did in the past.

15. The scenes of the Aymara school in the video program reveal that it has

    a. glass in the windows and central heating.
    b. poor lighting, seating, and educational curriculum.
    c. modern desks and schoolbooks.
    d. a *mestizo* teacher who is harsh with the children.

Short-Answer Essay Questions

1. Are there any indications in this lesson that the Aymara can change their class status? What are the conditions that block upward mobility for the Aymara?

2. The film footage of the fiesta, of the National Flag Day celebration, and of several other occasions where the *mestizos* and Aymara interact depicts several displays of class attitudes. What are some of these attitudes? How do they ignore the dependence of each group on the other?

Suggested Activities

1. Read and prepare a brief review of *The Bolivian Aymara*, by Hans C. Buechler and Judith-Maria Buechler (New York: Holt, Rinehart and Winston, 1971).

2. What similarities do you see in the situation of the Aymara as presented in the video program and the situations of one or more of the minority groups in the United States? Use your local library resources to compare, in particular, the literacy levels of various minority groups in the United States with those of the two Bolivian social groups described in Background Notes 17A.

3. The Bolivian revolution of 1952 inaugurated extensive land reforms that changed a feudal ownership system extending back more than 400 years. However, the changes made after the revolution have not had a great effect on the social stratification of the Aymara. Read additional information on the revolution and evaluate its effect on opportunities for social mobility for the Aymara.

Answer Key

STUDY ACTIVITIES

Vocabulary Check

1. c	4. d	7. j
2. a	5. e	8. f
3. i	6. h	

Completion

1. language, agricultural, religious, feudal, forced
2. middle-class, urban, educational, professional
3. landownership, education (either order); distrust, lazy, fiestas

SELF-TEST

Objective Questions

(Page numbers refer to the textbook.)

1. c (Objective 1; video program; Background Notes 17A)
2. a (Objective 1; video program; Background Notes 17A)
3. c (Objective 2; pages 309–313; video program; Background Notes 17A)
4. a (Objective 2; video program; Background Notes 17A)
5. d (Objective 2; video program; Background Notes 17A)
6. c (Objective 2; pages 309–313; video program; Background Notes 17A)
7. b (Objective 3; video program; Background Notes 17A)
8. a (Objective 3; video program; Background Notes 17A)
9. d (Objective 4; video program; Background Notes 17A)
10. b (Objective 4; video program; Background Notes 17A)
11. b (Objective 5; video program; Background Notes 17A)
12. c (Objective 5; video program; Background Notes 17A)
13. a (Objective 5; Background Notes 17A)
14. c (Objective 6; video program)
15. b (Objective 6; video program)

Short-Answer Essay Questions

1. Are there any indications in this lesson that the Aymara can change their class status? What are the conditions that block upward mobility for the Aymara?

    Your answer should include:

    - Two examples of possible upward mobility are shown in the program: the police chief of Ayata, the mestizo town, is an Aymara, as is Hugo, the schoolteacher. In both cases, their professional education has allowed the men to assume higher-class jobs.

    - However, both these examples are limited in that they are exceptions to the common pattern.

    - Serious obstacles to upward mobility facing the Aymara include poverty, poor health, limited access to education, a high illiteracy rate, and primitive farming techniques. There are no indications of other economic potential for the Aymara, and opportunities for work other than farming in a rural area are limited.

2. The film footage of the fiesta, of the National Flag Day celebration, and of several other occasions where the mestizos and Aymara interact depicts several displays of class attitudes. What are some of these attitudes? How do they ignore the dependence of each group on the other?

    Your answer should include:

    - All participants seem aware of the differences in status reflected by clothing and appearance.

    - The members of each group do not really "mix"; the *mestizo* children play separately from the Aymara.

    - Attitudes of the *mestizo* adults toward the Aymara seem condescending; expressions of resentment are heard from the Aymara.

    - The *mestizos* appear to ignore the extent to which they depend on the Aymara for labor and the performance of menial tasks, as well as for agricultural products.

    - The Aymara resent the *mestizos*, yet they depend on them for employment, for certain religious services, and for professional services such as health care. They also depend on the government, which actually arises from groups identified with the *mestizos*.

Political **18** Organization

Assignments

Before viewing the video program	• Read the Overview and the Learning Objectives for this lesson. Use the Learning Objectives to guide your reading, viewing, and thinking. • Read textbook Chapter 12, "Political Organization and Social Control," pages 326–338 and 355–356. (The balance of the chapter will be assigned in the next lesson.)

View video program 18, "Political Organization"

After viewing the video program	• Review the terms used in this lesson. In addition to those terms in the Learning Objectives, you should be familiar with these: nation theocracy • Review the reading assignments for this lesson. • Complete each of the Study Activities and the Self-Test in this study-guide lesson; check your answers with the Answer Key at the end of this lesson. • According to your instructor's assignment or your own interests, complete one or more of the Suggested Activities. You may also be interested in the readings listed at the end of Chapter 12 in the textbook.

Overview

Why do human societies develop political organizations? Perhaps it seems that the politics seen in U.S. society always pits the "insiders" against the "outsiders." In other words, a quest for power. But what is done with that power?

Political organizations can be a way that people effect social change: grass roots movements, political action committees, support for "reform" ticket candidates in local elections, and so on. However, what about those parts of society that no one particularly wants changed? What keeps them stable?

The political organization in a society helps ensure that certain behaviors will provide for the common good, whatever the common good is perceived to be. Perhaps an example of "common good" is simply a hunting-gathering society moving its camp. It may be raising an army to deter or repel invaders. It may be the building or maintenance of a particular institution. Actually, even the simplest society has a number of concerns that fall under the heading of common good, and anthropologists are sometimes fascinated in discovering the mechanisms that reinforce the common good. It is intriguing to discover where the power resides, who supports those with power, how leaders are chosen, and how the power of leaders is limited.

For all of their differences, basic similarities are found in the political organizations of all societies. Political systems have leaders with special names or titles. These systems provide the mechanisms by which societies maintain internal social order, cope with public affairs, and manage relations with external groups, whether they are other political organizations or other societies. All political systems employ some method of social control, which may be as subtle as gossip or as overt as physical force.

Political organizations take one of four general forms, distinguished by their complexity: bands, tribes, chiefdoms, and states. In general, a more complex society gives rise to a more complex form of political organization, which may or may not include a government. The relationship between a society's patterns of subsistence, stratification, and economics and its political systems is further evidence of how cultures are integrated and how each feature of a culture complements and supports many of its other facets. Thus, family organizations, social organizations, economic systems, and political organizations tend to be mutually supportive.

This four-part model of political organization has been the subject of much discussion among anthropologists in recent years, since it refers to homogenous societies that, in the wake of colonialism, have come under the jurisdiction of larger political entities anthropologists call "nation-states." The United States is a nation-state, as are the countries of Europe and the rapidly emerging goverments of Africa, such as Zaire and Namibia. In fact, all the countries that make up that international organization, the United Nations, are nation-states.

A number of groups anthropologists traditionally described as "tribal" now express a preference for being called "nations," so that one can refer to the "Hopi nation" or the "Sioux nation." This use of the term "nation" should not be confused with the popular usage of the term, which designates countries or nation-states. The use of the term "nation" in the name "United Nations" conforms to popular usage.

This lesson explores the four kinds of political organizations that traditional societies have developed to meet their basic social needs. In Lesson 19, you will learn more about the methods of social control employed by political organizations. One additional thought is suggested for this lesson: While studying the cultural examples presented here, be alert to any hints about those qualities of personality and character that society expects of its "politicians," whether they be high officials in a complex governmental system or informal leaders in a village or camp. What traits do these politicians have in common? How do they differ?

Video Program: This program examines the four major forms of political organization: bands, tribes, chiefdoms, and states. The oldest and simplest form of political organization, the band, is illustrated with footage of the nomadic Ju/'hoansi ! (Kung) of southwestern Africa, who group together in small bands in their search for food. Tribal rule is depicted by the Mendi of New Guinea, whose economic and political activities are organized around clans, usually under the leadership of "Big Men" who have some authority based on their skills at collecting and giving away wealth to form alliances. Even more complex in political organization are chiefdoms, such as that of the Kpelle of Liberia. Their centralized government includes a chief and leaders of lesser rank, whose wealth and control are directly related to their position in the hierarchy. The final form of political organization the program covers is the state, a political organization with centralized power based on legitimacy, a formal code of law, and the authority to enforce that law. The theocratic government of Tibet, in exile in India, exemplifies the concept of the state.

As you view the program, look for:

- how a Mendi "Big Man" gains his influence.
- the population size and political structure of a !Kung band and the role of the headman.
- the power of the paramount chief of the Kpelle of Liberia.
- different attitudes about the source of government legitimacy in the United States and Tibet.

Learning Objectives

When you have completed all assignments in this lesson, you should be able to:

1. Recognize that all societies have some form of political organization. TEXTBOOK PAGE 328; VIDEO PROGRAM

2. Describe the basic function of political organizations. TEXTBOOK PAGE 328; VIDEO PROGRAM

3. Name the four basic kinds of political systems identified by anthropologists, and identify each as uncentralized or centralized. TEXTBOOK PAGES 328–338; VIDEO PROGRAM

4. Describe the general features of band organization, including a description of the Ju/'hoansi (!Kung) as an example. TEXTBOOK PAGES 328–330; VIDEO PROGRAM

5. Describe the general features of tribal organization and discuss specific forms of tribal organization in the following societies: Nuer (kinship segmentary lineage); Tiriki (age-grade); Cheyenne (common-interest); Kapauku ("Big Man"). TEXTBOOK PAGES 328–334

6. Describe the general features of a chiefdom, including a description of Kpelle society as an example. TEXTBOOK PAGES 334–336; VIDEO PROGRAM

7. Describe the general features of a state political system. TEXTBOOK PAGES 336–338; VIDEO PROGRAM

8. Explain the concept of legitimacy and its role in maintaining political power. TEXTBOOK PAGE 355

9. Explain how religion may be used to legitimize political power and cite examples. TEXTBOOK PAGES 355–356; VIDEO PROGRAM

Study Activities

Vocabulary Check

Check your understanding of terms by writing the letter of the appropriate definition in the space next to the corresponding term. Check your choices with the Answer Key at the end of the lesson.

_____ 1. political organization
_____ 2. band
_____ 3. tribe
_____ 4. age-grade organization
_____ 5. centralized political systems

_____ 6. chiefdom
_____ 7. state
_____ 8. legitimacy
_____ 9. segmentary lineage system

a. found in societies with larger populations and surplus of production
b. a regional polity in which two or more local groups are organized under one person
c. a means for maintaining social order and reducing social disorder
d. political organization that cuts across territorial and kin groupings
e. support for the political system based on important values of the society
f. form of political organization in which a larger group is divided into clans and then into lineages
g. political organization in which a clan is subdivided along family descent lines
h. a centralized system that has the power to coerce
i. any type of society in which the leader does not have actual authority for final decisions
j. a group of bands or villages integrated by several unifying factors, including language and culture
k. a small, autonomous group of related people occupying a single region

Completion

Fill in the blank squares with information from the Haviland textbook.

Comparison of Four Political Organizations

Political Organization (Listed from simplest to most complex)	Degree of Centralization	Description of Region Occupied (Size)	Degree of Stratification	Subsistence Pattern/ Economy	Example of Leadership
Band					
Tribe					
Chiefdom					
State					

Self-Test

Objective Questions

Select the one best answer.

1. Political organizations are found in
    a. hunting-gathering bands.
    b. tribes organized around descent groups.
    c. societies encompassing many clans.
    d. all of the above groups.

2. The fundamental means by which societies maintain public order is by
    a. political organization.
    b. military and police power.
    c. coercion.
    d. religious belief.

3. Of the following terms, the one that is used by anthropologists to describe one kind of political system is

   a. lineage.
   b. clan.
   c. tribe.
   d. kindred.

4. The band represents

   a. probably the oldest form of political organization.
   b. the simplest centralized type of political organization.
   c. the political integration of several clans.
   d. delegation of authority.

5. Among the Ju/'hoansi (!Kung) of the Kalahari, the *kxau*, or headman,

   a. owns the land settled by his people.
   b. holds authority by descent.
   c. controls the surplus grown by his group.
   d. loses his position if he leaves the territory.

6. The Tiriki political system features

   a. a series of common-interest groups.
   b. a king and nobility.
   c. age grades that advance through warrior and elder grades.
   d. a chief and several high-ranking persons who have authority over specific territories.

7. The leader of the Kapauku of western New Guinea holds his position because of

   a. heredity.
   b. wealth and generosity.
   c. influence and coercion.
   d. the support of subchiefs.

8. In a chiefdom,

    a. each male member of the society is basically equal.
    b. each kinship group is basically equal.
    c. the leaders are considered one class, the rest of the population another class.
    d. every member of the society has a unique position in the hierarchy.

9. The Kpelle society's leadership is provided by

    a. several paramount chiefs.
    b. a king.
    c. a "Big Man."
    d. an informal "owner."

10. Which of the following is NOT characteristic of the state pattern of political organization?

    a. delegation of authority to maintain order
    b. varied social classes and associations
    c. tendency toward egalitarianism
    d. market economy and unequal distribution of wealth

11. The highest level of authority in Swazi political organizations is

    a. the council of elders.
    b. a dual monarchy.
    c. the *libanda,* or council of state.
    d. a hereditary chief.

12. The Tibetan political structure is that of a

    a. feudal chiefdom.
    b. stratified chiefdom.
    c. common-interest association.
    d. theocracy.

13. The concept of legitimacy is an important aspect of
    a. ownership of land.
    b. support for the political system.
    c. coercion.
    d. hereditary ranking.

14. Religion is used to legitimize political structures and leadership
    a. rarely.
    b. chiefly in industrial societies.
    c. chiefly in uncentralized political systems.
    d. in a wide range of societies.

Short-Answer Essay Questions

1. Briefly describe the functions of these four organizational systems in achieving a political integration of their respective societies: **(a)** segmented lineage for the Nuer; **(b)** age-grade organization for the Tiriki; **(c)** common-interest associations for the Cheyenne; and **(d)** the "Big Man" for the Kapauku.

2. How do the political organizations of the band and the tribe differ?

3. How do the political organizations of the chiefdom and the state differ?

4. Give examples of the use of religion to legitimize political power. What other factors may be employed to foster a claim to legitimacy?

Suggested Activities

1. The Haviland textbook suggests several personality and character traits required of leaders in societies that select their leaders informally. What similarities and differences do you see in the traits desired of a leader in band and tribal societies and the traits often desired in a complex political system, such as that of the United States?

2. Review Haviland's definition of political systems. Then relate his definition to the smallest unit of general government that affects you (such as a city, town, or county, rather than a specialized unit such as a school or sanitation district). Review the activities of the governing body through the minutes, agenda, or other summary of its last three or four meetings and explain how each of the expressed concerns relates to "social order and public policy."

Answer Key

STUDY ACTIVITIES

Vocabulary Check

1. c	4. d	7. h
2. k	5. a	8. e
3. j	6. b	9. f

Completion

Comparison of Four Political Organizations

Political Organization (Listed from simplest to most complex)	Degree of Centralization	Description of Region Occupied (Size)	Degree of Stratification	Subsistence Pattern/ Economy	Example of Leadership
Band	uncentralized	single region	society of equals (egalitarian)	food-foraging	"headman" Ju/'hoansi
Tribe	uncentralized	a specific region	little or none; varies depending on leadership and subsistence pattern	horticulture or pastoralism; food-foraging (sometimes)	"Big Man" (Kaupauku) "Leopard-Skin Chief" (Nuer)
Chiefdom	centralized	any size	ranked society	horticulture or intensive agriculture; produces a surplus	"paramount chief" (Kpelle)
State	centralized	large enough to hold a hetero-geneous society and have a market economy	social classes or castes	market economy; intensive agriculture; produces a surplus	king (Swazi)

SELF-TEST

Objective Questions

(Page numbers refer to the textbook.)

1. d (Objective 1; page 328; video program)
2. a (Objective 2; page 328)
3. c (Objective 3; page 330; video program)
4. a (Objective 4; page 329; video program)
5. d (Objective 4; page 330; video program)
6. c (Objective 5; page 334)
7. b (Objective 5; page 331)
8. c (Objective 6; page 335; video program)
9. a (Objective 6; page 335)
10. c (Objective 7; pages 336–338)
11. b (Objective 7; page 338)
12. d (Objective 7; video program)
13. b (Objective 8; page 355)
14. d (Objective 9; pages 355–356; video program)

Short-Answer Essay Questions

1. Briefly describe the functions of these four organizational systems to achieve a political integration of their respective societies: **(a)** segmented lineage for the Nuer; **(b)** age-grade organization for the Tiriki; **(c)** common-interest associations for the Cheyenne; and **(d)** the "Big Man" for the Kapauku.

   Your answer should include:

   - The segmented lineages of the Nuer serve as links with other groups in their own maximal and major lineages, the clans that join lineages, and the tribe. The relationships are better described as alliances that become active only during times of conflict between minimal lineage segments.

   - The age-grade system of the Tiriki assigns specific roles to each age-level grouping. As a group goes through each of four age grades, its members carry out key functions within the society, beginning with warrior and ending with ritual elder duties.

- In the Cheyenne society, a young man might have been invited to join any one of seven military societies, which had a variety of military, ceremonial, and social roles. Since identical societies with identical names existed within each band, membership cut across band lines and helped to integrate the entire society.

- The "Big Man" of the Kapauku achieves his leadership status through wealth, generosity, and other desirable traits. He is thus "accepted" rather than elected, and may lose his position through, for example, loss of wealth. As "Big Man," however, he is recognized as a negotiator, judge, and leader in a variety of social situations. Hence, he is a "focus" for social integration.

2. How do the political organizations of the band and the tribe differ?

    Your answer should include:

- Many tribal systems involve significantly more people than bands do; tribes typically involve more than one band.

- The band itself is adequate organization for its political system. Decisions are usually made on the basis of a democratic consensus. Tribes often contain organizations of other groups smaller than the tribe, such as age grades or common-interest associations, which also serve political functions.

- Bands usually recognize the leadership of one individual, such as the Ju/'hoansi (!Kung) headman, who has no actual power. Tribal leadership is also informal, and the leadership of the headman or chief depends more on his persuasive ability and community support than upon any power to coerce. He serves as a decision maker in some matters of policy, can function as an arbitrator or judge in disputes, and may represent the tribe in dealings with outside groups.

3.   How do the political organizations of the chiefdom and the state differ?

Your answer should include:

- In a chiefdom, the chief is the greatest and final authority in all political and economic matters. In turn, lesser authorities control major and minor subdivisions of the chiefdom in a kind of chain-of-command structure.

- Although no state is ever permanent, each involves the idea of a permanent government, a "central power," rather than just a single individual. The state also has a formal legal code. Organization of the state is more complex than that of the chiefdom; power is delegated for specific functions, such as police and foreign ministries, rather than over territorial subdivisions, as it is in a chiefdom.

4.   Give examples of the use of religion to legitimize political power. What other factors may be employed to foster a claim to legitimacy?

Your answer should include:

- In religious states, or theocracies, the political leader is also the religious leader, as in present-day Iran, the Tibetan government-in-exile, and the Inca society before the coming of the Spanish.

- In medieval Europe, religion played a key role. Appropriate religious approval of governments was sought, and many enterprises, from constructing buildings to waging wars, were motivated by religious belief.

- In the United States, religion remains an aspect of support for the political system. The Declaration of Independence refers to a Supreme Being, and prayers and mottos reflecting religious values are employed by the federal, state, and local governments.

- Claims to legitimacy are based on the values a society holds most important. The textbook mentions other values that have served to establish legitimacy in different cultures, including "divine right," wealth, and age.

Social Control 19

Assignments

Before viewing the video program	• Read the Overview and the Learning Objectives for this lesson. Use the Learning Objectives to guide your reading, viewing, and thinking. • Read textbook Chapter 12, "Political Organization and Social Control," pages 338–355. • Review textbook Chapter 12, pages 326–338 and 355–356.

View video program 19, "Social Control"

After viewing the video program	• Review the terms used in this lesson. In addition to those terms in the Learning Objectives, you should be familiar with these:
	
	    crime naturalistic worldview
	    exploitative worldview tort
	
	• Review the reading assignment for this lesson.
	• Complete each of the Study Activities and the Self-Test in this study-guide lesson; check your answers with the Answer Key at the end of this lesson.
	• According to your instructor's assignment or your own interests, complete one or more of the Suggested Activities. You may also be interested in the readings listed at the end of Chapter 12 in the textbook.

Overview

In Lesson 18, it may have looked as if the mechanisms for social control are relatively easy to recognize. The political organization is evident in many societies, particularly in chiefdoms and states, for example. One might need a discerning eye to spot the "Big Man" or elder male of a society more informally organized—yet, the leadership is evidently there, and the organization that supports the leader may be expected to support the good order of the community.

This lesson explores how many of the forces of social control spring not from the highest positions of political organization but rather from the standards set by the society itself, as if by general agreement. Some social controls are as subtle as the lessons taught to the young, who learn them so well that the controls become incorporated as part of each individual's internal values, which are beyond question or doubt. Other social-control mechanisms are as open and powerful as gossip or protest demonstrations and boycotts.

In most societies, social controls are frequently *not* based on laws or rules, in the sense that an impersonal standard is clearly established and penalties for violation are clearly defined and applied. Social controls are usually present in every society even without stated rules. In North American society, controls are quite strong in matters where the rule of law does not apply. For example, do you generally cover your mouth if you cough or yawn when someone else is nearby? Do you eat with silverware, not your hands? Do you wear a dress or suit to church instead of a swimsuit? Do you usually wear colors and designs that match or coordinate? Two socks of the same color? You would not be arrested or sued for doing or not doing any of these things, but when you behave in these ways you are responding to a very real kind of social control.

This lesson discusses methods of social control, ranging from gossip to warfare. Some methods are nearly universal, while others appear only in more complex societies with centralization of power.

Video Program: From the religious traditions and internal controls of an Amish community to the mediatory methods of dispute settlements among the Nundewala tribe of India and the Barabaig of Tanzania, this program examines forms of social control, including internal and external, and types of sanctions designed to maintain order within a society. Anthropologist James Gibbs analyzes the trial-by-ordeal form of adjudication practiced in a Kpelle village and observes that it bears strong similarities to the use of a lie detector in Western countries. The program concludes with consideration of theories about the cause of conflict between groups and attempts to achieve order and cooperation among the many peoples of the world.

As you view the program, look for:

- scenes of Amish society in the United States. Identify the kinds of social control illustrated by this subculture.

- the formal external social control exemplified by a trial in a U.S. courtroom.

- examples of various forms of dispute settlements, including song duels among the Netsilik, negotiation among the Nuer, mediation among the Nundewalas of India, adjudication among the Barabaig tribe of Tanzania, and trial by ordeal among the Kpelle of Liberia.

- warfare among Masai groups in Africa and why an exploitative worldview may be a prerequisite to warfare.

Learning Objectives

When you have completed all assignments in this lesson, you should be able to:

1. Recognize that one of the basic functions of any political system is to maintain social control. TEXTBOOK PAGE 340; VIDEO PROGRAM

2. Distinguish between internalized and externalized controls as methods of maintaining social order. TEXTBOOK PAGES 341–343, 346; VIDEO PROGRAM

3. Describe the use of internalized controls by the traditional Wape culture of New Guinea. TEXTBOOK PAGES 340–341

4. Define *positive, negative, formal,* and *informal sanctions* as forms of externalized control. TEXTBOOK PAGES 341–343, 346; VIDEO PROGRAM

5. Discuss the role of women in exerting social control in various societies. TEXTBOOK PAGES 338–340, 343–345

6. Define *law* and list three basic functions of this kind of social control. TEXTBOOK PAGES 346–351

7. Recognize that one way to understand the nature of "law" and "crime" in non-Western societies is to analyze the ways in which disputes are resolved. TEXTBOOK PAGES 348–351; VIDEO PROGRAM

8. Define *negotiation, mediation,* and *adjudication.* TEXTBOOK PAGE 350; VIDEO PROGRAM

9. Recognize the use of trial by ordeal as an example of adjudication in some traditional societies and briefly describe the use of trial by ordeal by the Kpelle in Liberia. TEXTBOOK PAGE 350; VIDEO PROGRAM

10. Compare the frequency of warfare in food-foraging societies with the frequency of warfare in farming, pastoral, and industrial societies; and describe some reasons for the difference in frequency. TEXTBOOK PAGES 351–355; VIDEO PROGRAM

11. Define *worldview* and explain in what sense food-foraging and food-producing populations may have differing worldviews. TEXTBOOK PAGE 353; VIDEO PROGRAM

Study Activities

Vocabulary Check

Check your understanding of terms by writing the letter of the appropriate definition in the space next to the corresponding term. Check your choices with the Answer Key at the end of the lesson.

_____ 1. social control
_____ 2. internalized controls
_____ 3. negative sanctions
_____ 4. formal sanctions
_____ 5. law

_____ 6. tort
_____ 7. mediation
_____ 8. adjudication
_____ 9. naturalistic worldview
_____ 10. exploitative worldview

a. form of externalized control that discourages certain behaviors
b. an external sanction that requires the threat or application of physical force by an individual or organization having the socially recognized privilege of so acting
c. the concept that nature exists only to be used by humans
d. the methods employed to ensure acceptable behavior by members of a society
e. a wrongful act or injury of an individual
f. requires a third party who has the power to render decisions
g. a concept based on respect for and dependence on nature
h. decisions made voluntarily by the parties involved
i. requires a third party, who does not have power to enforce decisions
j. controls designed to regulate behavior precisely and explicitly
k. beliefs so strongly held that the individual controls his or her own conduct

Completion

Fill each blank with the most appropriate term from the list immediately following that paragraph.

1. External social controls developed by a society to encourage desirable behaviors are known as _____. Such actions as a simple smile of approval from a neighbor or the presentation of an award for perfect attendance to a student are examples of _____ sanctions. Actions that threaten something unpleasant, such as a large fine for a traffic infraction, are _____ sanctions, which can be imposed if the person does not conform to social _____.

    negative   positive

    norms   sanctions

2. The forms of social control called sanctions may be formal or informal. Informal sanctions are _____ expressions by members of the community. They have a powerful effect, because most people want to be _____ in their community. Formal sanctions are _____, quite specific, and exact. Both formal and informal sanctions may be either positive or negative.

    accepted   spontaneous

    organized

3. Many societies do not have formal laws. The textbook suggests that a worthwhile approach to understanding the nature of law is to study the way in which _____ are settled in the absence of formal legal systems. Negotiation involves argument and _____ between the parties involved. Mediation brings in a _____ party, who can assist in settling the problem, but does not have authority to enforce a decision. In another way of settling disputes, a third party is authorized to make a decision to which the parties in the dispute are bound, a process known as _____.

    adjudication   disputes   third

    compromise   second

4. The textbook describes law as having three primary functions: Law defines the _____ among members of the society and the proper behavior under specific circumstances; it grants authority to individuals or organizations to use _____ to enforce the law; and it redefines social relations and ensures social _____.

      coercion   relationships

      flexibility

Self-Test

Objective Questions

Select the one best answer.

1. One of the most important basic functions of a political system is to

   a. set up a system of laws for its subjects to follow.
   b. ensure that people behave in certain ways.
   c. oppose threats to its territorial sovereignty.
   d. ensure that the values and beliefs of the society are passed on to succeeding generations.

2. Internalized controls are best defined as

   a. values and beliefs that the individual subscribes to in his or her own mind.
   b. formal methods used by society to ensure an acceptable behavior pattern among its members.
   c. methods of control that involve rewards or approval.
   d. spontaneous sanctions.

3. The Wape society of New Guinea seeks to avoid or settle quarrels because

   a. quarrels are severely punished by community leaders.
   b. they fear that quarrels will lead to warfare.
   c. they believe quarrels adversely affect their supply of game.
   d. any quarrel brings rapid individual retaliation.

4. To maintain social order, the Amish of Pennsylvania mostly rely on

   a. external controls and internal controls.
   b. internal controls and formal sanctions.
   c. formal sanctions and informal sanctions.
   d. internal controls and informal sanctions.

5. *Sanction* is best defined as

   a. an externalized social control.
   b. a formal control.
   c. a negative control.
   d. an internalized control.

6. A formal sanction is always

   a. spontaneous.
   b. organized.
   c. in the form of punishment or threat.
   d. written in law.

7. Approval of a marriage arrangement by neighbors would be classified as a

   a. positive formal sanction.
   b. negative formal sanction.
   c. negative informal sanction.
   d. positive informal sanction.

8. Viewing societies as a whole, it has been found that women reach high positions of political leadership

   a. frequently.
   b. rarely.
   c. as often as men.
   d. in most food-foraging societies.

9. In a large number of traditional societies, women's influence on social control is

   a. greater than men's.
   b. almost nonexistent.
   c. equal to men's.
   d. less than men's.

10. In Bedouin society, the woman's role in exerting social control includes

   a. veto power over orders of a male leader.
   b. the right to "make war" on a tyrannical leader.
   c. stubborn resistance to a command by a man.
   d. removal of an unsatisfactory leader.

11. The definition of law included in the textbook includes

   a. a formal hearing before a court or judge.
   b. the threat or use of physical force.
   c. a religious basis for the sanction.
   d. a written code that defines the specific conduct.

12. A basic function of law includes all of the following except

   a. defining relationships among members of society.
   b. redefining social relations and ensuring social flexibility.
   c. protecting land or territory from misappropriation.
   d. defining who has authority to employ coercion.

13. The term *crime* has different meanings in Western and non-Western societies because

   a. in many non-Western societies, all offenses are considered to be against individuals.
   b. in most non-Western societies, a careful distinction is made between offenses against individuals and crimes against the social order.
   c. some non-Western cultures do not attempt to maintain social control.
   d. the kinds of punishments applied vary from one society to another.

14. The Nuer bride price dispute shown in the video program is an example of

   a. mediation.
   b. negotiation.
   c. trial by ordeal.
   d. adjudication.

15. The assumption basic to the concept of trial by ordeal is that

   a. the stronger person deserves the support of the community.
   b. fear of punishment will prevent most offenses.
   c. supernatural forces will protect the innocent and punish the guilty.
   d. a guilty person will be afraid to undergo any kind of test.

16. One of the differences between food foragers and agricultural or pastoral peoples that may account for different attitudes of these groups toward warfare is the

   a. size of individual families.
   b. commitment to specific areas of land.
   c. manner in which children are nurtured.
   d. quality of food consumed by the various societies.

17. The worldview of farming and pastoral societies tends to be

   a. naturalistic.
   b. legalistic.
   c. cooperative.
   d. exploitative.

18. A naturalistic worldview is best summed up as a

   a. tendency to live in close harmony with nature.
   b. belief that extracting what is needed from the environment is a "right."
   c. desire for combat with one's neighbors.
   d. belief that all living things are controlled by spirits.

Short-Answer Essay Questions

1. Explain how the beliefs and behaviors of the Wape illustrate the power of internalized controls.

2. Discuss limitations that are placed on women's influence on social control, and give examples of women overcoming these limitations.

3. Contrast food-foraging societies with pastoral and agricultural societies, identifying those factors that might influence different attitudes toward warfare.

Suggested Activities

1. For further reading and the basis for a written report, you may be interested in one of the following books. They deal with topics covered in Lesson 18 and Lesson 19.

    Harris, Marvin. *Cannibals and Kings: The Origins of Cultures*. New York: Random House, 1978. Consideration of warfare and state development of control over resources and population.

    Hoebel, E. A. *The Cheyennes: Indians of the Great Plains*. 2d ed. New York: Holt, Rinehart and Winston, 1978. A classic ethnographic study of a society with a tribal system of political organization.

    Kuper, Hilda. *The Swazi: A South African Kingdom*, 2d ed. Fort Worth, Texas: Harcourt Brace College Publishers, 1986. An ethnographic study of a nation with a state system of political organization.

2. For one day, try to keep track of all of the behaviors you engage in that result from strictly informal sanctions. Refer again to suggestions made in the Overview for this lesson and to the reading assignment in the Haviland textbook.

3. Discuss the implications of Hoebel's definition of law in relation to organizations other than government that establish written rules or "laws," whether it be an institution such as a bank or a "social" organization such as the Elks. Do the constitution and bylaws of such entities qualify as "law," according to Hoebel's definition?

Answer Key

STUDY ACTIVITIES

Vocabulary Check

1. d	5. b	8. f
2. k	6. e	9. g
3. a	7. i	10. c
4. j		

Completion

1. sanctions, positive, negative, norms
2. spontaneous, accepted, organized
3. disputes, compromise, third, adjudication
4. relationships, coercion, flexibility

SELF-TEST

Objective Questions

(Page numbers refer to the textbook.)

1. b (Objective 1; page 340; video program)
2. a (Objective 2; page 341; video program)
3. c (Objective 3; page 340)
4. d (Objective 4; video program)
5. a (Objective 4; page 341)
6. b (Objective 4; page 342)
7. d (Objective 4; pages 341–343)
8. b (Objective 5; page 338)
9. c (Objective 5; page 338)
10. c (Objective 5; pages 344–345)
11. b (Objective 6; page 347)
12. c (Objective 6; pages 348–349)

13. a (Objective 7; page 349; video program)
14. b (Objective 8; page 350; video program)
15. c (Objective 9; page 350; video program)
16. b (Objective 10; pages 352–353; video program)
17. d (Objective 11; page 353; video program)
18. a (Objective 11; page 353)

Short-Answer Essay Questions

1. Explain how the beliefs and behaviors of the Wape illustrate the power of internalized controls.

    Your answer should include:

    - The Wape believe that their gunman's lack of success is due to intervention of ancestral ghosts, who can adversely affect the supply of game and the gunman's aim. These ghosts will act, they believe, if their specific (living) descendants have a quarrel with the gunman.

    - This belief that a quarrel or resentment leads to poor success in hunting serves to minimize quarrels in the community.

    - This belief is deeply ingrained among the Wape, and it strongly influences their behavior, both encouraging the avoidance of quarrels and the settling of differences when they occur. This belief is a good example of internalized control.

2. Discuss limitations that are placed on women's influence on social control, and give examples of women overcoming these limitations.

    Your answer should include:

    - In most societies, women rarely hold the highest leadership positions in political organizations. There are instances where women have reached high status, however. The textbook points out that, frequently, women achieve such power as a result of a relationship to a man, and that those women who have achieved top leadership positions in Western society (such as Margaret Thatcher, former Prime Minister of Great Britain) have had to display characteristics commonly associated with men, such as toughness and firmness.

- Women in traditional societies have great political influence, even though many men may hold all the major visible positions. Among the Igbo, for example, women could bring great pressure to bear on a man who was behaving improperly. In the Iroquois, men held all the high offices, but they were appointed by women and could be removed by women. The textbook points out that Western colonizing powers who took over regions with traditional societies frequently failed to recognize the political power women actually held, establishing systems that greatly weakened the role of women.

- In Bedouin society, which was dominated politically by men, women could resist tyrannical social control, but only at considerable risk. Continuous active resistance to commands of a husband or father would gain the respect of the community in some cases. However, in other cases, resistance would have to be continued to the point of suicide.

3. Contrast food-foraging societies with pastoral and agricultural societies, identifying those factors that might influence different attitudes toward warfare.

   Your answer should include:

- In general, food-foraging societies do not have centralized political systems. Their territorial borders are not sharply defined, bands may range over wide areas, and members may move individually from one band to another. Marriage patterns increase the likelihood that kinfolk may live in nearby bands, thereby reducing the chance of violence. Populations in food-foraging societies tend to remain relatively small, so that regions do not become overcrowded.

- The worldview of food-foraging societies frequently is naturalistic; these societies view themselves as a part of nature, working in cooperation with nature.

- Farming and pastoral societies are more likely to develop centralized governments. Often, individual or family ownership of property is common. Their territories are not flexible, and expansion may be limited by the presence of neighboring groups. Agricultural production may accompany growth in population, which leads to a need for more land and to conflict with neighbors over land and resources.

- The worldview of food-producing societies is likely to be more exploitative: an attitude that one must take from nature, and that nature exists to be used.

- On the one hand, the pressures that might develop in farming and pastoral societies could account for the tendency of such societies to engage in wars. On the other hand, the worldview typical of such societies lends itself to taking what is needed or wanted from nature or from others.

- The causes of war are many and complex. It is not possible to single out one "primary cause" of conflict.

Religion and Magic 20

Assignments

Before viewing the video program	• Read the Overview and the Learning Objectives for this lesson. Use the Learning Objectives to guide your reading, viewing, and thinking. • Read textbook Chapter 13, "Religion and the Supernatural," pages 360–387.

View video program 20, "Religion and Magic"

After viewing the video program	• Review the terms used in this lesson. In addition to those terms in the Learning Objectives, you should be familiar with these:

ancestral spirits	incorporation	separation
contagious magic	nature spirits	shaman
divination	pantheon	supernatural
imitative magic	ritual	transition

• Review the reading assignments for this lesson.
• Complete each of the Study Activities and the Self-Test in this study-guide lesson; check your answers with the Answer Key at the end of this lesson.
• According to your instructor's assignment or your own interests, complete one or more of the Suggested Activities. You may also be interested in the readings listed at the end of Chapter 13 in the textbook.

Overview

In December, 1968, Apollo VIII made humankind's first journey to the moon. Apollo VIII did not land on the moon's surface, but a television broadcast was beamed back to Earth as the craft orbited the moon. During the broadcast, the three U.S. astronauts aboard Apollo VIII took turns reading the story of the Creation from the Bible. (The video program for this lesson concludes with a recording from this event.) It was a moment that joined one of the United States' most visionary technical achievements with religious traditions that originated thousands of years ago. To many people, this combination of science and religion was logical and appropriate. To others, it was startling and thought provoking, because U.S. society, like most complex industrialized ones, has largely separated religious activities from everyday life.

In traditional and Western cultures, religion seeks to deal with ultimate questions of human purpose and meaning. As Haviland points out, religion embodies many "truths" about humanity, its cultures, and its social practices. Religion meets important needs for both individuals and society. The importance of these needs is dramatically illustrated by the fact that every society known to have existed has engaged in some form of religious activity. Among cultures around the world, however, there is enormous diversity in religious practices and beliefs and in the functions these religions serve.

The major question explored in this lesson deals with the many important social and psychological functions religion serves. It's important to keep in mind that neither this course nor the field of anthropology can draw conclusions regarding the existence of supernatural forces. Nor does anthropology attempt to judge whether any metaphysical "truths" are indeed true. Why study religion, then? The answer is that, as noted earlier, every culture practices some form of religion because it serves needs critical to the culture. Thus, religious practices can be seen as another form of adaptive behavior. And anthropology is interested in *all* human behavior.

This lesson also examines the meaning and practice of magic and explores the similarities and differences between magic and religion. As you read the textbook chapter and view the video program, see if you can distinguish clearly between religion and magic. Where do they overlap? In what ways are they different?

Video Program: The great variety of religious beliefs and practices in the world is illustrated with numerous examples. The program begins with footage of American Indians describing their worldview and their belief in the Great Spirit and how that worldview is reflected in their religion. The program includes scenes of religious practices among the Highland Maya, who have combined ancient beliefs and Roman Catholicism; the ritual of *Eka Dasa Rudra*, a once-a-century ceremony by the Balinese that links their three worlds of gods, people, and demons; modern Hare Krishnas in Los Angeles; and revitalization movements, such as those of the Mormons. The end of the program briefly considers the role of religion in an increasingly "scientific" world and how the quest for meaning will continue.

As you view the program, look for:

- an explanation of American Indian belief in the spirits of nature.

- how the carving of a medicine mask from a living tree is an attempt to restore physical and spiritual harmony.

- Maya religion today, a mixture of Roman Catholic and traditional Maya. In particular, take note of the role of the shaman and the employment of magic.

- the *Eka Dasa Rudra* ceremony of the Balinese people and its function in Balinese society.

- the development of Mormonism, a revitalization movement.

Learning Objectives

When you have completed all assignments in this lesson, you should be able to:

1. Define religion from the viewpoint of anthropology. TEXTBOOK PAGES 361–364; VIDEO PROGRAM

2. Recognize that some form of religion is found in all human cultures. TEXTBOOK PAGES 362–364; VIDEO PROGRAM

3. Explain the differences between *gods* and *goddesses* and *ancestral spirits*. TEXTBOOK PAGES 365–367

4. Explain the differences between *animism* and *animatism* and describe the importance of impersonal supernatural powers to believers. TEXTBOOK PAGES 367–369; VIDEO PROGRAM

5. Define and describe the differences between *priests* and *priestesses* and *shamans*. TEXTBOOK PAGES 369–371, 373; VIDEO PROGRAM

6. Identify the general function of religious rituals and define and describe *rites of passage* and *rites of intensification*. TEXTBOOK PAGES 375–378; VIDEO PROGRAM

7. Define *magic* and identify the relationship between religion and magic from the viewpoint of anthropology. TEXTBOOK PAGES 378–379; VIDEO PROGRAM

8. Define *witchcraft* and describe at least one social and one psychological function served by belief in witchcraft. TEXTBOOK PAGES 379–382

9. Describe at least five psychological and social functions of religion. TEXTBOOK PAGES 382–383; VIDEO PROGRAM

10. Define and cite examples of revitalization movements. TEXTBOOK PAGES 384–385; VIDEO PROGRAM

Study Activities

Vocabulary Check

Check your understanding of terms by writing the letter of the appropriate definition in the space next to the corresponding term. Check your choices with the Answer Key at the end of the lesson.

_____ 1. religion	_____ 7. shaman
_____ 2. magic	_____ 8. divination
_____ 3. ritual	_____ 9. rites of passage
_____ 4. pantheon	_____ 10. rites of intensification
_____ 5. ancestral spirits	_____ 11. witchcraft
_____ 6. animism	

a. belief that spirit beings animate nature
b. rituals marking important stages in the life of an individual
c. a collection of the gods and goddesses of a people
d. any form of manipulation of supernatural beings and powers
e. procedure for determining the cause of an event or predicting the future
f. belief that impersonal supernatural powers animate nature
g. the use of specified rituals and formulas to compel supernatural forces to behave in desired ways
h. one who develops special religious powers through his or her own initiative
i. religious specialist usually found in more complex societies
j. believed to display many of the traits of living humans
k. a belief that some persons have innate psychic power to cause harm
l. a means through which an individual relates to the sacred
m. rituals marking crises in the life of the group

Completion

Fill each blank with the most appropriate term from the list immediately following that paragraph.

1. From an anthropological view, religion is an attempt to deal with serious problems by calling on _____ beings and powers, especially when technology or social organizations cannot solve such problems. There is much variation in religious practices and beliefs among societies, but some form of religion is found in _____ known cultures. In traditional societies whose members tend to see themselves as part of nature, religious activity is likely to be a part of _____ ; while in industrial societies, such activity tends to be limited to _____. In societies that do not have occupational specialization, the religious practitioners are usually _____. In contrast, societies that have developed specializations usually have religious specialists formally inducted into the offices of _____.

all	most	special occasions
daily life	priest and priestess	supernatural
gods and goddesses	shamans	

2. Rituals are described as religious activities that mark important events and through which people relate to the _____. By using rituals, people seek to manipulate supernatural beings to obtain desired results. One type of ceremony, illustrated by the Australian aborigine initiation into manhood, is classified as a rite of _____. Such rites deal with crucial times in the life of individuals, and usually involve three stages, _____ , _____ , and _____. Other rites, such as the *Eka Dasa Rudra* of Bali, are classified as rites of _____ , and occur at times of potential or actual crisis for the entire society.

incorporation	passage	separation
intensification	sacred	transition

3. Several factors seem to contribute to the strength of a society's belief in supernatural beings and powers. One important factor in maintaining belief is the manifestation of _____, by which is meant that people may see success or failure resulting not so much from their own efforts and skills as from the supernatural influences that aided or hindered them. Another factor that maintains belief in the supernatural is that supernatural beings tend to have _____ that are familiar to the believers. A third factor is the role of _____, the stories that rationalize religious beliefs and practices. Belief in the supernatural does not necessarily decline as science advances. Both "mainline" and "fundamentalist" religions attract new believers in Western societies, and the number of newspapers carrying astrology columns has _____ over the past 30 years.

attributes	grown	power
decreased	mythology	

4. Revitalization movements are attempts to _____ a society through a new religious movement. Many of these movements are so removed from reality that they fail. Other movements meet such basic social needs that they survive and flourish. An example is _____, a movement that began in the 1840s in New England, spread west, and has experienced continuous growth ever since.

Mormonism

reform

5. Sir James George Frazer drew a contrast between religion, which he defined as "propitiation or conciliation" of supernatural powers, and magic, which he saw as an attempt to manipulate certain perceived "laws" of _____. Magic involves attempts to _____ supernatural forces by employing specified _____. Witchcraft and sorcery involve the capability and skills to do _____ through supernatural means. Seeking out the cause and the agent of such harm through magical means is called _____. Witchcraft serves a number of functions for individuals and societies. It provides an excuse for misfortune, an opportunity to vent anger, and a means of social control by discouraging behaviors that might suggest to others that one is a witch.

control	formulas	nature
divination	harm	

Self-Test

Objective Questions

Select the one best answer.

1. According to anthropological definition, religion always involves
   a. the use of known technology to solve problems.
   b. rituals to mobilize supernatural forces to achieve or prevent transformations.
   c. employment of specific formulas to compel desired actions.
   d. any kind of gathering that promotes social solidarity.

2. Comparison of religious activity in most Western societies with that in most food-foraging societies shows that
   a. Western societies are more likely to include religious activity in their daily routine.
   b. food-foraging societies have few religious activities.
   c. Western societies are more likely to experience decreasing interest in religious activities.
   d. food-foraging societies are more likely to include religious activity in their daily routine.

3. Because religion fulfills many social and psychological needs, some form of religion has been found in all
   a. food-foraging societies and most agricultural societies.
   b. farming societies and most pastoral societies.
   c. industrial societies and a few food-foraging societies.
   d. societies.

4. Supernatural beings, often with humanlike qualities, who seem rather remote yet control the universe and take an interest in human affairs, are called
   a. gods and goddesses.
   b. ancestral spirits.
   c. nature spirits.
   d. *mana.*

5. Whether groups worship gods or goddesses or both depends mostly upon

    a. how men and women relate to each other in the society.
    b. whether the society is primarily agricultural or pastoral.
    c. the region of the world that gave rise to the culture.
    d. none of the above.

6. *Animism* refers to belief in

    a. gods with animal shapes.
    b. gods and goddesses.
    c. spirit beings that live in natural objects.
    d. impersonal supernatural powers.

7. *Mana* is a name given to

    a. an impersonal abstract force and is an example of animatism.
    b. a goddess in a pantheon and is an example of animism.
    c. nature spirits and is an example of animism.
    d. ancestral spirits and is an example of animatism.

8. A person who undergoes formal initiation into a religious role and holds a socially recognized office is a

    a. witch.
    b. shaman.
    c. priest or priestess.
    d. sorcerer.

9. Shamans gain their powers through

    a. formal instruction and perform services on behalf of supernatural powers.
    b. individual effort and perform services on behalf of human clients.
    c. formal instruction and perform services on behalf of human clients.
    d. individual effort and perform services on behalf of supernatural powers.

10. Religious rituals function generally as a means of

    a. reaffirming the status of priests and shamans.
    b. enabling people to relate to the sacred.
    c. controlling supernatural forces.
    d. honoring spirit beings.

11. A ceremony marking a crucial point in the life of an individual is called a rite of

    a. passage.
    b. intensification.
    c. transition.
    d. incorporation.

12. The most significant element of the male initiation rites among Australian aborigines is

    a. removal of the young man from society.
    b. introduction of the new adult into society.
    c. oral instruction in tribal traditions.
    d. a physical operation.

13. The female initiation practiced by the Mende is best described as preparing the young person for

    a. adulthood.
    b. womanhood.
    c. warrior rank.
    d. religious service.

14. Marriage is classified as a rite of

    a. intensification.
    b. incorporation.
    c. passage.
    d. separation.

15. The *Eka Dasa Rudra* of the Balinese is best described as a

    a. funeral rite.
    b. rite of intensification.
    c. rite of passage.
    d. rite of incorporation.

16. From the viewpoint of anthropology, magic is the

    a. belief in any supernatural power or force.
    b. belief in any ancestral or nature spirit.
    c. use of supernatural means to cause harm or injury.
    d. use of specific formulas to compel supernatural forces to act in certain ways.

17. The Navajo belief in witchcraft serves the psychological function of providing

    a. a means for the ordinary person to gain control over difficult problems.
    b. an acceptable outlet for feelings of hostility that are otherwise suppressed.
    c. a means for making the preferred personal and social decisions.
    d. status for the witch and a convenient means of expression for unstable personalities.

18. *Divination* is defined, in part, as

    a. determination of the cause of an event by magical means.
    b. the study of spirits associated with objects and living things.
    c. the entire group of gods and goddesses recognized by a particular society.
    d. a way to cause harm, such as illness, through the use of magical formulas.

19. According to the textbook, the *psychological* functions of religion include all of the following EXCEPT

    a. validating the political and social organization of a culture.
    b. reducing anxiety by explaining the unknown.
    c. the promise of supernatural aid.
    d. transferring responsibility for decision making from the individual to the supernatural.

20. According to the textbook, the *social* functions of religion include all of the following EXCEPT

    a. setting precedents for acceptable behavior.
    b. sanctioning an acceptable range of conduct.
    c. helping to maintain social solidarity.
    d. providing an outlet for unstable personalities.

21. A deliberate effort by members of a society to construct a more satisfying culture results in

    a. a type of animism.
    b. development of pantheons.
    c. attempts to apply magical formulas.
    d. revitalization movements.

Short-Answer Essay Questions

1. According to anthropologists, how does religion differ from magic?

2. Describe the categories of supernatural beings and powers that are discussed in textbook Chapter 13 and in the video program for this lesson.

3. Summarize several significant social and psychological functions of religion.

Suggested Activities

1. Many organizations and groups today offer to teach new "truths," whether revealed from supernatural sources, through meditation, or from a claimed scientific discovery. Find a magazine or newspaper advertisement from such a group and read one or more accounts describing the group. Try to determine if the organization is religious by anthropological definition and if the organization could be classified as a revitalization movement.

2. Many cultures have creation myths that explain the formation of the world or universe and define, in part, the relationship of humans to the supernatural. Use your local library to find the myths of a society other than your own, and write a brief report.

3. Attend a religious service as if you were an anthropologist studying a culture about which you have little previous knowledge. Write a summary of what you see and hear. Include the details of the ceremony itself, the structure and layout of the place of worship, visible symbols and artifacts employed in the service, and descriptions of worshipers, especially those performing rituals or leading the service.

Answer Key

STUDY ACTIVITIES

Vocabulary Check

1. d	5. j	9. b
2. g	6. a	10. m
3. l	7. h	11. k
4. c	8. e	

Completion

1. supernatural, all, daily life, special occasions, shamans, priest and priestess
2. sacred, passage, separation, transition, incorporation, intensification
3. power, attributes, mythology, grown
4. reform, Mormonism
5. nature, control, formulas, harm, divination

SELF-TEST

Objective Questions

(Page numbers refer to the textbook.)

1. b (Objective 1; pages 363–364; video program)
2. d (Objective 2; page 364)
3. d (Objective 2; page 364)
4. a (Objective 3; page 365)
5. a (Objective 3; page 365)
6. c (Objective 4; pages 367–368; video program)
7. a (Objective 4; pages 368–369)
8. c (Objective 5; pages 369–370)
9. b (Objective 5; page 371; video program)
10. b (Objective 6; page 375)
11. a (Objective 6; page 375)
12. a (Objective 6; page 376)
13. b (Objective 6; page 376)
14. c (Objective 6; page 375)
15. b (Objective 6; pages 377–378; video program)
16. d (Objective 7; page 378)
17. b (Objective 8; page 382)
18. a (Objective 8; page 382; video program)
19. a (Objective 9; pages 382–383)
20. d (Objective 9; pages 382–383)
21. d (Objective 10; page 385)

Short-Answer Essay Questions

1. According to anthropologists, how does religion differ from magic?

   Your answer should include:

   - The classical definition of magic is the use of specified formulas for the purpose of compelling supernatural powers to act in specified ways.

- In contrast, religious rituals are done with the goal of entreating supernatural powers to act in specific ways.
- Sir James George Frazer further defined magic, in contrast to religion, as an attempt to manipulate certain laws of nature. From this perspective, magic beliefs and practices are a kind of pseudoscience.

2. Describe the categories of supernatural beings and powers that are discussed in textbook Chapter 13 and in the video program for this lesson.

Your answer should include:

- **Gods and goddesses:** Rather remote beings, usually with many familiar (human) characteristics, who are believed to take interest in and influence human affairs. They are believed to have the power to control the universe.

- **Ancestral spirits:** Believed to be the vital spirits of those who have died. Frequently, such spirits are believed to retain an interest in society and most of the personality and character traits of living humans.

- **Nature spirits (animism):** Those spirits associated with animals, plants, or inanimate objects such as mountains and springs. They are usually believed to be involved in daily affairs and may have any of a wide range of attitudes toward human activities.

- **Impersonal supernatural power (animatism):** The *mana* of the Melanesians or the *orenda* of the Iroquois. Though not associated with a personality, like gods or spirits, animatism is responsible for good fortune, luck, success, or failure.

3. Summarize several significant social and psychological functions of religion.

Your answer should include:

- **Social functions:** Religion sanctions a wide range of conduct by prescribing "right" and "wrong." It sets precedents for acceptable behavior. It aids in maintaining social solidarity through the sharing of common beliefs and rituals. It serves education, particularly in transmitting oral traditions.

- **Psychological functions:** Religion reduces anxiety, explaining the unknown by providing an orderly model of the universe. It promises supernatural aid. It transfers the burden and responsibility for certain decisions from the individual to the supernatural.

The Asmat of New Guinea: A Case Study in Religion & Magic **21**

Assignments

Before viewing the video program	• Read the Overview and the Learning Objectives for this lesson. Use the Learning Objectives to guide your reading, viewing, and thinking. • Read Background Notes 21A, "Religion and Magic in Asmat Society," in this study-guide lesson. • Review textbook Chapter 13, "Religion and the Supernatural," paying particular attention to the sections on "Ancestral Spirits" and "Animism," pages 366–368; "Shamans," pages 370–371, 373; and "Religion, Magic, and Witchcraft," pages 378–382.

View video program 21, "The Asmat of New Guinea: A Case Study in Religion and Magic"

After viewing the video program	• Review the terms used in this lesson. In addition to the Asmat names mentioned in the video program, you should be familiar with these terms:

      animism   myth   shaman
      magic   ritual

• Review the reading assignments for this lesson.
• Complete each of the Study Activities and the Self-Test in this study-guide lesson; check your answers with the Answer Key at the end of this lesson.
• According to your instructor's assignment or your own interests, complete one or more of the Suggested Activities.

Overview

Where do we—and everything else—come from? Who are we? What are we? What is good? What is bad? Why is the world the way it is? Finally, what happens after we die?

As children, we ask questions like these time and again, but answers do not usually come easily; we generally *learn* the answers we seek as we grow up, as we absorb the values and beliefs of the cultures and subcultures to which we belong. Human societies attempt to answer many such questions through religious beliefs and practices, and some also turn to the practice of magic. As you will remember from Lesson 20, religion exists in all cultures to meet many social and psychological needs.

In this lesson, you will see how religion and the practice of magic can become effective survival mechanisms for a culture that believes itself to be surrounded by danger and death. The video program takes a detailed look at the religious beliefs and customs of the Asmat of western New Guinea. Their religion and magic are an essential part of their adaptation to a challenging environment; and these beliefs support their predominantly food-foraging subsistence pattern. Their beliefs are a fascinating example of animism because, for the Asmat, ancestral spirits and other spirit beings exist all around them. The Asmat perceive their world as being hostile, made dangerous by nature, physical enemies, and ancestral spirits. Their religious beliefs respond to the hostility they perceive in nature and in other humans. And their perception of nature includes much more than meets the eye.

Be prepared for surprises at your first introduction to the Asmat. For example, violence against an enemy is a part of an Asmat religious rite, as well as a form of magic; the Asmat believe that trees and plants are powerful in their own right; and the spirits of the dead, though honored, can cause problems for the living. But as strange as the Asmat religious beliefs and practices may seem at first, you will come to see how consistent and functional these beliefs and practices are within the Asmat cultural pattern.

Video Program: This detailed study of the Asmat, a once-cannibalistic society of western New Guinea, shows their use of religion and magic as tools for survival in a world they perceive as hostile and threatening. The centrality of trees in their religion is shown by scenes in which the Asmat carve a sacred *Bis* pole from a mangrove tree to release spirits of the dead, and butcher and skin a sago palm as if it were human to release the starch that is the mainstay of their diet. The program explores many facets of Asmat society and daily life linked to religious beliefs. Concluding segments of the program consider how economic development and modernization, including the government's ban on headhunting, will affect the Asmat's religious beliefs and practices, which are such an integral part of their total culture.

As you view the program, look for:

- the brief descriptions of creation myths concerning *Neso-ipitj*, "the man of the wound"; and *Fumerew-ipitj*, "the carver of wood."

- the *Bis* ceremony, its elaborate preparations, and the religious and magical beliefs that underlie it.

- the practical and symbolic importance of trees, particularly the sago palm and the mangrove tree.

- how children learn headhunting skills from the games they play.

- the Asmat beliefs that give special meaning to ancestor poles, dancing, coconuts, and the praying mantis.

- the impact of western culture on Asmat religious practices.

Learning Objectives

When you have completed all assignments in this lesson, you should be able to:

1. Describe the Asmat beliefs in supernatural beings and powers. TEXTBOOK PAGES 366–368; VIDEO PROGRAM; BACKGROUND NOTES 21A

2. Explain the relationship between revenge killing, ancestral spirits, and ancestor poles. TEXTBOOK PAGES 366–368; VIDEO PROGRAM; BACKGROUND NOTES 21A

3. Describe the Asmat myth of creation and how it justifies revenge killings. VIDEO PROGRAM

4. Cite two examples of the Asmat use of magic. TEXTBOOK PAGES 378–380; VIDEO PROGRAM; BACKGROUND NOTES 21A

5. Describe the significance of trees, especially the sago palm, to the Asmat. VIDEO PROGRAM; BACKGROUND NOTES 21A

6. Describe the carver's role and authority in Asmat society. VIDEO PROGRAM; BACKGROUND NOTES 21A

7. Describe some of the religious symbols of Asmat society and explain their significance and function. VIDEO PROGRAM; BACKGROUND NOTES 21A

RELIGION AND MAGIC IN ASMAT SOCIETY

The Asmat live in a world dominated by the ebb and flow of the tides and by a tropical rain forest. The territory where the Asmat live is in the western half of the island of New Guinea, in Irian Jaya, a province of Indonesia (see map on textbook page 202). The territory is a wide mud flat crisscrossed by many rivers and includes two distinct environmental zones. Near the ocean, at high tide, the rivers can become very broad and the area can be covered with water. At low tide, the rivers may dry out completely. Farther inland, the land is a swampy forest. The Asmat, who are headhunters by tradition, perceive their unusual environment as a hostile one, made even more hostile by the threat of attack from neighboring villages.

The different environmental zones provide two general subsistence areas. Saltwater swamps near the ocean are rich in marine protein, while upstream, in the freshwater swamps, grow the sago palms that the Asmat need for other food and materials. According to anthropologist David Eyde, the fierce warfare associated with headhunting and cannibalism, which is characteristic of traditional Asmat society, is related to the unequal distribution of resources in the two zones. People living upstream need access to the animal protein in the form of marine resources near the ocean, and people near the ocean need the starches and carbohydrates of the sago palms that grow upstream.

Many Asmat, who are probably closely related to the aborigines of nearby Australia (see map on textbook page 202), are quite blond when young and have a variety of skin tones. They live in wooden houses built on low piles in villages of about 400 people. The dwelling houses are made of thatched sections, each with its own doorway and fireplace or hearth. Each doorway usually corresponds to a family grouping of husband, wife, and children. The Asmat travel by dugout canoes that are tied in front of the houses when not in use. When walking through the forest, the people use footpaths of fallen trees and loose branches to keep from sinking into the mud. Each village claims control of the surrounding forest, although territorial limits really are determined by the ability of each village to assert control over its territory against the claims of a neighboring village.

The sago palm is the most important item in the Asmat diet. It is gathered in expeditions away from the village, when people stay in temporary shelters. The tree is chopped open and the pith is chopped up. Traditionally, women chop up the pith while men stand guard by forming a circle around them. The pith is rinsed with water and the sago starch settles to the bottom of the hollowed-out trunk. The congealed starch is cut into sections and cooked before eating. For ritual feasts, an especially fine sago tree is dressed in a skirt of sago leaves. Then it is chopped down and left to lie so the capricorn beetle will lay eggs in it. The larvae of the capricorn beetle are a great delicacy and provide a basis for ritual feasting.

Fish and shrimp are caught by the women who use small hand nets or, in groups, stretch nets across the rivers. The men sometimes kill a wild pig with bows and arrows. The Asmat grow a few crops around their houses, including coconut and sago palms, breadfruit (a tropical fruit that looks and tastes like bread when baked), and yams. But they depend mainly on hunting and gathering.

The Asmat use wood for building houses and canoes, making weapons, and as fuel for fire. Because there is no stone in the area, the Asmat trade for stone axes. Since the introduction of metal tools, stone axes are now used primarily for ritual purposes.

Unmarried men live in men's houses, large rectangular houses built on pilings about 18 feet high. The houses are built facing the rivers and serve as guardhouses in case of attack. Since the Asmat travel primarily by boat, attacks are most likely to come by way of the rivers. Each men's house has an upstream and a downstream half, marked by the central hearth. A men's house contains a number of other hearths, each belonging to a patrilocal family group. Thus, membership in the men's house is determined patrilocally.

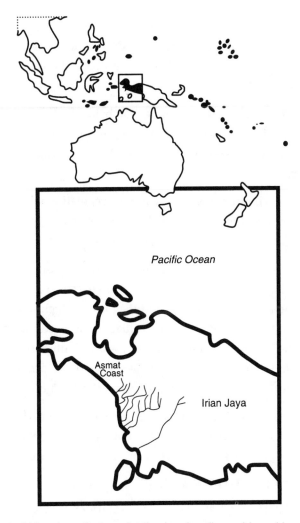

Figure 21.1: The Asmat of Irian Jaya (Indonesia) live in a hostile world, a wide mud flat dominated by the tides and a tropical rain forest.

This hearth group is also related to the maintenance of cutting rights, or family "plots," in the sago forest. Family plots are, in turn, divided among individual members of the group. Each individual knows the plants in his area and gives a name to each young sago palm as he finds it. Paths through the forest are known by the name of the owner.

Each hearth consists of a rectangular mud slab baked by the fire, with a post at each corner. A drying rack is fastened between the posts. One post is associated with an ancestor figure. It may be carved in the form of a human figure and be given that ancestor's name.

In front of the men's house is a space cleared of vegetation where the men carve their canoes, hold dances, and bury their dead. The men's house is a ceremonial center, and women do not enter it except on important ceremonial occasions.

The men's house is also a kind of community center, serving as a focus for patrilineal groups, and a training center for young men, where they learn Asmat customs. They are taught to drum, to dance, and to sing, and they learn which sacred songs go with particular ceremonial feasts. Young men are initiated into headhunting and cannibalism customs in the men's house and learn about the distribution of power, both within the village and in relation to neighboring villages. Leadership among the Asmat is not hereditary, but is related to superiority in warfare and economic life.

In the men's house, the young men listen to legends about early heroes. Through interaction with lineage leaders and village elders in the men's house, adolescent males learn what will be expected of them as fully participating adults.

THE SIGNIFICANCE OF WOODCARVING

The Asmat are skilled woodcarvers, and woodcarving is associated with important ceremonial occasions. Woodcarving is usually done by specialists, who learn by observing and helping established woodcarvers. Selection of the young men to be trained as woodcarvers appears to be based on skill and desire to learn, rather than on descent.

The woodcarver is not released from regular subsistence duties, except when he has been commissioned to do a carving for a major ceremonial event. His employer then takes over his subsistence duties, such as pounding sago, hunting, or fishing. The carver may also receive extra delicacies from the ceremonial feast, but he earns no other compensation for this work. The woodcarving becomes the property of the man who commissioned it. However, a respected woodcarver shares the status of a successful headhunter.

Ancestral poles are important objects of the woodcarver's art. These poles are very tall, with one human figure carved on top of another. The bottoms of the poles usually end in carvings shaped like boats. All of them have a large, open-work, pennant-shaped projection at the top. The Asmat also carve the prows of their canoes, paddles, spears, shields, and a wide variety of human figures.

The art motifs expressed in the ancestor poles and other items have special significance. Many motifs depict creatures that display the qualities of a good headhunter. One common motif, for example, is the praying mantis. The female mantis eats her mate's head during copulation, an act the Asmat equate with a headhunter eating his victim's brains.

HEADHUNTING AS RELIGIOUS RITUAL

Until headhunting was outlawed by the Dutch colonial government, almost all major rituals or public ceremonies were associated with headhunting raids. The initiation of a young male into adulthood was marked by the preparation of a newly taken human head.

During the initiation rite, the young man was smeared with the burnt hair and blood of the victim and given the dead man's name. This ritual established a kin tie between the initiate and relatives of the dead man. When he later met these relatives, they called him by the name of their dead kin, gave him presents, and protected him during his stay in their village. The Reverend Gerard A. Zegwaard, who lived among the Asmat for some time, writes, "It is strictly forbidden to kill people from other villages who, because of their ritual names, are related to one's village" ("Headhunting Practices of the Asmat of Netherlands New Guinea," *American Anthropologist* 61 (1959):1027).

An objective of most Asmat rituals, including headhunting, was to drive away the spirits of the dead, especially the decapitated dead. The deceased was replaced by assigning his name to someone else or to an object. Zegwaard writes, "The names of these spirits are passed on to other persons who will take over their duties and functions, and thus it is made quite clear to them that they are no longer needed" (p. 1029). New canoes, houses, spears, and paddles are among the objects named after the dead.

But the spirits are also driven away by other rituals and ceremonies, such as those shown in the video program. Spirits are allowed to remain in the village for only a limited time. When faced with a new, frightening, or potentially dangerous situation, the Asmat cope by boasting about their exploits. So, to drive away the spirits of the dead, the Asmat boast about the deeds of the living headhunters.

Headhunting is related to safeguarding the territory and therefore the food supply, according to Zegwaard. Since the Asmat do not cultivate extensively, they are entirely dependent on the forest resources surrounding the village and their territorial rights over it. Zegwaard writes, ". . . according to the origin myths, the prime function of the ancestors is the protection of the tribe's economic prerogatives . . . they . . . emphasize the fact that the ancestor selected a definite territory for himself and his progeny" (p. 1032). For the Asmat, headhunting is consistent with their "charter" handed down in the legends of great heroes. Headhunting is also a means by which young men gain status and open their way to becoming respected elders.

As with other religious systems, Asmat religion frames a coherent explanation for their experience of the world. To the Asmat, death is always very near in the form of ancestor spirits and headhunting. The ancestor spirits must be driven away by threats and intimidation. If a man is to survive the onslaught of ancestors and headhunting, he must constantly show that he is very fierce. When the Asmat man dies and rejoins his ancestors, they will demand to know how he has died. He will respond with stories about men he has killed and heads he has taken in battle. He will show them his scars and tell them how he acquired each one. His status in the afterworld will be determined by how well he conveys a sense of his own ferocity and valor. For the Asmat, life with the ancestors, as with life on Earth, demands courage. Their religious and magic practices promote such courage as well as provide protection from the spirits.

Study Activities

Vocabulary Check

Check your understanding of terms by writing the letter of the appropriate definition in the space next to the corresponding term. Check your choices with the Answer Key at the end of the lesson.

_____ 1. *Neso-ipitj*   _____ 6. magic
_____ 2. *Fumerew-ipitj*   _____ 7. tree people
_____ 3. *Bis*   _____ 8. animism
_____ 4. sago   _____ 9. *Safan*
_____ 5. praying mantis

a. the realm of the dead
b. beliefs and patterns of behavior by which people try to control the area of the universe that is beyond control
c. a common motif in Asmat art
d. the meaning of "Asmat"
e. mythical figure from whose severed head the stars spilled out to fill the universe
f. belief in spirit beings that give life to nature
g. practice of using specified formulas to compel certain acts by supernatural powers
h. member of the palm family that provides much of the Asmat diet
i. mythical figure of the great carver who made men and women
j. take place at important stages in the lives of individuals
k. ceremony by which Asmat drive out threatening ancestral spirits to the land of the dead

Completion

Fill each blank with the most appropriate term from the list immediately following that paragraph.

1. To the Asmat, both the visible and invisible worlds are extremely hostile. Other villages are considered enemies; there are also _____ of Asmat ancestors waiting for an opportunity to create mischief; and there are other evil spirits in the _____. The Asmat try to calm some of the plant spirits with offerings left in the forest, but more often, the spirits must be frightened off. In the video program, the men _____ and the women attack with _____ to frighten away the spirits.

    plants   spears

    sing   spirits

2. According to traditional Asmat belief, the spirit of a dead person remains on Earth for a time. The Asmat employ several practices designed to make the spirit leave. For example, the dead man's name is taken by the one who _____ him; the name may be given to inanimate objects as well. The _____ ceremony is performed to chase these spirits away and to build fervor for _____. To free the spirit, however, his death must be _____.

    avenged   headhunting

    Bis   killed

3. The universe was created, according to Asmat myth, from the severed _____ of *Neso-ipitj*. The human race was formed by *Fumerew-ipitj*, who carved human figures from _____ and gave them life. By beheading an enemy, the Asmat reenact the _____ of the universe.

    creation   head   trees

    hand   stone

4. The woodcarver also participates in a mythological event when he carves _____ for the *Bis* ceremony. His skills and artistry make it possible for the village to _____ the spirits, for each figure represents someone who has recently died.

    ancestor poles

    honor

Self-Test

Objective Questions

Select the one best answer.

1. To the Asmat, forest plants and trees are

    a. sacred objects to be protected from harm.
    b. animated by spirit beings.
    c. resources to be exploited at will by humans.
    d. animated by impersonal supernatural powers.

2. The Asmat belief concerning life after death is that

    a. souls are reborn into another body.
    b. spirits go immediately to *Safan*.
    c. spirits of the dead inhabit trees.
    d. spirits of the dead may remain and cause trouble.

3. Dances are performed at the climax of the *Bis* ceremony to

    a. drive away ancestral spirits and to build courage for headhunting.
    b. gain the aid of ancestral spirits as the men prepare to go on a raid.
    c. frighten the spirits of trees that have been cut down.
    d. recount the brave deeds of those who have died.

4. Revenge killing is an important Asmat religious belief because

    a. killing an enemy is supposed to strengthen defenses against nature spirits.
    b. a young man is not given a name until he has killed someone.
    c. the spirit of someone killed by an enemy is earthbound until an enemy is killed.
    d. important trees will cease to grow if attacks on the village are not punished.

5. According to Asmat religious belief, the stars and the universe were created

    a. by a great woodcarver, who designed all the world.
    b. from the severed head of an ancient mythical figure.
    c. from the first sago palm, its edible parts becoming the material of the universe.
    d. from a great flood that covered the world.

6. The Asmat identify revenge killings with their myth of creation because

   a. the enemy represents dark forces that opposed and almost prevented creation.
   b. creation, according to the Asmat myth, was an act of revenge.
   c. the killings are demanded by the gods responsible for the creation.
   d. the killings are reenactments of the creation myth.

7. The Asmat dance and sing in order to

   a. compel spirits to depart, or at least leave humans alone.
   b. calm spirits so that they will assist in a good hunt.
   c. frighten potential enemies who live in nearby villages.
   d. provide a meaningful activity to replace headhunting.

8. Which one of the following actions is NOT an example of magic as practiced by the Asmat?

   a. assigning a slain enemy's name to a member of the village
   b. beheading an enemy to revenge a villager's death
   c. growing crops in the village area
   d. carving the ancestor poles

9. Trees are important to the Asmat for all of the following reasons EXCEPT that trees

   a. provide most of the environmental resources used by the Asmat.
   b. are regarded as important religious symbols by the Asmat.
   c. are used as a major export product.
   d. contain spirits.

10. The sago palm plays such an important part in the daily life of the Asmat because

    a. its fronds are an important religious symbol.
    b. its fruit is eaten at important feasts.
    c. it contributes the major part of their regular diet.
    d. its wood is used for carving religious symbols.

11. According to the Asmat myth, Earth was populated from the

    a. original sago palm.
    b. severed head of a mythical figure.
    c. figures done by a woodcarver.
    d. nature spirits.

12. A chief responsibility of the woodcarver is to
    a. be the shaman for the village.
    b. carve important religious symbols, as well as other objects.
    c. preserve the history of the village in pictorial form.
    d. carve decorations for the lodges, as well as for festivals.

13. The position of a woodcarver in the Asmat village is equal to that of
    a. the village chief, although he does not lead headhunting raids.
    b. a successful headhunter, although he does not take part in raids.
    c. a successful headhunter, although he must still prove himself to be courageous.
    d. the women of the village.

14. The religious function of the ancestor poles is to
    a. provide a temporary dwelling place for spirits of the dead.
    b. serve as a pictorial history of the patrilineal descent.
    c. decorate the hearth in the men's lodge.
    d. record the names of enemies who have been beheaded.

15. A symbol that is related to Asmat beliefs about both plants and headhunting is the
    a. new moon.
    b. praying mantis.
    c. facial details in the ancestor pole.
    d. boat carving at the end of the ancestor pole.

Short-Answer Essay Questions

1. Why do certain practices of the Asmat fall into the category of magic rather than religion?

2. In what ways are trees an important environmental resource to the Asmat? How is the use of trees as a resource related to the role that trees play in the Asmat religion?

3. Explain the religious significance of dancing, the ancestor pole, the praying mantis, and the coconut.

Suggested Activities

1. From what you have learned about Asmat practices and beliefs, it should be apparent that a basic consistency and harmony underlies Asmat religion and magic. Write an essay suggesting how the aspects of Asmat culture presented in this lesson reinforce and support each other. Also explain how these aspects may have contributed to the survival of this society.

2. The video program briefly describes the changes and cross-cultural contact occurring in the forests of New Guinea. Summarize the changes and speculate about how they will affect the religious traditions of the Asmat described in this lesson.

3. The Asmat perception of the world is one of hostile forces, whether from physical enemies, ancestral spirits, or nature spirits. Their religious customs seem designed to protect the people from the omnipresent hostility and danger they perceive. Yet, the Asmat religion fulfills larger functions. Review the functions of religion as presented in Lesson 20 and textbook Chapter 13, and describe briefly how the Asmat religion performs each of these functions for the society.

Answer Key

STUDY ACTIVITIES

Vocabulary Check

1. e	4. h	7. d
2. i	5. c	8. f
3. k	6. g	9. a

Completion

1. spirits, plants, sing, spears
2. killed, *Bis*, headhunting, avenged
3. head, trees, creation
4. ancestor poles, honor

SELF-TEST

Objective Questions

(Page numbers refer to the textbook.)

1. b (Objective 1; video program)
2. d (Objective 2; pages 367–368; video program; Background Notes 21A)
3. a (Objective 2; video program)
4. c (Objective 2; video program; Background Notes 21A)
5. b (Objective 3; video program)
6. d (Objective 3; video program)
7. a (Objective 4; video program)
8. c (Objective 4; pages 378–379 video program; Background Notes 21A)
9. c (Objective 5; video program; Background Notes 21A)
10. c (Objective 5; Background Notes 21A)
11. c (Objective 6; video program)
12. b (Objective 6; video program; Background Notes 21A)
13. c (Objective 6; video program; Background Notes 21A)
14. a (Objective 7; video program; Background Notes 21A)
15. b (Objective 7; video program; Background Notes 21A)

Short-Answer Essay Questions

1. Why do certain practices of the Asmat fall into the category of magic rather than religion?

   Your answer should include:

   - Magic is an attempt to manipulate supposed "natural laws" by using specific formulas to compel supernatural powers to behave in certain ways.

   - All attempts to frighten ancestral or nature spirits, such as dancing or attacking them, are examples of magic. The yelling, chasing, and dancing are supposed to force the spirits to depart, or at least stay away.

- Beheading an enemy is, in part, a kind of magic, since it is supposed to free an earthbound spirit by avenging that spirit's death.

- The *Bis* ceremony is a ritual designed to force the ancestral spirits to leave. The ancestor poles become the dwelling place for the spirits. The final ceremonies are rituals designed to send the spirits down the river to *Safan*, the final resting place.

2. In what ways are trees an important environmental resource to the Asmat? How is the use of trees as a resource related to the role that trees play in Asmat religion?

    Your answer should include:

    - Most of the resources the Asmat take from their environment come from trees: fuel, building materials, weapons, and food.

    - The sago palm provides about 90 percent of the Asmat diet.

    - Asmat religious beliefs serve to reinforce the importance of trees and, at the same time, integrate them into Asmat mythology and into the combative headhunting behavior that was long a part of their cultural pattern.

    - Trees are believed to have spirits just as humans do. The sago palm is believed to have the same spirit as a headhunter.

    - When a mangrove tree is taken for an ancestor pole or a sago palm for feasting, it is "attacked" and overcome, not just cut down. Offerings are left for tree spirits.

3. Explain the religious significance of dancing, the ancestor pole, the praying mantis, and the coconut.

    Your answer should include:

    - Dancing is a magic ritual designed to frighten spirits. The costumes worn during the *Bis* preparation reflect the characteristics of plants that the Asmat admire.

    - The ancestor pole is a symbol of those killed in headhunting raids. It is believed that, after appropriate ritual, the pole holds the spirits of those killed.

    - Due to its resemblance to plants, the praying mantis symbolizes a living plant. The mantis also symbolizes headhunting, cannibalism, and courage because the female bites off the head of her mate during mating.

    - The coconut symbolizes the tree-victim's "head," and eating it is symbolic of eating the brains of an enemy.

The **22** Arts

Assignments

View video program 22, "The Arts"

After viewing the video program
- Review the terms used in this lesson. In addition to those terms in the Learning Objectives, you should be familiar with these:

abstract	iconic images
aesthetic approach	interpretive approach
construal	motif
entopic phenomena	narrative approach
epic	representational
ethnomusicology	symbol
folklore	tonality
folkloristics	

- Review the reading assignments for this lesson.
- Complete each of the Study Activities and the Self-Test in this study-guide lesson; check your answers with the Answer Key at the end of this lesson.
- According to your instructor's assignment or your own interests, complete one or more of the Suggested Activities. You may also be interested in the readings listed at the end of Chapter 14 in the textbook.

Overview

Whatever you may consider art to be, join with the textbook for this lesson in accepting art as the "creative use of the human imagination to interpret, understand, and enjoy life."

Too often, Western societies tend to look upon art as a means of escaping from (or forgetting) the problems and concerns of everyday life. A musical composition, a motion picture, or a short story (particularly adventure or romance) is thought of as an "escape" from ordinary routines.

For both the artist and the anthropologist, art is neither an escape nor a simple pleasure. To the artist, his or her work may well be an intensification of life, a part of a quest for truth or beauty (or both). For the anthropologist, the many forms of art in a culture may each reveal something about what is most important to the society.

The video program explores a wide range of human creative activities and offers a collage of art forms and creative expression. Some are inspired by religions, others by a sense of strong social identity. Still others reveal the sense of freedom held by the artist or reflect the artist's convictions or beliefs. The textbook provides an anthropological perspective on three art forms: verbal arts, music, and pictorial arts. The textbook explains that art fulfills several needs encompassed by the definition of "art" and that art may contribute to social cohesiveness.

Through the arts, you may experience new pleasure. You may also discover new facets of life that enlarge your understanding and appreciation. For the purposes of this course, you may develop new insights into deeper, almost unspoken, aspects of a culture by appreciating the achievements the arts have inspired.

Video Program: Some form of artistic expression exists in *all* cultures. This program presents many kinds of art and explores the variety of functions served by the arts: fulfillment of the need for individual creative expression, expression of people's conceptions of the unknown or spiritual world, and reflection of cultural values and ideas. Among the arts and cultures featured in the program are the rich objects found in Tutankhamen's tomb, the mandalas of Tibetan Buddhist monks, the offerings of light of the *Vesak* Buddhist holiday in Sri Lanka, Balinese temple dancing, body decoration among the indigenous peoples of the southern Amazon and in the United States, and Tex-Mex music of the southwestern United States. Also shown in the program are several contemporary Western artists, including a performance artist, and various artistic creations, such as the AIDS quilt and Christo's "Running Fence."

As you view the program, look for:

- the diversity of art forms found in societies around the world.

- the close link between artistic expression and religious beliefs demonstrated by artifacts from the tombs of the Egyptian Empire and the arts of Buddhist Tibet.

- the functions of Balinese temple dancing.

- the celebration of *Vesak* in Sri Lanka, the occasion it marks, and the art forms used there.

- the function of Tex-Mex music.

- the expression of social values in art.

Learning Objectives

When you have completed all assignments in this lesson, you should be able to:

1. Define *art* from an anthropological perspective and explain how the study of a culture's arts contributes to an understanding of that culture. TEXTBOOK PAGES 389–392; VIDEO PROGRAM

2. Recognize that some form of artistic expression is found in all societies, describe the contribution of the arts to a society, and give examples that illustrate the diversity of art forms throughout the world. TEXTBOOK PAGES 389–393, 399–400, 402–405; VIDEO PROGRAM

3. Identify myths, legends, and tales as three major forms of the verbal art of narrative and describe the content and function of each form. TEXTBOOK PAGES 392–400

4. Identify the distinctive characteristics of human music and describe the function of music in a society. TEXTBOOK PAGES 400–404; VIDEO PROGRAM

5. Describe the continuum of pictorial art. TEXTBOOK PAGES 404–405

6. Explain southern African rock art through three different approaches: aesthetic, narrative, and interpretive. TEXTBOOK PAGES 405–412

Study Activities

Vocabulary Check

Check your understanding of terms by writing the letter of the appropriate definition in the space next to the corresponding term. Check your choices with the Answer Key at the end of the lesson.

_____	1. epic	_____	6. tale
_____	2. myth	_____	7. motif
_____	3. folklore	_____	8. ethnomusicology
_____	4. tonality	_____	9. iconic images
_____	5. legend	_____	10. folkloristics

a. scale systems and their modifications
b. a traditional narrative providing explanation of ultimate questions about human existence
c. a long oral narrative that recounts the life of a real or legendary person
d. study of verbal art forms
e. a story situation in a folktale
f. beings "seen" in the deepest stage of a trance
g. a long oral narrative recounting glorious events in someone's life
h. a sacred narrative explaining how the world came to be
i. a creative, fictional narrative
j. traditional oral stories and sayings
k. a story told as true, set in the postcreation world
l. the study of a society's music in relation to its cultural setting
m. bright, pulsating geometric forms "seen" during a trance

Completion

Fill each blank with the most appropriate term from the list immediately following that paragraph.

1. One example of art is a traditional song that has grown through the contribution and improvements by many people over many years. Another example is the product of a single artist, such as Michelangelo's larger-than-life marble statue *David*. Both of these, however, reflect one essential quality of art, the expression of human _____. Each has a symbolic message for its society and contributes in a unique way to feelings of _____. This latter aspect of art has also been served by arts that had practical functions, such as sea chanteys, which set the _____ for cooperative work aboard sailing ships.

    creativity   social cohesiveness

    pace

2. To the anthropologist, art is _____ use of imagination that helps the artist and others to interpret, understand, and _____ life. Art includes a wide range of forms, from picture and design to dance, song, _____, and the use of language. Arts using language are called the _____ arts.

    body decoration   enjoy

    creative   verbal

3. Works of art may fulfill different functions at different times. The articles found in Tutankhamen's tomb were designed to accompany the dead king to the _____. Legends in some societies relate stories of past events and peoples, a function fulfilled in Western societies by _____ books. However, the textbook points out that written works in this field may not be free of bias, and that facts may be selectively omitted or _____, just as they were, on occasion, in legends.

    afterworld   modified

    history   tasks

4.   Art fulfills several functions in a society. Myths, for example, set _____ for behavior and define the _____. Through legends, history may be preserved. In all the verbal arts and in words of _____, important customs and values may be communicated. Music communicates _____ that can be shared. Any art, whether painstakingly developed like formal sculpture or dance, or hastily completed like graffiti on a wall, may contribute to a sense of _____ and unity for a society.

cohesiveness   songs   universe

feelings   standards

Self-Test

Objective Questions

Select the one best answer.

1.   The principal reason anthropologists study a culture's arts is that the arts

     a. reflect the values and concerns of the people who create them.
     b. are the only way to understand the culture's religion.
     c. provide insight into practical matters.
     d. are the only nonsymbolic form of communication.

2.   Art always includes an aspect of

     a. practical use.
     b. symbolic communication.
     c. religious belief.
     d. humor.

3.   The textbook says that art contributes to

     a. interpretation, understanding, and enjoyment of life.
     b. preservation of historical information.
     c. illustrations of moral principles or practical advice.
     d. an explanation of a society's worldview.

4. Artistic expression has been found by anthropologists

   a. chiefly in literate and semiliterate societies.
   b. primarily in hunting-gathering and complex industrial societies.
   c. in some form in all human societies.
   d. primarily in Western countries.

5. The Sri Lankan festival of *Vesak* includes art that combines

   a. paper lanterns and electric lights.
   b. dance and music.
   c. mandalas and prayers.
   d. body painting and dance.

6. In the textbook, Haviland tentatively suggests that art is universal because art

   a. is derived from religion.
   b. began as an attempt to communicate with spirits.
   c. began as an attempt to organize people's activities.
   d. is a necessary kind of social behavior.

7. A true myth is basically a

   a. sacred narrative explaining how the world came to be in its present form.
   b. story told as true, set in the postcreation world.
   c. long oral narrative recounting the glorious events in the life of a legendary person.
   d. fictional narrative, told for entertainment.

8. In nonliterate societies, legends serve a function that, in Western societies, has been taken over by the formal study of

   a. science.
   b. religion.
   c. history.
   d. sociology.

9. An epic can be described as a

   a. long semihistorical narrative.
   b. story generally accepted as fiction.
   c. narrative that explains creation.
   d. short account of a fictional event.

10. A verbal art form recognized as fiction, but conveying a moral or practical advice is

    a. a myth.
    b. a tale.
    c. a legend.
    d. an epic.

11. An example of a social function of music shown in the video program was

    a. Tutankhamen's tomb.
    b. Tibetan creation of a Buddhist mandala.
    c. Christo's running fence.
    d. Tex-Mex music.

12. Human music is perceived in terms of

    a. sounds that are "in tune" to everyone who hears them.
    b. a random imitation of natural music.
    c. a formless range of possible sounds.
    d. a repertory of tones at regular intervals.

13. As a type of symbolic expression, pictorial art can be described as ranging from

    a. naturalistic to exploitative.
    b. representational to abstract.
    c. ugly to beautiful.
    d. stylistic to exaggerated.

14. In studying Bushman rock art, the most useful approach has been the

    a. aesthetic.
    b. narrative.
    c. interpretive.
    d. naturalistic.

Short-Answer Essay Questions

1. From each of the three art forms (verbal arts, music, and pictorial art) discussed in this lesson's reading, or from the video program, give examples of art as a form of symbolic communication.

2. List several reasons anthropologists are interested in the arts.

Suggested Activities

1. Read a myth from Greek, Nordic, American Indian, or other culture that gives an account of the creation of the world. Attempt to answer these questions: How did humans come into being? What beings were instrumental in the creation of that culture? How do the creator's powers compare with those of later members of the culture? What features of the actual culture does the myth attempt to explain? Does the myth seem to have influence on the life of the culture at the time it was told?

2. Read the lyrics of a few currently popular country-western, pop-rock, and rap songs. What do you think each one reveals about values or attitudes in areas such as individualism, love, sex, patriotism, or loyalty?

Answer Key

STUDY ACTIVITIES

Vocabulary Check

1. c	5. k	8. l
2. h	6. i	9. f
3. j	7. e	10. d
4. a		

Completion

1. creativity, social cohesiveness, pace
2. creative, enjoy, body decoration, verbal
3. afterworld, history, modified
4. standards, universe, songs, feelings, cohesiveness

SELF-TEST

Objective Questions

(Page numbers refer to the textbook.)

1. a (Objective 1; page 392; video program)
2. b (Objective 1; page 391)
3. a (Objective 2; page 389; video program)
4. c (Objective 2; pages 390–392)
5. a (Objective 2; video program)
6. d (Objective 2; page 390)
7. a (Objective 3; page 393)
8. c (Objective 3; page 396)
9. a (Objective 3; page 396)
10. b (Objective 3; page 397)
11. d (Objective 4; video program)
12. d (Objective 4; pages 400–401)
13. b (Objective 5, page 405)
14. c (Objective 6; pages 405–410)

Short-Answer Essay Questions

1. From each of the three art forms (verbal arts, music, and pictorial art) discussed in this lesson's reading, or from the video program, give examples of art as a form of symbolic communication.

   Your answer should include:

   - In verbal art, the subject of the myth and the story of the myth may symbolize the worldview of the people. The hero of an epic or tale may provide a symbol of heroism or other quality that members of that society are expected to emulate. Tales may offer practical advice about behavior.

   - Music, both in song and other forms, may serve as a symbol for feelings shared by the group.

   - The rock art of southern Africa depicts animals and incorporates various patterns intimately connected with the practices and beliefs of shamanism. The images are believed to have innate power because of their supernatural origin.

2. List several reasons anthropologists are interested in the arts.

   Your answer should include:

   - The arts reflect the cultural values and concerns of a people.

   - They are based in symbolic communication.

   - Much can be learned about a society's worldview from its myths, about history from legends and epics, and about values and standards from all of the verbal arts.

   - Pictorial art, too, often reflects the worldview of the society.

   - Anthropologists may find clues about communication between cultures from the distribution of similar tales, music, and other arts among societies.

New Orleans Black Indians: A Case Study in the Arts 23

Assignments

Before viewing the video program	• Read the Overview and the Learning Objectives for this lesson. Use the Learning Objectives to guide your reading, viewing, and thinking. • Read Background Notes 23A, "The Black Indian Mardi Gras," in this study-guide lesson. • Review textbook Chapter 14, "The Arts," paying particular attention to the sections on verbal arts and music, pages 392–404.

View video program 23, "New Orleans Black Indians: A Case Study in the Arts"

After viewing the video program	• Review the meanings of these terms:

battlefield	legend	second line
Big Chief	Lent	Spyboy
folk art	Mardi Gras	tribes
folklore	mutual-aid societies	verbal arts
krewe		

• Review Background Notes 23A for this lesson.
• Complete each of the Study Activities and the Self-Test in this study-guide lesson; check your answers with the Answer Key at the end of this lesson.
• According to your instructor's assignment or your own interests, complete one or more of the Suggested Activities.

Overview

All societies have aesthetic traditions. Men and women decorate their bodies, the tools they use, and their surroundings. Dancing and music are universal, or nearly so. In small-scale societies, everyone participates in creating art forms. Even in complex, stratified societies, art often begins in the streets among the poor and only gradually becomes accepted at all levels of society. Shakespeare aimed his plays at the masses of his day. Classical composers incorporated peasant melodies and themes into their music.

Art and aesthetic forms like dance and music are a vitalizing force in a society. They allow people to act out, invent, and reinvent cultural forms. Art can be a medium for telling stories about people or about significant events. Or it can simply be decorative. Drama and dance can be ways of reflecting upon, rehearsing, and transcending real-life roles. Or they can simply be entertaining. But even entertainment tells about the culture that produces it and the people who find it entertaining. All societies have decorative forms, but what is considered to be decorative may differ from culture to culture.

You may have had the impression that the arts of non-Western cultures, particularly those of cultures that are relatively isolated, come from ordinary people, while the arts of industrial societies in the Western world come from professionals who compose music or create another kind of art as their major occupation. Many people share this impression.

Even in Western societies, however, only a *fraction* of the art produced is the creation of professional artists. By far the largest volume of artistic expression in Western societies results from the work of "ordinary people." Although the art they produce is usually created for pleasure, much of it has aesthetic or artistic merit and qualifies as "folk art."

Folk art often serves broader purposes than mere pleasure. In a multicultural society like the United States, for example, an ethnic group can employ folk art to express its ethnicity, enhance group cohesiveness, and promote solidarity. Such art can also chronicle notable events in the life of the group, serving as a kind of living history to be passed from one generation to the next. The Black Indian tribes of New Orleans have developed such a folk art, one that not only affords them the pleasure of artistic expression, but also pays homage to their heritage and revitalizes group feelings of pride and solidarity.

Black Indians are descendants of American Indians and blacks, some of whom were West Africans brought to New Orleans as slaves. In this lesson, you will meet these people and take an absorbing look at their art and its unusual forms during the famous and colorful Mardi Gras celebrations held in New Orleans every spring. You will learn about the historical roots of the black Mardi Gras and the importance of its traditions to the people themselves. And you will understand that the Black Indian tribes, through their unique art, are doing more than merely entertaining themselves and others. They are making an intense and deeply personal statement.

Video Program: This documentary begins by tracing the roots of the Black Indian tribes and the origins of the Black Indian Mardi Gras celebration. Much of the program focuses on the distinctive features of the Mardi Gras—the songs, dances, and costumes—and on the social significance of these artistic expressions to the Black Indians. The program includes comments by the participants to convey the intense and deeply personal meaning of the many traditions of the Black Indian Mardi Gras. Several of these comments help to illuminate the importance of these folk art forms to the community, and parts of the comments are reproduced here as an aid to your study.

As you view the program, look and listen for:

- the contrast between the "white" and "black" celebrations of the Mardi Gras.

- the woman explaining, while she watches a Mardi Gras parade in a black neighborhood, "If you want to be white today, you can be white today . . . Superman, Batman, Robin Hood. You can be anything you want to be today, but *not* tomorrow. You got to be a nigger tomorrow, 'cause that's what you is!"

- a costume maker explaining something of the Indian tradition and describing the feelings he associates with Mardi Gras, "... Mardi Gras is just something you got to be a part of ... the feeling of what it's all about. It's just part of our heritage. You sittin' down, and ... the tambourines start ringin' up. Some people call it funk, you know, it's strictly us, second-line to us. Everything that's got that kind of beat is second-line, something to get your blood warmed up and make your feet begin to move, and you start being part of yourself, the *real* you. And the beautiful part of it is that no two people can express themselves the same way. Everyone is feelin' what *they* feel. And it's all basically a proud thing, and a happy thing. It's a sad thing. It's a joyous thing. It's all these things combined."

- the historical roots of the Black Indians, illustrated through photographs and drawings.

- costume makers describing how costumes are designed. One concludes that "no one goes to school to learn this ... this is something you just have to automatically pick up."

- the appearance of "Spyboy," brief glimpses of the many other participants in Black Indian parades, and two Black Indians describing how the tribes meet and confront each other in modern parades.

- a father expressing the importance of the tradition, "This Indian thing is ... something I feel every black man should be into, you know. And I have kids right now, and my kids is coming up, and I want to get all my kids into it. When it gets to the point where I have to drop out, I want my kids to take over for me."

- names of some of the Black Indian tribes (White Eagles, Yellow Pocahontas, Wild Tchoupitoulas, Creole Wild West, Golden Blades, Seventh Ward Hunters).

Learning Objectives

When you have completed all assignments in this lesson, you should be able to:

1. Describe the social and artistic activities of the Black Indian tribes of New Orleans. VIDEO PROGRAM, BACKGROUND NOTES 23A

2. Briefly describe the origins of art forms created by the Black Indian tribes, noting the influence of American Indian, African, and Haitian cultures. VIDEO PROGRAM, BACKGROUND NOTES 23A

3. Identify the significance of the costumes and music of the Black Indians' Mardi Gras celebrations. VIDEO PROGRAM, BACKGROUND NOTES 23A

4. Describe in what ways the Black Indian tribes and their ceremonies reflect the status of blacks in the United States. VIDEO PROGRAM, BACKGROUND NOTES 23A

THE BLACK INDIAN MARDI GRAS

The Mardi Gras celebrations of New Orleans combine several decorative forms, among them music, dancing, and the making of costumes, as you will see during the video program for this lesson. Mardi Gras began with the first French settlers in New Orleans in the early 1700s and is tied to the Roman Catholic calendar as a festival that precedes the season of Lent. Lent is, for Christians, a time of atonement and fasting in preparation for Easter. Mardi Gras is French for "Fat Tuesday," the last day for feasting before Lenten fasting begins.

The Mardi Gras celebration began to develop its modern form in 1857 with the formation of the Mistik Krewe of Comus, a prestigious secret society. The Mistik Krewe's parade and ball are still a highlight of Mardi Gras, but now a number of other krewes have been formed, representing many segments of New Orleans society.

The krewes spend $10,000 or more on floats and sponsor elaborate balls. To be named king or queen of a krewe and preside over its ball is considered a great honor. Families of socially prominent debutantes use their influence to have their daughters named queens of the more prestigious balls. Thus, Mardi Gras reflects the New Orleans class structure and is a way of asserting status. The secrecy of the major krewes excludes all but the chosen from their membership, and, in this way, Mardi Gras emphasizes and reinforces class differences.

A Black Indian of New Orleans could never hope to become king or queen of one of the major balls. As descendants of slaves and perhaps also of Indians who were driven from their lands, they are doubly disenfranchised. Black Indians are poor, and they are excluded from the society of those who control most Mardi Gras festivities. But the Black Indians hold their own Mardi Gras celebration, one that affirms their cultural heritage and asserts their claim on the artistic expression of the city. Under the guise of Mardi Gras, the Black Indians can openly pay homage to their cultural heritage.

Figure 23.1: The Black Indians brought new forms to the Mardi Gras celebration in New Orleans. Their culture is the product of black slaves and Indians who met while working for whites in the nineteenth century and intermarried.

New Orleans Black Indians: A Case Study in the Arts   373

Black Indians represent a unique cultural blend. In the middle of the nineteenth century, black slaves met and mingled with Indians of various tribes (primarily Choctaw) when they went to the French Market to buy goods for white households. Indians also hid runaway slaves. Thus, the Indians became associated with freedom for the slaves. There was also intermarriage between blacks and Indians.

In the 1870s, after the Civil War, "free persons of color" began to form mutual-aid societies to support members at times of life crises, such as birth, death, and marriage. For example, blacks weren't accepted by white-owned insurance agencies, so blacks provided their own kind of insurance. Writing in the New Orleans newspaper *The Courier*, Don Lee Keith asserts that these organizations provided "in reality what Lincoln's emancipation provided in theory." These organizations may have grown out of earlier African tribal associations, which held dancing and drumming competitions in New Orleans's Congo Square on Sunday afternoons, the slaves' day off. These competitions were banned before the Civil War because of rebellions by slaves, but they went underground and thereafter were permitted only on Mardi Gras. After the Civil War, when these associations resurfaced, they quickly became oriented toward Mardi Gras. In the 1880s, Chief Becate presented the first Black Indian tribe for Mardi Gras. Early tribes paraded through the black sections of New Orleans in American Indian costumes decorated with eggshells, turkey feathers, and broken glass.

In 1894, a dance teacher founded the Illinois Club, modeled after white social clubs. Now divided into two clubs, the members of this group hold Mardi Gras balls similar to those held by whites, even to the presentation of debutantes in expensive gowns.

The most famous black Mardi Gras organization is the Zulu Social Aid and Pleasure Club, which was founded in 1909 by laborers who had seen a vaudeville skit about Zulus. The club holds a ball and stages a parade through the black community. A main feature of early Zulu parades was a drunken king. Today, the society is upwardly mobile and has taken on many characteristics of white clubs, but during its early existence the Zulu Club made fun of white Americans who tried to behave like aristocrats.

But the most colorful and authentically black Mardi Gras celebrations are the Black Indian parades, featuring elaborate Indian costumes and music. These processions are put on by a number of "tribes," having names such as Wild Magnolias, Seventh Ward Hunters, Wild Tchoupitoulas, White Eagles, Golden Sioux, and Yellow Pocahontas. Each tribe has its own parade route, songs, and costume traditions. Beginning several months before Mardi Gras, practice singing sessions are held in bars every Sunday evening after church. These practices have become part of the Mardi Gras tradition, and each tribe practices in a particular bar. The chief of the tribe opens practice sessions by saying "Ma-Day, Cootie Fiyo." All present answer: "Tee-Nah Aeeey." Then tribe members practice the songs they will sing on Mardi Gras. The music is primarily West African, with elements from Haiti and Trinidad. Some older songs have elements of American Indian music. The songs often tell stories about previous Mardi Gras celebrations or about the hardships of life and the resilience of the human spirit.

Each member of the tribe has a title and a specific role to play on Mardi Gras. Spyboy (the scout) starts the march. Next comes Flagboy, carrying the tribal banner. He may be accompanied by Gang Flag, who carries a flag or emblem on a "spear," or stick. Next comes Wildman, who may also be called "Witch Doctor" or "Medicine Man" and is supposed to keep the crowds back. Wildman may be followed by the second and third chiefs. A woman "queen" or perhaps several "princesses" may accompany these chiefs. Big Chief, the tribal leader, follows this group and, sometimes, a Trail Chief completes the procession. This central group may be followed by the "second line," hundreds of noncostumed adherents who sing and dance with the parade.

Until about the middle of the twentieth century, Spyboy's role in the parade was more than ceremonial. He was supposed to keep watch for rival tribes, because the parades were occasions for conflicts fought with knives and guns to resolve disputes and prove one gang to be the most powerful in the city. When rival tribes met, one chief would order the other to "humba," or bow down in deference. If the opposing chief refused the order, the tribes would fight. The Mardi Gras parade route thus came to be called the "battlefield." Two traditional Black Indian songs, "Meet de Boys on de Battlefront" and "Corey Died on the Battlefield," describe those early battles. "Corey" was a spyboy, possibly legendary, whose courage made him run far ahead of his tribe, eventually to be attacked by members of another tribe. By the time his own tribe caught up with him, he had been killed.

Early hostilities are still observed ritually. When two tribes meet on their parade routes, the chiefs begin a complex encounter ritual, dancing around each other and shouting threats. However, this hostility is purely for display, and the tribes try to outdo each other in the art of costume design, not with knives and guns. The style of sewing and materials used in costume construction vary from tribe to tribe, but all costumes are elaborate and display fine workmanship. Writing in *Black New Orleans*, Maurice M. Martinez notes, "The biggest disgrace to self and others is a 'raggedy' Indian whose costume displays 'short cuttin', something slapped together in a hurry with glue and paste." Making a costume requires skill and years of practice in sewing. Costume makers use velvet, ostrich feathers, rhinestones, and sequins. The "crown" is the most prized part of the costume. It is worn over a black wig with braids. It is made of feathers or ostrich-plumed marabou formed like a chieftain's headdress. Numerous fine examples of costumes are shown in the video program. The "apron" covers the body from the waist to below the knees. Usually the design is sketched on canvas and then "drawn out" by stitching on beads and stones. "Wings" are arm coverings that spread out like plumage when the wearer's arms are raised.

As with folk art in other parts of the world, the various forms represented among the Black Indians in Mardi Gras—music, costuming, and dancing—are more than decorative. They are a social statement and a revitalizing force for the participants. In the case of the Black Indians, the social statement is about (1) class and racial consciousness, (2) feelings of powerlessness, and (3) the importance of maintaining social identity. For example, even among the Black Indian tribes, distinctions are made between "uptown" and "downtown." Groups that perform "uptown" are considered by downtowners to be more "commercial" and less true to the racial and class origins of the art form than are the groups that perform "downtown." The downtown neighborhood groups are concerned that the costumes and music remain within their neighborhood boundaries, be performed by group members, and be performed for their own pleasure and enjoyment.

All black Mardi Gras celebrations reflect a form of rebellion. The Zulu Social Aid and Pleasure Club began as a parody of white pretensions and gradually conformed to the white institutions it had previously mocked. The Illinois Clubs were always modeled after white institutions.

Black Indian traditions also began as defiance, growing out of underground black societies and reflecting the social realities of their times. As social reality changed, so did Black Indian celebrations. Real-life hostilities among tribes became ritualized and transformed into aesthetic competition. Some tribes have now released albums of their Mardi Gras songs, and most participate in the annual Jazz and Heritage Festival, which is a newly developed showcase for Black Indian music. In early parades, men carried flaming torches to light night parades, but black high school marching bands have recently replaced traditional flambeaux carriers in the parades. These are now ceremonial flambeaux carriers that serve no functional purpose.

In stratified societies, folk art often begins as an act of rebellion or alternative form of expression among the disenfranchised, but it revitalizes the society as a whole. Expressive forms developed in black neighborhoods of New Orleans have found their way into the mainstream cultural patterns. But, because it is a living art form, folk art is continually being reinvented and transformed by the lives and experiences of those who produce it.

Like conventional art, however, folk art has rules and cultural traditions. A spyboy cannot dress or behave like a chief, for example. As in conventional art, folk art requires a body of knowledge and skills that must be transmitted to each successive generation. But, unlike conventional art, it is not produced by a class of artists for collectors and museums. It is art by and for the people.

Study Activities

Vocabulary Check

Check your understanding of terms by writing the letter of the appropriate definition in the space next to the corresponding term. Check your choices with the Answer Key at the end of the lesson.

_____ 1.	folklore	_____ 6.	mutual-aid societies
_____ 2.	legends	_____ 7.	battlefield
_____ 3.	Lent	_____ 8.	second line
_____ 4.	krewe	_____ 9.	Spyboy
_____ 5.	tribes		

a.   large groups, often without costumes, that follow behind tribal leaders in a parade

b.   organizations of members of the black community for traditional celebrations of Mardi Gras

c.   a name for Mardi Gras parade routes

d.   organizations of members of the white community for traditional celebrations of Mardi Gras

e.   ritual encounter in which loud threats are exchanged

f.   starts the march and heads the procession

g.   oral traditions and verbal arts found in all societies

h.   in Christian religions, the period of fasting and penance that precedes Easter

i.   French for "Fat Tuesday"

j.   semihistorical narratives that tell the stories of past heroes, the movements of peoples, and the establishment of local customs

k.   organized as a form of insurance protection

Completion

Fill each blank with the most appropriate term from the list immediately following that paragraph.

1. New Orleans Black Indian tribes meet regularly in neighborhood _____ to practice traditional _____ throughout much of the year. The leader, known as the _____, conducts the practice sessions and occupies a place of honor in the parade. One of his functions is to _____ leaders of other tribes in the Mardi Gras parades.

bars	mutual-aid societies
Big Chief	songs
challenge	Spyboy

2. The interest of the black community in Indians began in the years before the _____ War. There was intermarriage among the peoples, and the Indians aided the blacks by hiding _____. The Indian influence on Mardi Gras festival art is seen chiefly in _____ and in the roles of tribe members.

Civil	Revolutionary
costumes	runaway slaves

Self-Test

Objective Questions

Select the one best answer.

1. Black Indian tribe activities reach their high point each year in the celebration of
    a. Lent.
    b. Mardi Gras.
    c. New Orleans day.
    d. Indian Summer.

2. Members of each tribe learn their songs for Mardi Gras while participating in

   a. high school band classes.
   b. practice sessions of social clubs.
   c. meetings held in members' homes.
   d. sessions held in a particular bar.

3. The Black Indian tribes of New Orleans identify with American Indians because

   a. Indian dances were seen by a group of blacks at a vaudeville show in the 1880s.
   b. blacks associated freely with Indians in the early twentieth century.
   c. both blacks and Indians were victims of oppression and had been moved from their homelands.
   d. the black tribes admired Indian costumes seen in early western movies.

4. The music of the Black Indians reflects influences from all of the following sources EXCEPT

   a. music from gatherings held during the slavery years.
   b. Spanish gypsy music.
   c. West African music.
   d. the music of Haiti.

5. The most prized part of a Black Indian Mardi Gras costume is the "crown," which resembles a

   a. pair of wings.
   b. royal tiara.
   c. chieftain's headdress.
   d. plumed hat.

6. Individual Black Indian costumes

   a. have remained the same, being passed down to participants from one year to the next.
   b. are usually purchased from professional designers each year.
   c. are identical except for color.
   d. are individually designed and prepared by costume makers in the community.

7. When used in Black Indian songs, the term "battlefield" refers to

   a. the parade route.
   b. the Civil War.
   c. battles between American Indians and soldiers.
   d. the First World War.

8. Spyboy's traditional role was to

   a. scout for the approach of a rival tribe.
   b. demand that a rival tribe bow to his tribe.
   c. discover the meanings of other tribal symbols.
   d. hold back the crowds during the parade.

9. The Black Indian tribes stage their parades in

   a. the center of New Orleans, on Canal Street.
   b. the black community area of New Orleans.
   c. both the black neighborhoods and the white communities.
   d. festivals held throughout the United States.

10. At the time of their first meetings with American Indians, blacks in Louisiana probably felt a strong similarity between themselves and the Indian because

    a. both blacks and American Indians felt powerless and under oppressive control of the dominant society.
    b. both groups had a long and warlike heritage.
    c. each society had a culture and folklore similar to the other.
    d. each society desired to return to its former lands.

11. The original Illinois Club of New Orleans patterned itself after

    a. northern social clubs.
    b. mutual-aid societies.
    c. white society social clubs.
    d. the Zulu Club.

12. The closest counterpart of the Black Indian tribes in white society is

    a. insurance companies.
    b. Mardi Gras.
    c. social clubs.
    d. krewes.

Short-Answer Essay Questions

1. Describe the origins and typical subjects of the music forms used by the Black Indian tribes today.

2. In what way could the formation of the Zulu and Illinois clubs be termed a form of rebellion against the dominant culture of New Orleans of that day?

3. In what ways can the costumes and music of the Black Indian tribes be seen as an example of folk art?

4. According to Background Notes 23A, what kind of social statement is made by the Black Indian tribes through their folk art?

Suggested Activities

1. In the video program, one brief section shows the "use" of art on American Indian shields and dwellings. The animal or god-animal pictured, for example, shared its "medicine" with the bearer. From suggestions given in the program and in Background Notes 23A, try to identify possible cultural values of the Indian symbols worn by the New Orleans Black Indians. Write a brief paper on this topic.

2. If a local pageant or festival is held in your area, gather information concerning the event, particularly information distributed by those responsible for staging the event. If possible, talk with someone associated with the festival to learn how it originated and the purpose it serves in the community. Write a report describing what you think is the cultural importance of this event. If you find evidence that the festival has changed over time, suggest reasons for such change.

Answer Key

Vocabulary Check

1. g	4. d	7. c
2. j	5. b	8. a
3. h	6. k	9. f

Completion

1. bars, songs, Big Chief, challenge
2. Civil, runaway slaves, costumes

SELF-TEST

Objective Questions

(Page numbers refer to the textbook.)

1. b (Objective 1; video program, Background Notes 23A)
2. d (Objective 1; video program, Background Notes 23A)
3. c (Objective 2; video program, Background Notes 23A)
4. b (Objective 2; video program, Background Notes 23A)
5. c (Objective 2; Background Notes 23A)
6. d (Objective 3; video program, Background Notes 23A)
7. a (Objective 3; video program, Background Notes 23A)
8. a (Objective 3; video program, Background Notes 23A)
9. b (Objective 4; video program, Background Notes 23A)
10. a (Objective 4; video program, Background Notes 23A)
11. c (Objective 4; Background Notes 23A)
12. d (Objective 4; Background Notes 23A)

Short-Answer Essay Questions

1. Describe the origins and typical subjects of the music forms used by the Black Indian tribes today.

    Your answer should include:

    *   Their music is based on West African rhythms brought to the United States by black slaves, with some influence from the music of Haiti and Trinidad. Blacks and Indians fleeing oppression in those areas in the late 1800s brought their music with them. There may also be some influence from American Indian music.

    *   The songs relate to earlier Mardi Gras festivals, especially those that recount the "battlefield" days when competing tribes fought upon meeting each other during parades. Other songs relate to life's conditions today, its problems, and the enduring resilience of the human spirit.

2. In what way could the formation of the Zulu and Illinois clubs be termed a form of rebellion against the dominant culture of New Orleans of that day?

    Your answer should include:

    *   The Zulu Club was a kind of black response to the white society's "krewes" and, at first, mocked white pretensions to nobility and courtly manners. The original Illinois Club patterned itself after the white social clubs, giving dances and providing its own "showcase" for debutantes. It developed opportunities for the black community that previously were available only to the dominant whites.

    *   Both groups have provided a means of self-expression and group identity for black society, since the organizations of the white society were closed to them.

3. In what ways can the costumes and music of the Black Indian tribes be seen as an example of folk art?

    Your answer should include:

    *   Black Indian tribe art is handed down to succeeding generations by learning "in the street," rather than through formal teaching in schools or academies.

    *   The arts and traditional ceremonies of these people have changed and adapted to the needs of the society.

- They qualify as art because they are products of creative activities that help one to enjoy, appreciate, and understand life better. They fulfill many functions that anthropologists have found in the arts: Communication of history, values, and standards of behavior are three of these functions. Perhaps most important, they strongly support a sense of cohesiveness and group solidarity among the New Orleans black community.

- The Black Indian traditions are a vitalizing force in the community.

4. According to Background Notes 23A, what kind of social statement is made by the Black Indian tribes through their folk art?

Your answer should include:

- The social statement expressed through the Black Indian tribes' art includes class consciousness, feelings of powerlessness, and maintaining social and ethnic identity.

Culture Change 24

Assignments

Before viewing the video program	• Read the Overview and the Learning Objectives for this lesson. Use the Learning Objectives to guide your reading, viewing, and thinking. • Read textbook Part V introduction, pages 416–417, and Chapter 15, "Cultural Change," pages 418–449. • Review textbook Chapter 13, pages 384–385, "Religion and Culture Change."

View video program 24, "Culture Change"

After viewing the video program	• Review the terms used in this lesson. In addition to those terms in the Learning Objectives, you should be familiar with these:

applied anthropology	revolutionary
culture of discontent	structural differentiation
integrative mechanism	syncretism
rebellion	tradition
revitalization movement	

• Review the reading assignment for this lesson.
• Complete each of the Study Activities and the Self-Test in this study-guide lesson; check your answers with the Answer Key at the end of this lesson.
• According to your instructor's assignment or your own interests, complete one or more of the Suggested Activities. You may also be interested in the readings listed at the end of Chapter 15 in the textbook.

Overview

In Lesson 2, you learned about the various characteristics of culture. Two of these characteristics are especially important to remember as you study this lesson: (1) cultures are integrated and (2) they are always changing. Change in one area of the culture will cause change in other areas, often unforeseen, because beliefs, activities, and traditions *are* integrated into one system. Even though many topics in this course may seem to suggest that culture is static, cultures are, in fact, dynamic. Although cultures may achieve considerable stability, change, not sameness, should be expected.

For most of us, change does not come easily. Perhaps you feel that *your* culture is more flexible than others you have learned about in this course. If you do, think for a moment about an example of "cultural stubbornness" that has made itself apparent in the last several decades. Despite social, legal, and scientific incentives, the population of the United States has shown strong resistance to a simple change that offers many advantages—the adoption of the metric system of measurement. Moreover, other Western societies have long since adopted this change without adverse results. In fact, only three countries now use nonmetric measurement systems.

Why are some changes adopted quickly and easily, yet others take a long time, cause turmoil, and are met with great resistance? Anthropologists have discovered that change is sometimes influenced by forces within the culture, sometimes by forces outside the culture, and sometimes by changes in the environment. William A. Haviland devotes much of Chapter 15 to the influences of other cultures on change within a society. Cross-cultural contact is not the only cause of culture change and does not necessarily cause harm to cultures involved. But you will probably agree that many of the severe culture crises in today's world result from the contact of Western industrial culture with less-industrialized societies. The video program presents vivid instances of the impact of Westerners and modern technology on indigenous peoples.

"Modern" technological society may not really hold a positive promise for the future, either for its own people or for those others who seek to imitate it. Change is not necessarily progress—and change, even when it is an attempt at improvement, can have unexpected, even disastrous, effects.

Video Program: A montage of examples of culture change opens this program. The remainder of the program reviews the many ways in which cultures can change and examines four cultures—the Balinese, the Ju/'hoansi, the Yanomamo, and the Maya—to illustrate how cultures change through innovation, invention, and diffusion. Particular attention is paid to colonialism and the loss of indigenous cultures. The program also includes updates by two anthropologists on recent changes in the lives of the Yanomamo and the Maya, two cultures studied earlier in the course.

As you view the program, look for:

- how Balinese rice farmers are integrating modern technology with traditional horticultural techniques.

- the impact of colonial rule on the Ju/'hoansi people and culture and how they are trying to regain control over their lands.

- how the Yanomamo are contending with a drastic form of culture change brought about by colonialism.

- Napoleon Chagnon's comments on the impact of mining on the health, the self-sufficiency, and the environment of the Yanomamo and one Yanomamo's comments about the miners.

- anthropologist Hubert Smith's description of culture change in the Maya of Chican, almost two decades after his original fieldwork.

Learning Objectives

When you have completed all assignments in this lesson, you should be able to:

1. Explain why cultures change, and identify mechanisms that may lead to cultural change. TEXTBOOK PAGES 419–426; VIDEO PROGRAM

2. Define *innovation* and explain the difference between *primary innovation* and *secondary innovation*. TEXTBOOK PAGES 421–423; VIDEO PROGRAM

3. Describe diffusion and identify examples of this process. TEXTBOOK PAGES 423–425; VIDEO PROGRAM

4. Describe cultural loss as an aspect of cultural change. TEXTBOOK PAGES 425–426; VIDEO PROGRAM

5. Explain what is meant by forcible change, and define *acculturation* and *genocide*. TEXTBOOK PAGES 426–429

6. Explain directed change and describe the role of applied anthropologists in directed change. TEXTBOOK PAGES 429–432

7. Briefly describe various reactions of peoples to forcible change. TEXTBOOK PAGES 432–437; VIDEO PROGRAM

8. Describe modernization and its four subprocesses and explain why this term is inappropriate. TEXTBOOK PAGES 437–439, 446–447

9. Summarize the effects of recent change on the Shuar Indians, the Skolt Lapps, the Ju/'hoansi, the Yanomamo, and the Maya of Xaibe village. TEXTBOOK PAGES 439–441; VIDEO PROGRAM

Study Activities

Vocabulary Check

Check your understanding of terms by writing the letter of the appropriate definition in the space next to the corresponding term. Check your choices with the Answer Key at the end of the lesson.

_____ 1. primary innovation   _____ 8. revolutionary
_____ 2. secondary innovation   _____ 9. structural differentiation
_____ 3. diffusion   _____ 10. modernization
_____ 4. acculturation   _____ 11. revitalization movement
_____ 5. applied anthropology   _____ 12. integrative mechanism
_____ 6. genocide   _____ 13. cultural loss
_____ 7. syncretism

a. division of a single traditional role into two more roles, each with a single function
b. a revitalization movement from within, directed primarily at the ideological system and social structure
c. the spread of customs or practices from one culture to another
d. the blending of indigenous and foreign traits to form a new system
e. a tendency in modernization that splits formerly combined functions
f. a chance discovery of a new principle
g. major culture changes that people are forced to make and that result from intensive contact between societies
h. cultural elements that oppose forces for differentiation
i. a deliberate attempt to construct a more satisfactory culture by rapid acceptance of multiple innovations
j. an attempt from within the culture to change the social structure of a society
k. a change in which a practice, skill, or belief ceases, with or without replacement
l. the total destruction of a cultural pattern by violence or environment
m. something new that comes from the deliberate application of known principles
n. extermination of one people by another
o. the use of anthropology to solve practical problems, often for a specific client
p. process by which traditional or developing societies acquire characteristics of Western industrialized societies

Completion

Fill each blank with the most appropriate term from the list immediately following that paragraph.

1. Changes can be introduced into a culture from forces outside the culture, such as contact with other _____ or by _____. Changes can also come from _____ the culture. Primary innovations are those that result from the discovery of _____ principles, while secondary innovations are those that come from the application of _____ principles.

accident	known	within
cultures	new	

2. Diffusion is cultural _____ under conditions in which the society has a _____ whether to adopt features from another culture. Usually, in diffusion, there are significant changes in practice or use of technology to make the adopted feature _____ with the existing culture. The adoption of clothing designs, such as the parka from the Inuit by North American settlers, is an example of _____.

   Acculturation, in contrast, lacks the element of _____. It always includes an element of actual or threatened _____ by the society that dominates another. Massive changes occur in one or both cultures as the result of prolonged intense contact. The two cultures may merge into a single one; a culture may keep its identity but lose its _____; or the society under threat may disappear.

autonomy	compatible
borrowing	diffusion
choice	force

3. Societies react in several ways to forcible change. Some seek to escape by retreating into wilderness areas; others try to _____. Some accept the new features forced upon them, but creatively blend them into their own traditions, creating a new system but remaining loyal to their own ways. This process is called _____. A movement from within the society to deliberately and rapidly introduce many innovations that will improve the society is called a _____ movement. A movement from within that seeks to change social structure and ideology is described as _____.

rebel	revolutionary
revitalization	syncretism

Self-Test

Objective Questions

Select the one best answer.

1. Significant changes in culture may result from

    a. accidents.
    b. innovations.
    c. forced or selective contact with other cultures.
    d. all of the above.

2. Left to itself, a society's cultural pattern will usually

    a. change gradually, consistent with its basic pattern.
    b. change rapidly and dramatically.
    c. degenerate rather quickly into small factions.
    d. rapidly but smoothly develop new practices and beliefs.

3. A new practice, tool, or principle that becomes widely accepted within a group is called

    a. a cultural challenge.
    b. a diffusion.
    c. an innovation.
    d. an acculturation.

4. Pottery manufacturing with fired clay is considered a primary innovation because it

    a. involved the chance discovery of new principles.
    b. caused formation of a substantially new culture.
    c. involved application of known techniques to new uses.
    d. was discovered by more than one culture.

5. Diffusion can be described as basically

    a. voluntary and disruptive.
    b. forced and selective.
    c. voluntary and selective.
    d. selective and disruptive.

6. Linton has suggested that cultural borrowing may account for

   a. 30 percent of a culture's content.
   b. 50 percent of a culture's content.
   c. 70 percent of a culture's content.
   d. 90 percent of a culture's content.

7. In the process of diffusion, an innovation is usually

   a. modified to fit into the borrowing culture.
   b. modified to fit into the originating culture.
   c. accepted so widely that the culture loses its identity.
   d. rejected completely to protect the values of the culture.

8. Adoption of a different practice or technology may lead to a culture loss because

   a. the former practice may be forgotten through disuse.
   b. any innovation usually leads to new innovations.
   c. Western technology and innovation may upset major segments of the society.
   d. the society may selectively reject the new ways.

9. An example of culture loss without replacement is

   a. Skolt Laplanders and snowmobiles.
   b. Canary Islanders and boat making.
   c. Balinese and rice farming.
   d. Eskimos and washing machines.

10. Acculturation is characterized by

    a. voluntary decisions and selective choice.
    b. threat of force and massive change.
    c. selective choice and massive change.
    d. voluntary decisions and massive change.

11. Systematic efforts that result in extermination of one people by another is termed

    a. acculturation.
    b. genocide.
    c. nativism.
    d. syncretism.

12. Applied anthropology most frequently involves

    a. assistance for a society that wants to modernize.
    b. helping a society preserve traditional arts and crafts.
    c. study of historical changes that earlier affected a society.
    d. assistance for a group that wants to impose changes on another group.

13. A situation that may lead to rebellion and revolution is

    a. the practice of shamanism in the society.
    b. increased expectations of material wealth.
    c. a change in environmental conditions.
    d. loss of prestige by an established authority.

14. All of the following groups are examples of revitalization movements EXCEPT

    a. Skolt Lapps.
    b. Mormons.
    c. Black Muslims.
    d. the "religious right."

15. *Syncretism* is best defined as

    a. rebellion without revolutionary change.
    b. blending of indigenous and foreign traits.
    c. disappearance of a cultural trait.
    d. rejection of new ways and return to old patterns.

16. The term *modernization* reflects the belief that

    a. anthropologists should assist societies that wish to change.
    b. food-foraging and pastoral societies are superior to other culture patterns.
    c. nonrenewable resources should be used carefully, if at all.
    d. Western industrial societies are superior to traditional societies.

17. The concept of modernization does NOT necessarily include

    a. technological development.
    b. population growth.
    c. agricultural development.
    d. urbanization.

18. As a result of the introduction of motorized equipment into the Skolt Lapps society,

    a. the average reindeer herd size has increased.
    b. new economic opportunities have developed.
    c. the cost of maintaining herds has decreased.
    d. fewer Lapp men can possess herds.

19. The Ju/'hoansi of southern Africa

    a. became culturally extinct when their lands were taken over.
    b. formed a federation to adapt to an industrial economy.
    c. have organized themselves into a farmers' cooperative.
    d. successfully rebelled against the government.

20. The Shuar Indians attempted to protect their way of life by

    a. forming a federation to guide and direct necessary changes.
    b. starting a rebellion against the government.
    c. moving to a government-protected reserve.
    d. adopting an urban-industrial economic pattern.

Short-Answer Essay Questions

1. Explain why directed change may be a form of forcible change and describe the ethical problem faced by applied anthropologists who work in such programs.

2. Summarize the concern expressed in the textbook about genocide, and list recent examples of such occurrences.

3. Define *modernization* and briefly describe the four subprocesses that take place in this kind of culture change. Explain why the term is inappropriate.

4. How have the Skolt Lapps and the Shuar Indians each responded to pressures toward modernization?

Suggested Activities

1. As you learned by reading the textbook, *modernization* is a term used to describe a particular type of acculturation that carries with it a suggestion of ethnocentrism. In your opinion, does this implied ethnocentric approach to culture change interfere with your understanding of what may actually be happening with formerly nonindustrial peoples, such as Lapps and newly emerging African nations? Can you suggest a different term to use for this present-day phenomenon that would be descriptive without implying ethnocentric attitudes?

2. In recent decades there have been rebellions or revolutions in many parts of the world. Obtain information on one country that is experiencing such upheavals or their aftermath. You might, for example, pick South Africa, Northern Ireland, Iran, or one of the Eastern European or Balkan countries. You may want to use one or more books or articles on the factors that led to the present conditions.

   Write a brief report that includes: (1) identification of factors, such as those listed on textbook page 436, that led to the actions against the present or former government and (2) assessment of the type of reaction (rebellion or revolution) illustrated by this country's recent history.

3. Colonialism usually presents a picture of "one-way" acculturation, in which the subordinate peoples adopt cultural attributes from the dominant society; yet colonialism has been shown to be a "two-way" process. Do research on an instance of colonialism (such as the Spanish in the Americas, the British in India, or the French in Africa) and indicate the cultural traits that colonial powers adopted from conquered or subordinate cultures.

Answer Key

STUDY ACTIVITIES

Vocabulary Check

1. f	6. n	10. p
2. m	7. d	11. i
3. c	8. b	12. h
4. g	9. a	13. k
5. o		

Completion

1. cultures, accident, within, new, known
2. borrowing, choice, compatible, diffusion, choice, force, autonomy
3. rebel, syncretism, revitalization, revolutionary

SELF-TEST

Objective Questions

(Page numbers refer to the textbook.)

1. d (Objective 1; pages 421–426; video program)
2. a (Objective 1; page 420; video program)
3. c (Objective 2; page 421; video program)
4. a (Objective 2; page 421)
5. c (Objective 3; pages 423–425; video program)
6. d (Objective 3; page 424)
7. a (Objective 3; pages 424–425; video program)
8. a (Objective 4; pages 425–426)
9. b (Objective 4; page 426)
10. b (Objective 5; pages 426–427)
11. b (Objective 5; page 428)
12. d (Objective 6; pages 431–432)

13. d (Objective 7; page 436)
14. a (Objective 7; pages 434–435)
15. b (Objective 7; page 432)
16. d (Objective 8; pages 437–438)
17. b (Objective 8; page 438)
18. d (Objective 9; pages 439–440)
19. c (Objective 9; video program)
20. a (Objective 9; pages 440–441)

Short-Answer Essay Questions

1. Explain why directed change may be a form of forcible change and describe the ethical problem faced by applied anthropologists who work in such programs.

    Your answer should include:

    *   Although directed change may be most carefully planned, the direction and the goals of such change are most often imposed on a society by another society or organization.

    *   Applied anthropology is a specialty that applies known principles toward the solution of "practical" problems. Often, an anthropologist's "client" in directed change is not the society involved, but another group (such as the government of the country or a colonial government) that desires the change.

    *   What an anthropologist should do when a given people do not want such changes, especially when they are unable to resist imposed change, poses a serious ethical problem: How much should the anthropologist do that may permanently change the way of life of these people?

2. Summarize the concern expressed in the textbook about genocide, and list recent examples of such occurrences.

    Your answer should include:

    *   Genocide, or the extermination of one people by another, continues to occur in many parts of the world. Sometimes, it is a deliberate policy. Other times, genocide may be an unforeseen result of practices intended to promote "progress." Anthropologists have found that genocide is often carried out through alliances between religious, economic, and political interests.

- Genocide continues, in spite of stated opposition to the practice. In the latter half of the twentieth century, instances of genocide occurred in Iraq (the Kurdish), in Guatemala, in Namibia while under South African control (Ju/'hoansi), and in Bosnia-Herzegovina (Muslims).

3. Define *modernization* and briefly describe the four subprocesses that take place in this kind of culture change. Explain why the term is inappropriate.

Your answer should include:

- Modernization is the acquisition of characteristics of Western industrialized societies by developing (or nonindustrialized) societies.

- The four subprocesses in modernization are (1) technological development, in which scientific knowledge and techniques replace traditional knowledge and techniques; (2) agricultural development, with a shift in emphasis from subsistence farming to commercial farming; (3) industrialization, with inanimate forms of energy replacing human and animal power; and (4) urbanization, in which populations move from rural areas to cities.

- The term modernization is inappropriate because it is ethnocentric, assuming that other societies must become more like Western industrialized societies. It also assumes that change is equivalent to improvement and progress.

- The Western world's standard of living is based on a high rate of consumption of nonrenewable resources. It is probably unrealistic to expect that most peoples of the world will ever be able to achieve a comparable standard of living.

4. How have the Skolt Lapps and the Shuar Indians each responded to pressures toward modernization?

Your answer should include:

- The Skolt Lapps voluntarily chose to adopt snowmobiles, a modern technology.

- Using snowmobiles for reindeer herd management had unforeseen consequences. The use of snowmobiles greatly changed the manner of herd management and the economics of herd ownership and has caused the herds to decline.

- In this instance, modernization is not an improvement. Reindeer herding is more expensive, so fewer Lapp males can own herds, and many who do have herds must work for wages to support the increased costs of snowmobile operation.

- The Shuar Indians, in danger of losing their traditional lands to settlers, formed a federation to negotiate with the national government and to work toward solutions for their problems.

- The federation has developed programs to secure lands for its people, to develop a viable economic base (cattle ranching), and to control their children's education.

- While a number of features of Shuar culture are changed, the leadership of the federation feels that the most essential elements—such as language, communal landownership, an economy that is basically egalitarian, and kin-based communities with maximum autonomy—are being retained.

- Although modernization and change were forced upon the Shuar, they have tried—through the federation—to control the direction and extent of change.

Cricket the Trobriand Way: A Case Study in Culture Change **25**

Assignments

Before viewing the video program	• Read the Overview and the Learning Objectives for this lesson. Use the Learning Objectives to guide your reading, viewing, and thinking. • Read Background Notes 25A, "The Trobriand Islanders of the South Pacific," in this study-guide lesson. • Review textbook Chapter 15, "Cultural Change," particularly the information on Trobriand culture, acculturation, and syncretism (textbook pages 432–434.) Also, because Trobriand cricket has become integrated into their culture, review information on the Trobriand Islanders in earlier lessons: yam production and exchange (pages 187–188), *Kula* ring trading (pages 198–200), courtship and marriage (pages 220–221, 239–240), and residency patterns (pages 262–263).

View video program 25, "Cricket the Trobriand Way: A Case Study in Culture Change"

After viewing the video program	• Review the meaning of these terms:

acculturation	*kayasa*	*soulava*
avunculocal	*Kula* ring	syncretism
exogamy	matrilineal	tradition

• Review the reading assignments for this lesson.
• Complete each of the Study Activities and the Self-Test in this study-guide lesson; check your answers with the Answer Key at the end of this lesson.
• According to your instructor's assignment or your own interests, complete one or more of the Suggested Activities. You may also be interested in the readings listed at the end of Chapter 15 in the textbook.

Overview

This lesson is not so much about the game of cricket as it is about culture change and the important aspects of culture that the people of the Trobriand Islands have creatively and vigorously retained despite the pressure of contact with other societies. Even so, you will see exciting moments in a cricket match in the video program.

The Trobriand Islanders live in a part of Papua New Guinea and are horticulturists. Historically, in the Trobriand culture, a man's power and prestige were based on several kinds of competition: success in growing yams, skill in the exchange of valuables, and prowess on the battlefield. However, when foreign missionaries and colonists from Britain and Australia arrived, the Islanders were forced to eliminate traditional warfare and make many other changes in their culture. For example, they were pressured to adopt cricket as a substitute for warfare. Missionaries and government officials hoped that cricket (and other sports) would influence the society to adopt British standards of dress, religion, and sportsmanship.

Later, during World War II, Allied military forces introduced the Trobrianders to still other cultural elements. In this intensive case study of the dynamics of culture change, you will see how the culture of the Trobriand Islanders changed in response to strong external pressures throughout the first half of the twentieth century. The Trobrianders, as you will understand, were able to blend elements from other cultures with their own customs, keeping faith with their own cultural traditions.

This lesson does not, and cannot, provide any final answers for problems caused by acculturation, but it does give a view of what appears to be a "success story" out of forcible change.

Video Program: This detailed study of the Trobriand Islanders shows how one culture adapted to change through the process of syncretism. The program contrasts scenes of a traditional game of British cricket with those of a Trobriand cricket match. The scenes vividly depict how the Trobrianders have changed the game drastically, including the addition of their own rules and rituals, war paint, chants, and dances. The game, as adapted by the Trobrianders, is an example of how a culture can blend its own cultural traditions with those from other cultures. The program includes footage of many practices that reflect the blending of two cultures, such as treating cricket bats with war magic and decorating them for conflict.

As you view the program, look for:

- the description of the game of cricket as played by the British.

- the motivations of colonial officers and missionaries for introducing competitive games and attempting to change traditional Trobriand practices.

- changes that Trobriand Islanders made in team organization and equipment for their version of cricket.

- integration of traditional elements such as chants, dancing, and costumes into the game of cricket.

- the many ways in which the Trobriand Islanders have incorporated magic into cricket.

- the traditional *kayasa* competition, how it has blended with cricket matches, and the influence it has in determining the winner.

Learning Objectives

When you have completed all assignments in this lesson, you should be able to:

1. Describe the circumstances of the introduction of cricket to the Trobrianders. TEXTBOOK PAGES 432–434; VIDEO PROGRAM; BACKGROUND NOTES 25A

2. Define *syncretism* and explain how the Trobriand adaptation of cricket represents an example of syncretism. TEXTBOOK PAGES 432–434; VIDEO PROGRAM; BACKGROUND NOTES 25A

3. Identify three examples of how the Trobrianders transformed the game of cricket. TEXTBOOK PAGES 432–434; VIDEO PROGRAM; BACKGROUND NOTES 25A

4. Explain the significance of the following features of cricket in terms of Trobriand culture: **(a)** the games take place during the harvest period; **(b)** the players wear "war dress"; **(c)** war magic is used; **(d)** dances and chants are used; and **(e)** the host team is always the winner. VIDEO PROGRAM; BACKGROUND NOTES 25A

5. Explain how the game of cricket reveals political and economic aspects of Trobriand culture. TEXTBOOK PAGES 187–188, 198–200, AND 432–434; VIDEO PROGRAM; BACKGROUND NOTES 25A

THE TROBRIAND ISLANDERS OF THE SOUTH PACIFIC

The history of cricket in the Trobriand Islands reflects the history and aftermath of colonialism. It illustrates how attempts by a dominating society to eliminate local customs led to a compromise between traditional and foreign cultural elements.

The Trobriands, located off the northeast coast of Papua New Guinea, are coral islands that circle a shallow lagoon. The islands lack freshwater rivers, but they do receive heavy rainfall throughout the year. Rainwater soaks through the coral and collects in underground caves, providing fresh drinking water. The islands also lack hard stone, clay, and metal, so the natives have to buy or trade for those materials.

The Trobriand Islanders are horticulturists, planting their crops where soil has collected in cracks and hollows in the coral. On Kiriwina, the main island, crops are grown on a ridge along the east coast. Their primary subsistence crop is yams, which play a key role in the exchange and prestige system. Breadfruit, taro, sweet potatoes, beans, bananas, and corn are also important food sources. The people raise pigs, and they fish for mullet in the lagoon and for sharks in the deep-sea waters. The Trobrianders are skilled navigators. They build outrigger canoes and can sail a hundred miles or more across the open sea to exchange goods with people on other islands in the area. Bronislaw Malinowski, the anthropologist who studied them extensively early in the twentieth century, called the Trobrianders the "argonauts of the Western Pacific" (*Argonauts of the Western Pacific*, London: Routledge and Kegan Paul, 1922).

Most of the Islanders live in raised wooden houses clustered in small villages. Parents, young children, and adolescent females occupy one house. Young males live in bachelor houses near their mother's brother. Every household has a yam house for storing yams for family use. The households are arranged around a central clearing, where ceremonies, dancing, and cricket games are held. Yam houses for displaying yams occupy a central place in the clearing.

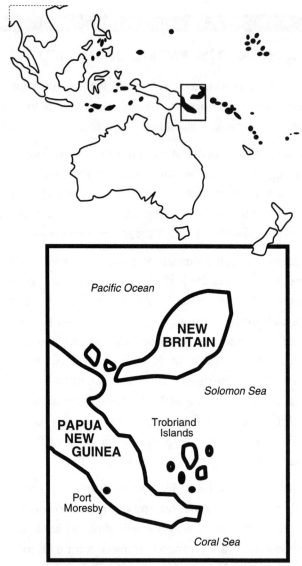

Figure 25.1: The game of cricket played by Trobriand Islanders demonstrates ways they have retained traditional practices while accepting new practices from foreign cultures.

The Trobrianders are matrilineal, but residence is patrilocal, except for chiefs or males who expect to inherit a position of high status. In the latter cases, residence is avunculocal. Young people must marry outside their own lineage. Upon marriage, the bride's family must give yams to her and her new husband. This sets up an elaborate system of exchange obligations between the two lineages.

Most households garden for themselves, but several households sometimes pool their labor. An individual can also summon people to work for him, after which he distributes food to them. Leaders of high rank use this method to mobilize followers to build yam houses or canoes or other large-scale projects. Such leaders accumulate food surpluses for this purpose through gifts from their kin. Each household grows a surplus of yams and gives away the best yams. Some yams are set aside as tribute to the village leader. Each man must also give yams to his sister, whose husband responds by giving a stone axe or clay pot to his brother-in-law. Because the Trobriand lineages are exogamous, yams move along paths of alliance among several lineages.

Only chiefs are entitled to marry more than one wife, and they can claim tribute from the kin group of each wife. Therefore, chiefs are able to accumulate a surplus of yams, which adds to their prestige and influence.

When a man dies, the women of his lineage (that is, his sister, mother, sister's daughter, and so on) give woven bundles and skirts made of banana leaves to his wife's lineage. Note that during his lifetime, a Trobriand man is continually paying out yams to his sister and receiving ceremonial objects in return. The stone axe blades or clay pots a man receives from his brother-in-law and the bundles and skirts given to his wife's lineage on his death are not put to practical use. However, the axe blades can be exchanged for pigs, magic spells, and yams.

A leader gains prestige and, therefore, influence by being able to give away large quantities of food at a mortuary feast or other ceremonial occasion. Traditionally, a chieftain would sponsor a feast, a war, or a work project as an occasion to add to his renown by distributing food and other valuables.

THE IMPORTANCE OF THE EXCHANGE SYSTEM

Inland villages exchange yams with villages along the coast that specialize in fishing. The exchanges take place as part of traditional alliances between villages.

Men may also belong to the *Kula* ring, an exchange network that links the Trobriands with other islands in the western Pacific. The *Kula* involves specific nonutilitarian trade goods, decorated necklaces, and armbands that are too elaborate for everyday use. Their worth is entirely symbolic. Some of the more prized necklaces and armbands have names and histories. In the *Kula*, a man publicly and ceremonially presents his partner on another island with a necklace. Some time later, the partner is obliged to give his benefactor an equally valuable arm shell. In this way, the necklaces, or *soulava*, travel in a clockwise direction around the islands, while the armbands, or *mwali*, travel in a counter-clockwise direction. A map on page 199 of the Haviland textbook shows trade routes in the *Kula* ring.

A man may have *Kula* partners, but each partnership lasts for a lifetime and a man may not exchange *Kula* valuables with anyone but his *Kula* partners. The *Kula* establishes alliances throughout the area and provides a setting for trading other goods, because other exchanges take place on *Kula* expeditions. But acquiring a particularly valuable *Kula* article is also a way of gaining prestige. A man may use magic and sometimes subterfuge to help him in his bargaining.

Exchange, both as a means of cementing social obligations and of acquiring prestige, is a central part of Trobriand life. The exchange system promotes distribution of goods in an area where no single group has access to all the material goods its people need. Thus, people in inland villages send yams to coastal villages and receive fish in return. The Trobrianders acquire stone and clay items through partnerships set up in *Kula* expeditions. Some anthropologists have also suggested that the exchange system encourages the Trobrianders to produce a surplus and establish alliances that could be useful in a fragile environment subject to natural climatic hazards.

CRICKET AS "WARFARE"

Some of the traditions underlying the exchange system were challenged around the beginning of the twentieth century when missionaries and colonial government officials traveled to the Trobriand Islands from Port Moresby on mainland Papua New Guinea. The missionaries hoped to eliminate what they considered to be pagan customs. In particular, they tried to stamp out warfare, the use of magic, and erotic native dances. Warfare was stopped by force, and mission games were introduced as a substitute. As noted in the video program, cricket was introduced by a missionary, the Reverend M. K. Gilmour, in 1903.

The aim of the missionaries in introducing cricket to the Trobrianders was to encourage them to conform to correct British comportment in dress, religion, and "sportsmanship." But the Islanders weren't used to the British style of "bowling" (pitching) or friendly competition. They preferred a bowling style closer to their traditional way of throwing a spear, and their version of competition, more aggressive than that of the British, sometimes ended in war.

Early games pitted the Islanders against mission teams of men from Fiji. But the Trobrianders gradually changed the game to conform to their earlier warfare system, as a means of settling disputes and adding to the prestige of powerful leaders. To the Australian and British game of cricket, the Trobrianders added battle dress and battle magic, and they reincorporated erotic dancing. Just as chieftains once called for warfare, they now scheduled cricket games. Following the game, the chieftains hold massive feasts, where they display their wealth to enhance their prestige. Cricket, in its altered form, fits in with traditional systems of prestige and exchange.

In the video program, the Trobriand elders say that cricket is now "our kind of competition—*kayasa*." Traditionally, a *kayasa* helped settle quarrels through competitive food display and distribution. A man's ability to produce a great deal of food for the *kayasa* indicated that he was powerful or had strong magic.

One of the people questioned by Malinowski during his fieldwork in the Trobriand Islands told him, "The reason for the custom of *kayasa* is that we should see that one man is the more powerful, his magic sharp" (*Coral Gardens and Their Magic*, Vol. 1 [London: George Allen and Unwin Ltd., 1935], p. 212). Thus, a man could win a dispute by demonstrating his ability to produce food.

Cricket has taken the place of warfare in settling disputes. It is a new type of *kayasa*, combining the British game of cricket with traditional battle customs and Trobriand practices of prestige and exchange.

Cricket played the Trobriand way is an example of *syncretism*. Syncretism is the fusion of two or more cultural elements. In groups that have been dominated by foreign cultures, it can be a way of preserving traditional practices and social relationships. Traditional ways of life are usually destroyed or severely disrupted when one culture is overpowered politically, socially, or militarily by another. People who were formerly autonomous generally become powerless, because they cannot be absorbed abruptly into the new system. In fact, they may resist such a fate, as did the Trobrianders. With syncretism, such people selectively integrate new beliefs and practices with ones to which they are accustomed, giving them a new identity and way of coping with change they have no other power to control. Trobriand spears may have been no match for British guns, but traditional competition as a way of establishing power and prestige survives in Trobriand cricket.

Study Activities

Vocabulary Check

Check your understanding of terms by writing the letter of the appropriate definition in the space next to the corresponding term. Check your choices with the Answer Key at the end of the lesson.

_____ 1. tradition
_____ 2. avunculocal
_____ 3. exchange obligations
_____ 4. acculturation
_____ 5. syncretism
_____ 6. exogamy

_____ 7. *soulava*
_____ 8. *kayasa*
_____ 9. Papua New Guinea
_____ 10. matrilineal
_____ 11. *Kula* ring

a. marriage outside the family
b. a cultural requirement that food and other goods be given to members of one's own lineage and the spouse's lineage
c. a display and gifts of food to demonstrate power and importance
d. major culture changes that people are forced to make
e. in a modernizing society, old cultural practices
f. South Pacific country of which the Trobriand Islands are a part
g. blending old cultural elements with new "outside" practices to form a new system
h. a trading system between islanders of the South Pacific, involving goods of symbolic value
i. residence of a married couple with the husband's mother's brother
j. the necklaces exchanged in the *Kula* ring
k. lines of descent traced through women
l. the spread of customs and practices from one culture to another
m. the armbands exchanged in the *Kula* ring

Completion

Fill each blank with the most appropriate term from the list immediately following that paragraph.

1. Warfare among Trobriand villages had been a series of highly _____ engagements, motivated chiefly by the desire for prestige and status. Missionaries and colonial officials, however, sought to end village _____, stamp out the "immoral" dances and _____ , and introduce British standards of religion, _____ , and _____ . The Trobrianders enthusiastically adopted cricket as a sport, but they incorporated the game into their own values and traditions, preserving significant aspects of their own culture in a new system of competition between villages.

chants	ritualized	wars
dress	sportsmanship	

2. Cricket, as it has been modified by the Trobrianders, is a confrontation of communities. The number of players may be as many as _____. The games are held in the harvest season, because the contests are a part of the food display and giving called _____. The Trobrianders adopted a different style of "bowling," more like _____ throwing. The winner is always the _____ team, because the _____ team shows respect for the sponsoring chief by losing.

desired	*kayasa*	visiting
host	spear	

3. As adapted and refined by the Trobrianders, cricket matches provide a means of achieving two important social needs. Team members and _____ are able to demonstrate their power and status, and all members of the community share in this status. The contests also make it possible to continue the tradition of distributing _____ and items of symbolic value, a pattern or style important to Trobriand culture long before cricket appeared. The system of exchange has probably developed over the centuries to meet the need for _____ resources and to establish _____.

alliances	food
distributing	village chiefs

Self-Test

Objective Questions

Select the one best answer.

1. Cricket was introduced to the Trobriand Islanders by

    a. missionaries in 1903.
    b. servicemen in 1942.
    c. government officers in 1903.
    d. missionaries in 1942.

2. Colonial government and missionary activities were able to stop

    a. erotic dances and chants.
    b. widespread exchange of food and symbolic goods.
    c. warfare between villages.
    d. use of magic spells and rituals.

3. The British and Australians introduced cricket to the Trobriand Islanders to

    a. provide the Trobrianders with a social means for acquainting themselves with other villagers.
    b. provide opponents for the colonists who enjoyed playing the games.
    c. encourage British standards of dress and behavior.
    d. allow the Trobrianders to retain most aspects of their culture.

4. Syncretism is a response to

    a. acculturation in which a substantial portion of former cultural traditions is lost.
    b. acculturation in which old patterns are blended with new ones.
    c. diffusion in which a society borrows only the behaviors or technology it desires.
    d. diffusion in which a society adopts many of the practices and customs of an entirely different culture.

5. A fundamental aspect of Trobriand culture that was threatened by the outside culture, but retained in part through the new cricket matches was

   a. marriage practices and taboos.
   b. horticultural practices.
   c. *Kula* ring trade.
   d. prestige and status determination.

6. Many of the activities and practices the Trobrianders have incorporated into cricket were formerly associated with

   a. marriage and mating festivals.
   b. intervillage warfare.
   c. selection of village chieftains.
   d. trade between islands.

7. As the Trobrianders turned cricket into their own game, they changed the rules governing team size by

   a. making the Trobriand teams smaller than British teams.
   b. making the Trobriand teams twice the size of British teams.
   c. allowing the Trobriand teams to have any number of players.
   d. not requiring opposing teams to have the same number of players.

8. Cricket, for the Trobrianders, is a type of *kayasa*, a cultural custom that primarily serves to

   a. provide the islanders with an alternative to warfare.
   b. furnish a means of demonstrating who has the greater prestige and magical power.
   c. determine the exchange obligations between families.
   d. represent the obligations of home team members to the visiting players.

9. Cricket matches are set up during the harvest period because

   a. the weather is more favorable during this time.
   b. harvest time is the traditional mating season.
   c. harvest time coincides with the *Kula* trading.
   d. yams for display and gifts are available at this time.

10. Missionaries objected to traditional Trobriand dances and chants because these traditions were associated with

    a. ritual warfare.
    b. pagan religion.
    c. explicit sexuality.
    d. anticolonial feelings.

11. The winner of a Trobriand cricket game is

    a. selected on the basis of audience approval of both dancing and playing skill.
    b. determined by scoring, which is recorded on a palm frond.
    c. traditionally the visiting team because they will distribute gifts.
    d. traditionally the host team because the chieftain will distribute gifts.

12. Of the following statements, the one that applies to both *kayasa* and *Kula* is

    a. exchange is a central part of Trobriand life.
    b. warfare between villages had both ritualistic and violent aspects.
    c. open sexuality is a vital part of Trobriand culture.
    d. yams have both practical and symbolic value.

13. By hosting cricket matches, a village chief

    a. earns approval from the present colonial government.
    b. receives increased prestige in the view of his village and of others as well.
    c. is invited to be the umpire for the next game.
    d. has an opportunity to display the battle potential of his male villagers.

Short-Answer Essay Questions

1. List several ways that Trobriand society has changed cricket into a different game.
2. Explain how the use of war dress, magic, dance, and song in their cricket matches helped the Trobrianders to maintain cultural integrity.

3.   The video program describes syncretism as "keeping important traditions alive by integrating them with elements borrowed from another culture." Background Notes 25A describes this process as a fusion of cultural elements, a selective blending of new beliefs with familiar ones. Briefly explain what element is not mentioned in these descriptions that is emphasized in the definition in the textbook. Explain how Trobriand cricket illustrates the process of syncretism. Finally, explain the difference between syncretism and diffusion.

Suggested Activities

1.   Gerry W. Leach, the anthropologist who studied the Trobrianders and their cricket matches, has observed that Trobriand cricket can be seen as a "creative adaptation of tradition to contemporary circumstances." In what way is their adaptation of the game "creative"? What were some aspects of their culture they were in danger of losing? Discuss these questions in a brief paper.

2.   Read more about the Trobriand Islanders in Bronislaw Malinowski's *Argonauts of the Western Pacific* (London: Routledge and Kegan Paul, 1922) and *Coral Gardens and Their Magic* (London: George Allen and Unwin Ltd., 1935).

3.   You have learned that tragic results may follow forcible change, whether from widespread depression and apathy among the helpless people or from outright genocide. You have also learned that some innovations, forced upon a people or not, have far-reaching effects on the way people in a society view themselves or others.

     Identify and describe aspects of Trobriand culture that were at risk when the British imposed changes on that society. Write a brief essay explaining what parts of the culture could have been affected if, for example, the British had been more forceful in directing changes, or if the Trobrianders themselves had not responded in creative ways to preserve their way of life.

Answer Key

STUDY ACTIVITIES

Vocabulary Check

1. e	5. g	9. f
2. i	6. a	10. k
3. b	7. j	11. h
4. d	8. c	

Completion

1. ritualized, wars, chants; dress, sportsmanship (either order)
2. desired, *kayasa*, spear, host, visiting
3. village chiefs, food, distributing, alliances

SELF-TEST

Objective Questions

(Page numbers refer to the textbook.)

1. a (Objective 1; page 432; video program; Background Notes 25A)
2. c (Objective 1; video program; Background Notes 25A)
3. c (Objective 1; pages 432–433; video program; Background Notes 25A)
4. b (Objective 2; page 432; video program; Background Notes 25A)
5. d (Objective 2; page 434; video program; Background Notes 25A)
6. b (Objective 2; pages 432–434 video program; Background Notes 25A)
7. c (Objective 3; video program)
8. b (Objective 3; video program; Background Notes 25A)
9. d (Objective 4; video program)
10. c (Objective 4; video program)
11. d (Objective 4; video program)
12. a (Objective 5; pages 187–188, 198–200, 434; video program; Background Notes 25A)
13. b (Objective 5; video program; Background Notes 25A)

Short-Answer Essay Questions

1. List several ways that Trobriand society has changed cricket into a different game.

   Your answer should include at least three of the following:

   - The Islanders have adapted their battle dress and facial paint to cricket matches.

   - Their version of the game incorporates traditional styles of dance and chants.

   - Magic rituals formerly associated with warfare are employed before and during the game.

   - The contests are associated with *kayasa* feasts.

   - Instead of twelve players, the number of players is unlimited; thus more members of the community may participate.

   - The balls, stumps, and bats have been modified, partly because of traditional Trobriander cultural skills.

   - The bowling style resembles the Trobriand spear-throwing technique.

   - Out of respect for the host chieftain, the host team always wins.

2. Explain how the use of war dress, magic, dance, and song in their cricket matches helped the Trobrianders to maintain cultural integrity.

   Your answer should include:

   - Trobriand Islanders transformed cricket into a competition that replaces warfare between villages.

   - The costumes and facial paint used in the games are associated with magic, which frees the players from inhibitions and bolsters courage—traits sought both in the former wars and in modern cricket.

   - Magic rituals formerly associated with weapons are now employed for the playing equipment; thus, the rituals themselves are retained.

   - Trobriand dancing was opposed by the missionaries, but the Trobriand Islanders preserved their dances by incorporating them into the cricket matches introduced by the missionaries.

   - Trobriand cricket and *kayasa* provide an avenue for gaining prestige.

3. The video program describes syncretism as "keeping important traditions alive by integrating them with elements borrowed from another culture." Background Notes 25A describes this process as a fusion of cultural elements, a selective blending of new beliefs with familiar ones. Briefly explain what element is not mentioned in these descriptions that is emphasized in the definition in the textbook. Explain how Trobriand cricket illustrates the process of syncretism. Finally, explain the difference between syncretism and diffusion.

    Your answer should include:

    - According to the textbook, syncretism occurs in acculturation, which involves an element of force. In syncretism, foreign traits are blended with those from the society, which is similar to "borrowing" or "fusion." However, the affected society does not have free choice to borrow or select—some degree of change is forced upon it. Syncretism involves the creative blending of traditional elements from the culture when foreign practices or beliefs are forced upon that society.

    - Trobriand cricket is an example of syncretism because the Trobrianders adapted a foreign practice to their own needs by blending in a number of important elements from their own cultural heritage, creating something new, but retaining their identity.

    - Syncretism is a term for creative adaptation under conditions of forcible change. Diffusion is a term for the spread of cultural traits from one society to another through voluntary borrowing.

The Future 26
of Humanity

Assignments

Before viewing the video program	• Read the Overview and the Learning Objectives for this lesson. Use the Learning Objectives to guide your reading, viewing, and thinking. • Read textbook Chapter 16, "The Future of Humanity," pages 450–479, and review Chapter 15, page 447, "Modernization: Must It Always Be Painful?"; and reread page 105, "Language Renewal among the Northern Ute," and page 283, "Federal Recognition for American Indians."

View video program 26, "The Future of Humanity"

After viewing the video program	• Review the terms used in this lesson. In addition to those terms in the Learning Objectives, you should be familiar with these:

ethnic resurgence   obsolescence
exploitative   pollution
fragmentation   replacement reproduction
futurist   separatist movements
green revolution

• Review the reading assignments for this lesson.
• Complete each of the Study Activities and the Self-Test in this study-guide lesson, check your answers with the Answer Key at the end of this lesson.
• According to your instructor's assignment or your own interests, complete one or more of the Suggested Activities. You may also be interested in the readings listed at the end of Chapter 16 in the textbook.

Overview

What do you think will determine the character and the quality of human societies during the twenty-first century? No doubt you have noticed imaginative predictions about the years to come. Some predictions involve nearly perfect worlds where all problems have been solved and people spend their days in happy pursuits. Other predictions include catastrophes that will usher in a new dark age or destroy life altogether. The truth, of course, is that the future is simply unknown. What happens in the future will depend on many factors, most of which cannot be foreseen at present.

The future of humanity, though, probably will be strongly influenced by some existing problems and conditions that can be identified now. To understand the future, it is of the greatest importance to recognize such key problems and conditions and to understand their significance, because decisions that are made in the next few years likely will have an important impact on the world 50 years from now. Most of these problems and conditions will not be new to you. Now, however, you will look at them from the perspective of anthropology. Culture-bound values and ethnocentrism, as you know, serve as "blinders," preventing an objective look at a complete picture. You now share in part the cross-cultural understandings that anthropologists have gained through comparative studies.

It should come as no surprise that anthropologists are concerned about the survival of every human society for which survival is still possible. Anthropologists are equally concerned that a record be kept of societies that do not survive and of practices that are discarded over time. For anthropologists, every human society that ever existed is of immense value. As Haviland, the author of the textbook, says: "When a song is forgotten or a ceremony ceases to be performed, a part of the human heritage is destroyed forever."

You will find, as well, that anthropologists are concerned with the rights of peoples who have a heritage of non-Western cultures. Many are actively concerned with protecting such rights; others are applying their knowledge to help such people preserve or restore important cultural elements that are endangered. Examples in the video program show how some indigenous peoples are working to preserve their cultural traditions.

You now understand that social and cultural change is inevitable. While studying this lesson, keep in mind three perspectives: First, you have already been introduced to traditional societies that have met the challenges of modernization and forcible change with apparent success. While their stories are still in progress, it is demonstrably possible for societies to accommodate tremendous changes if given the time and space to do so. Second, societies can be driven to extinction by the forces of change, particularly by forcible change—and such is happening on a far larger scale than most people realize. Third, the problems facing Western societies are huge and may be developing at a rate far too rapid to find workable cultural solutions.

This lesson does not glow with optimism for the future, nor is it a dark prophesy of catastrophe. The world today presents exciting and challenging problems for anthropologists and for all citizens concerned with the survival of humanity. During this lesson you may wish to take a broad look at the science of anthropology as you now understand it after 26 lessons. Those who prepared the materials for *Faces of Culture* feel that the readings and video programs give you new frames of reference for understanding your own culture and new perspectives for appreciating the broad panorama of humankind's search for solutions to its problems. You have encountered dramatic moments in the lives of individuals and peoples. May you find excitement and challenge in your own life and greater satisfaction in the achievements of other societies as well as your own.

Video Program: This final program addresses the compelling problem of preserving the diversity of human cultures in a world that often appears to be rushing toward a one-world culture. The program includes examples of how contact with Western industrial societies has harmed traditional societies and of how indigenous peoples are making the future their own by taking back the past. A Kwakiutl woman describes how her society is working to preserve its culture. The Yanomamo are featured in another segment, which shows how they are learning to defend their lands against outsiders and includes comments by Napoleon Chagnon on his concerns for the Yanomamo's survival. Throughout the program, many representatives of indigenous peoples express their concerns and desires for protecting their societies.

As you view the program, look for:

- examples of how changes in technology have altered the fabric of human life.

- the destruction caused by mining in the Amazon and in Kentucky.

- the confrontation between the Mohawks and Canadian government.

- how the Yanomamo are learning to defend their lands against outsiders.

- Napoleon Chagnon's comments on the concept of a biosphere reserve as a means of guaranteeing the survival of indigenous peoples.

- the Kwakiutl woman describing how her people negotiated the return of masks and other artifacts from Canada's National Museum of Man and built a "Box of Treasures" to house the items and serve as a center for preserving Kwakiutl cultural traditions.

- examples of how older generations can help to preserve cultural traditions by passing them on to younger generations.

Learning Objectives

When you have completed all assignments in this lesson, you should be able to:

1. Define *one-world culture* and list some of the difficulties that block its realization. TEXTBOOK PAGES 453–455, 458–460; VIDEO PROGRAM

2. Discuss the rise of multinational corporations and their role in influencing cultural and social change. TEXTBOOK PAGES 455–458

3. Cite examples of how indigenous peoples are reasserting their distinctive identities, and describe the possible role of anthropologists in preserving traditional cultures. TEXTBOOK PAGES 105, 283, AND 458–461; VIDEO PROGRAM

4. Describe *cultural pluralism* and list some of the difficulties that prevent its realization. TEXTBOOK PAGES 461–464 AND 467–468

5. Define and explain *global apartheid*. TEXTBOOK PAGES 469–470

6. Define *structural violence* and list some global conditions associated with it. TEXTBOOK PAGES 470–476

7. Describe some of the problems associated with overpopulation. TEXTBOOK PAGES 475–476

8. Summarize the factors that cause a widespread culture of discontent. TEXTBOOK PAGES 447, 477; VIDEO PROGRAM

Study Activities

Vocabulary Check

Check your understanding of terms by writing the letter of the appropriate definition in the space next to the corresponding term. Check your choices with the Answer Key at the end of the lesson.

_____	1.	obsolete	_____	6.	nonrenewable resources
_____	2.	green revolution	_____	7.	one-world culture
_____	3.	replacement reproduction	_____	8.	cultural pluralism
_____	4.	pollution	_____	9.	structural violence
_____	5.	ethnic resurgence	_____	10.	culture of discontent

a.   worldwide tendency for Western societies to have greater power than those of non-Western societies

b.   thought possible by those who believe that "old" cultures are destined to give way to new

c.   an attempt, often not successful, to use new technologies to increase food crop yields

d.   devastation brought about by anonymous situations, institutions, and social, political, and economic structures

e.   judgment that may be made by one society about the relevance of another society

f.   Western societies consume more than 50 percent of them

g.   when the birth rate is in equilibrium with the death rate

h.   a worldview that considers nature as something to be used

i.   condition in which aspirations far exceed opportunities

j.   results when people with different ways of living and thinking live within the same society

k.   one cause is chemicals and additives used in food production

l.   self-determination movements of indigenous peoples

Completion

Fill each blank with the most appropriate term from the list immediately following that paragraph.

1.   "One-world culture" is a phrase reflecting the belief that present-day
     communication and transportation will sooner or later lead to a worldwide
     _____ society. Two factors strongly oppose such a development, however.
     First, large states, both past and present, have tended to _____ throughout
     history. Second, there is a trend toward ethnic resurgence in which _____
     groups seek independence from a country or a dominant culture.

     Peaceful cultural pluralism seems effective in some countries, such as Switzerland
     and Canada. In the past, however, the United States has considered itself to be a
     cultural _____ rather than a pluralistic society. Where cultures are very
     dissimilar, as in Guatemala, one society tends to _____ the other, even to the
     point of extermination.

dominate	homogeneous	melting pot
fragment	indigenous	

2.   Anthropologists are showing increasing concern for the well-being of peoples who
     are adversely affected by _____ societies. Territories formerly the home of
     traditional societies have become sites of development and exploitation; examples
     are the Amazon Basin of South America and parts of Alaska and Canada.
     Frequently, little provision is made for helping such people to _____ to new
     social and environmental conditions. They seem condemned not only to remain on
     the _____ rung of the socioeconomic ladder, but to lose their cultural practices,
     values, identity, and even lives.

adapt	lowest
industrialized	

3.   One example of the "culture of discontent" is the plight of formerly _____
     peoples now living in urban slums who cannot be absorbed into _____ jobs.
     An example of greater magnitude is the situation of developing countries that desire
     the wealth and power of industrialized countries but lack the _____ for
     industrialization. The future does not seem to promise better conditions, because
     _____ resources are being used up.

industrial	resources
nonrenewable	rural

Self-Test

Objective Questions

Select the one best answer.

1. A tendency toward a one-world culture is seen in the present-day
   a. widespread adoption of the practices of Western societies.
   b. widespread adoption of the beliefs of traditional societies.
   c. resurgence of movements toward ethnic independence.
   d. countries that contain more than one distinct society.

2. The union of smaller units into larger political and social units on a worldwide basis
   a. occurs today at an increasing rate.
   b. has never been a tendency of human societies.
   c. now seems to be balanced by a tendency of large units to fragment.
   d. can be expected to occur more frequently, since no forces work against it.

3. Today's multinational corporations are best described as
   a. being almost totally dependent upon the goodwill of host governments.
   b. having decreased in number since 1950.
   c. frequently ignoring policies of the host government.
   d. being limited in their activities by governmental controls.

4. In the development of the Amazon region in Brazil, multinational corporations have
   a. generally opposed Brazilian government policies.
   b. improved the standard of living for the majority of persons already in the region.
   c. modified farming technology for suitability to the region.
   d. participated in the displacement of indigenous peoples and settlers.

5. Anthropologists generally hold a strong belief in the
   a. desirability of progress.
   b. need for modernization.
   c. value of every human society.
   d. need to return to egalitarianism.

6. For indigenous peoples, Cultural Survival, Inc., provides
   a. projects designed and established in indigenous societies with the approval of the national government involved.
   b. financial aid for development.
   c. advice and assistance upon request.
   d. preservation of records on disappearing cultures.

7. Generally, Cultural Survival, Inc., works toward the goal of helping societies to
   a. integrate themselves into the national "mainstream."
   b. isolate themselves from forces that promote change.
   c. work out their own adjustments to change.
   d. relocate to isolated preserves for further study.

8. The textbook points out that global spreading of any single idea may be harmful, regardless of the value of the concept, because it may eliminate
   a. diversity.
   b. technology.
   c. change.
   d. tolerance.

9. When two or more cultures exist in a given society, the term *cultural pluralism* implies that
   a. the two will eventually blend into one.
   b. one culture's values and goals will determine the course of the society.
   c. each culture will seek to form an independent society.
   d. each culture will respect the traditions and practices of the others.

10. Although two distinct cultures can be identified in Guatemala,
    a. the minority culture wields virtually all political and military power.
    b. both groups participate equally in political and social affairs.
    c. the Indian population is gradually assuming a dominant role.
    d. the country is becoming a "melting pot" blend of cultures.

11. *Apartheid* is a policy that originated in

   a. the United States and promoted the blending of minorities.
   b. South Africa and perpetuated the dominance of a white minority over a nonwhite majority.
   c. Germany and guided the extermination of minorities.
   d. Switzerland and led to equality.

12. The nonwhite human races make up about

   a. one-third of the world population.
   b. one-half of the world population.
   c. two-thirds of the world population.
   d. seven-eighths of the world population.

13. Which one of the following was NOT listed in the textbook as a problem of structural violence?

   a. overpopulation
   b. pollution
   c. revolution
   d. world hunger

14. Structural violence differs from other types of violence because

   a. it occurs as a side effect of deliberate acts of war.
   b. the source of the violence is anonymous or impersonal.
   c. it occurs only in highly industrialized countries.
   d. it is directed against political and social structures rather than against people.

15. The present world population is between

   a. 3 billion and 4 billion.
   b. 4 billion and 5 billion.
   c. 5 billion and 6 billion.
   d. 6 billion and 7 billion.

16. According to the textbook, overpopulation should be considered

    a. a worldwide problem that prevents solutions to many other major problems.
    b. a minor problem if world hunger and pollution can be corrected quickly.
    c. the only important global problem, since all other serious problems would disappear if it were controlled.
    d. a problem that cannot be corrected by any known measures.

17. Fewer nonrenewable resources will be available to developing nations in the future because

    a. Western industrialized nations already possess most of them.
    b. developing nations are using them to develop their own industry.
    c. their use inevitably causes pollution.
    d. nonrenewable resources such as oil are being used up to feed the present world population.

18. The term *culture of discontent* refers to

    a. revolutionary groups who seek freedom from oppressive governments.
    b. religious extremists who believe massive cultural changes will ensure a better world.
    c. employees and consumers who depend on large multinational corporations.
    d. groups who desire the standard of living of Western industrial societies but have little opportunity to achieve it.

19. Implementing solutions to many global problems is made more difficult by the worldview that

    a. nonrenewable resources must be preserved at all costs.
    b. humanity is distinctly superior to nature.
    c. humanity is one part of nature.
    d. every human society possesses great value.

Short-Answer Essay Questions

1. In what ways do multinational corporations exert a global unifying force? In what ways do they tend to weaken the autonomy of individual societies?

2. Summarize conditions that have been identified as contributing to a *global apartheid*.

3. List three categories of structural violence discussed in the textbook and give at least one example of each.

Suggested Activities

1. For more information on the effects of modernization or cross-cultural contacts in the last two years, consult the *Readers' Guide to Periodical Literature* for recent articles on some of the societies studied in this course. You may be particularly interested in the fortunes of the Yanomamo, the Kwakiutl, the Trobrianders, the Shuar, or the Maya of Guatemala. When you report on the content of the articles, list insights or understandings you have gained from this course that help you appreciate the significance of information in the article.

2. Obtain information from your library on Cultural Survival, Inc., or on the World Council of Indigenous Peoples (both described in Chapter 16 of the textbook). What particular society (or societies) are of special concern to either of these organizations at present? Try to obtain enough information to describe briefly the problems faced by the people seeking help from these organizations. You may wish to comment, in a brief report, on how the problems you learn about in this activity relate to the domination of one society by another, the influence of multinational corporations, or the occurrence of structural violence.

3. Review the bibliography at the end of the textbook and select two or three books to read in the coming months. List the books you selected and explain briefly what aspects of anthropological studies particularly interest you.

4. Review the general course goals on pages *v-vi* of this study guide. Write a short, informal evaluation of the course based on these objectives.

Answer Key

Vocabulary Check

1. e	5. l	8. j
2. c	6. f	9. d
3. g	7. b	10. i
4. k		

Completion

1. homogeneous, fragment, indigenous, melting pot, dominate
2. industrialized, adapt, lowest
3. rural, industrial, resources, nonrenewable

SELF-TEST

Objective Questions

(Page numbers refer to the textbook.)

1. a (Objective 1; page 453; video program)
2. c (Objective 1; pages 453–454)
3. c (Objective 2; page 456)
4. d (Objective 2; page 456)
5. c (Objective 3; page 458; video program)
6. c (Objective 3; page 459)
7. c (Objective 3; page 459)
8. a (Objective 3; page 458)
9. d (Objective 4; pages 460–461)
10. a (Objective 4; page 463)
11. b (Objective 5; page 469)
12. c (Objective 5; page 469)
13. c (Objective 6; pages 470–476)

14. b (Objective 6; page 470)
15. c (Objective 7; page 476)
16. a (Objective 7; page 475)
17. d (Objective 8; pages 447, 477)
18. d (Objective 8; pages 447, 477)
19. b (Objective 8; page 477; video program)

Short-Answer Essay Questions

1. In what ways do multinational corporations exert a global unifying force? In what ways do they tend to weaken the autonomy of individual societies?

    Your answer should include:

    - The top management of a multinational corporation can control industrial activities in many countries. This control is a unifying influence that cuts across national, social, and cultural boundaries.

    - Multinational corporations have demonstrated power to carry out their decisions without the consent of affected governments, to ignore governmental foreign policies, and to hold back information needed by the governments to make intelligent decisions. In cooperation with some governments, as in Brazil, corporations have participated in development programs that take land and autonomy away from traditional societies.

2. Summarize conditions that have been identified as contributing to a *global apartheid*.

    Your answer should include:

    - On a worldwide scale, societies that are predominantly white are affluent, while the societies composed of nonwhite peoples tend to live under conditions of poverty, even though they make up the majority of the world's population.

    - Several barriers impede social integration of the two groups.

    - Despite such separation of the affluent and the poor, the two groups are economically dependent on each other.

    - The white affluent societies possess most of the political, economic, and military power.

3. List three categories of structural violence discussed in the textbook and give at least one example of each.

Your answer should include:

- **World hunger**: One example is the problem of worldwide distribution. In the United States, millions of dollars' worth of edible food is thrown away every day, while millions of people in the world remain hungry. Another example is the widespread practice in developing countries of using farmland for crops grown for export rather than for food to be consumed by their own peoples.

- **Pollution**: One example is acid rain produced by industrial air pollution, which affects the health of other regions and nations. Another example is the dumping, by European countries, of toxic and low-grade radioactive wastes in Benin. Still another is the use of chemicals in intensive agriculture that accumulate as poisons in the soil and in water supplies.

- **Population growth**: One example is the high birth rates in many of the world's poorest countries despite efforts at dissemination of birth-control information. Another example is population-control policies, such as those in China, that are in conflict with other policies and societal traditions.